11th Workshop on Natural Language Processing for Computer Assisted Language Learning (NLP4CALL 2022)

Louvain-la-Neuve, Belgium and Online
9 December 2022

Editors:

David Alfter
Elena Volodina
Thomas Francois
Piet Desmet
Frederik Cornillie
Arne Jonsson
Evelina Rennes

ISBN: 978-1-7138-9143-7

Printed from e-media with permission by:

Curran Associates, Inc.
57 Morehouse Lane
Red Hook, NY 12571

Some format issues inherent in the e-media version may also appear in this print version.

Association for Computational Linguistics
209 N. Eighth Street
Stroudsburg, Pennsylvania 18360

Phone: 1-570-476-8006
Fax: 1-570-476-0860

acl@aclweb.org

Additional copies of this publication are available from:

Curran Associates, Inc.
57 Morehouse Lane
Red Hook, NY 12571 USA
Phone: 845-758-0400
Fax: 845-758-2633
Email: curran@proceedings.com
Web: www.proceedings.com

Proceedings of the 11th Workshop on Natural Language Processing for Computer Assisted Language Learning (NLP4CALL 2022)

C N
AL L
P

Linköping Electronic Conference Proceedings 190
eISSN 1650-3740 (Online) • ISSN 1650-3686 (Print) 2022

Proceedings of the

11th Workshop on Natural Language Processing for Computer Assisted Language Learning (NLP4CALL 2022)

edited by
David Alfter, Elena Volodina, Thomas François, Piet Desmet,
Frederik Cornillie, Arne Jönsson and Evelina Rennes

Linköping Electronic Conference Proceedings 190

Preface

The workshop series on Natural Language Processing (NLP) for Computer-Assisted Language Learning (NLP4CALL) is a meeting place for researchers working on the integration of Natural Language Processing and Speech Technologies in CALL systems and exploring the theoretical and methodological issues arising in this connection. The latter includes, among others, the integration of insights from Second Language Acquisition (SLA) research, and the promotion of "Computational SLA" through setting up Second Language research infrastructures.

The intersection of Natural Language Processing (or Language Technology / Computational Linguistics) and Speech Technology with Computer-Assisted Language Learning (CALL) brings "understanding" of language to CALL tools, thus making CALL intelligent. This fact has given the name for this area of research – Intelligent CALL, or for short, ICALL. As the definition suggests, apart from having excellent knowledge of Natural Language Processing and/or Speech Technology, ICALL researchers need good insights into second language acquisition theories and practices, as well as knowledge of second language pedagogy and didactics. This workshop therefore invites a wide range of ICALL-relevant research, including studies where NLP-enriched tools are used for testing SLA and pedagogical theories, and vice versa, where SLA theories, pedagogical practices or empirical data and modelled in ICALL tools. The NLP4CALL workshop series is aimed at bringing together competences from these areas for sharing experiences and brainstorming around the future of the field.

We invited submissions:

- that describe research directly aimed at ICALL
- that demonstrate actual or discuss the potential use of existing Language and Speech Technologies or resources for language learning
- that describe the ongoing development of resources and tools with potential usage in ICALL, either directly in interactive applications, or indirectly in materials, application, or curriculum development, e.g. learning material generation, assessment of learner texts and responses, individualized learning solutions, provision of feedback
- that discuss challenges and/or research agenda for ICALL
- that describe empirical studies on language learner data

This year a special focus was given to work done on second language vocabulary and grammar profiling, as well as the use of crowdsourcing for creating, collecting, and curating data in NLP projects. We encouraged paper presentations and software demonstrations describing the above-mentioned themes primarily, but not exclusively, for the Nordic languages.

A special feature in this year's workshop is the *research notes* session. This session included short talks about PhD projects and ongoing unfinished research that collaborating teams were eager to discuss with the community and get feedback. We tested this feature for the second time with an intention to evaluate its impact and utility for future uses. This time around, we circulated a separate call for expression of interest.

This year, we had the pleasure to welcome two invited speakers: Christopher Bryant (Reverso and University of Cambridge) and Marije Michel (University of Groningen).

Dr **Christopher J. Bryant** is a Principal Applied Research Scientist at the AI-powered translation and language tool service Reverso, and a Research Associate in the Institute for Automated Language Teaching and Assessment (ALTA) at the University of Cambridge. His main research interests include automatic grammatical error detection and correction (GED/GEC), automatic corpus annotation, and the robust evaluation of grammatical error correction systems, along with computer-aided language learning in general. He completed his PhD on "Automatic annotation for grammatical error correction" in 2019 and is the lead developer of the associated ERRor ANnotation Toolkit (ERRANT) which is

David Alfter, Elena Volodina, Thomas François, Piet Desmet, Frederik Cornillie, Arne Jönsson and Evelina Rennes. Preface. *Proceedings of the 11th Workshop on Natural Language Processing for Computer Assisted Language Learning (NLP4CALL 2022)*. Linköping Electronic Conference Proceedings 190: i–iv.

widely used to benchmark progress in the field. He led the most recent shared task on GEC in 2019 (BEA-2019) and currently researches artificial error generation for GEC and develops the Ginger grammar checker at Reverso.

In his talk, *The Evolution of Automatic Grammatical Error Correction*, he provided an overview of the field and introduced the datasets, approaches and evaluation methods that are commonly used to build Grammatic Error Correction systems. He concluded with recent trends and remaining challenges.

Dr **Marije Michel** is chair of Language Learning at Groningen University in the Netherlands. Her research and teaching focus on second language acquisition and processing with specific attention to task-based language pedagogy, digitally-mediated interaction and writing in a second language.

In her talk, *TELL: Tasks Engaging Language Learners*, she reviewed the most important principles of designing engaging learning tasks, highlighted examples of practice-induced L2 research using digital tools, and showcased some of her own work on task design for L2 learning during digitally mediated communication and L2 writing.

Previous workshops

This workshop follows a series of workshops on NLP4CALL organized by the NEALT Special Interest Group on Intelligent Computer-Assisted Language Learning (SIG-ICALL[1]). The workshop series has previously been financed by the Center for Language Technology at the University of Gothenburg, the SweLL project[2], the Swedish Research Council's conference grant, Språkbanken Text[3] and the L2 profiling project[4]. This year's workshop is jointly financed by itec[5] and the CENTAL[6].

Submissions to the eleven workshop editions have targeted a wide range of languages, ranging from well-resourced languages (Chinese, German, English, French, Portuguese, Russian, Spanish) to lesser-resourced languages (Erzya, Arabic, Estonian, Irish, Komi-Zyrian, Meadow Mari, Saami, Udmurt, Võro). Among these, several Nordic languages have been targeted, namely Danish, Estonian, Finnish, Icelandic, Norwegian, Saami, Swedish and Võro. The wide scope of the workshop is also evident in the affiliations of the participating authors as illustrated in Table 1.

Country	2012-2022 (# speaker/co-author affiliations)
Algeria	1
Australia	2
Belgium	9
Canada	4
Cyprus	2
Denmark	3
Egypt	1
Estonia	3
Finland	10
France	10
Germany	103
Iceland	6

[1] https://spraakbanken.gu.se/en/research/themes/icall/sig-icall

[2] https://spraakbanken.gu.se/en/projects/swell

[3] https://spraakbanken.gu.se

[4] https://spraakbanken.gu.se/en/projects/l2profiles

[5] https://itec.kuleuven-kulak.be

[6] https://cental.uclouvain.be

Ireland	2
Italy	7
Japan	7
Lithuania	1
Netherlands	4
Norway	13
Portugal	6
Romania	1
Russia	10
Slovakia	1
Spain	4
Sweden	71
Switzerland	11
UK	16
US	8

Table 1. NLP4CALL speakers' and co-authors' affiliations, 2012-2022

The acceptance rate has varied between 50% and 77%, the average being 63% (see Table 2).

Although the acceptance rate is rather high, the reviewing process has always been very rigorous with two to three double-blind reviews per submission. This indicates that submissions to the workshop have usually been of high quality.

Workshop year	Submitted	Accepted	Acceptance rate
2012	12	8	67%
2013	8	4	50%
2014	13	10	77%
2015	9	6	67%
2016	14	10	72%
2017	13	7	54%
2018	16	11	69%
2019	16	10	63%
2020	7	4	57%
2021	11	6	54%
2022	23	13	56%

Table 2: Submissions and acceptance rates, 2012-2021

We would like to thank our Program Committee for providing detailed feedback for the reviewed papers:

- David Alfter, Université catholique de Louvain, Belgium and University of Gothenburg, Sweden
- Serge Bibauw, Universidad Central del Ecuador, Ecuador
- Claudia Borg, University of Malta, Malta
- António Branco, Universidade de Lisboa, Portugal
- Andrew Caines, University of Cambridge, UK
- Xiaobin Chen, Universität Tübingen, Germany
- Frederik Cornillie, University of Leuven, Belgium
- Kordula de Kuthy, Universität Tübingen, Germany
- Piet Desmet, University of Leuven, Belgium
- Thomas François, Université catholique de Louvain, Belgium
- Johannes Graën, University of Zurich, Switzerland
- Andrea Horbach, FernUniversität Hagen, Germany
- Arne Jönsson, Linköping University, Sweden

- Ronja Laarmann-Quante, FernUniversität Hagen, Germany
- Herbert Lange, University of Hamburg, Germany
- Peter Ljunglöf, University of Gothenburg, Sweden and Chalmers Institute of Technology, Sweden
- Margot Mieskes, University of Applied Sciences Darmstadt, Germany
- Lionel Nicolas, EURAC research, Italy
- Ulrike Pado, Hochschule für Technik Stuttgart, Germany
- Magali Paquot, Université catholique de Louvain, Belgium
- Evelina Rennes, Linköping University, Sweden
- Egon Stemle, EURAC research, Italy
- Francis M. Tyers, Indiana University Bloomington, US
- Sowmya Vajjala, National Research Council, Canada
- Elena Volodina, University of Gothenburg, Sweden
- Zarah Weiss, Universität Tübingen, Germany
- Rodrigo Wilkens, Université catholique de Louvain, Belgium
- Torsten Zesch, FernUniversität Hagen, Germany
- Ramon Ziai, Universität Tübingen, Germany
- Robert Östling, Stockholm University, Sweden

We intend to continue this workshop series, which so far has been the only ICALL-relevant recurring event based in the Nordic countries. Our intention is to co-locate the workshop series with the two major LT events in Scandinavia, SLTC (the Swedish Language Technology Conference) and NoDaLiDa (Nordic Conference on Computational Linguistics), thus making this workshop an annual event. Through this workshop, we intend to profile ICALL research in Nordic countries as well as beyond, and we aim at providing a dissemination venue for researchers active in this area.

Workshop website:

https://spraakbanken.gu.se/forskning/teman/icall/nlp4call-workshop-series/nlp4call2022

Workshop organizers

David Alfter[1,2], Elena Volodina[2], Thomas François[1], Piet Desmet[3], Frederik Cornillie[3], Arne Jönsson[4], Evelina Rennes[4]

[1] Cental, Université catholique de Louvain, Belgium

[2] Språkbanken, University of Gothenburg, Sweden

[3] Itec, Department of Linguistics at KU Leuven & imec, Belgium

[4] Department of Computer and Information Science, Linköping University, Sweden

Acknowledgements

We gratefully acknowledge the financial support from *Cental*, *itec*, and the Language and Communication Institute (IL&C) - Research Center in Linguistics (PLIN) of the UCLouvain.

Content

Comparing Native and Learner Englishes Using a Large Pre-trained Language Model

Tatsuya Aoyama
Georgetown University
ta571@georgetown.edu

Abstract

The use of lexical items by L2 speakers of English has been analyzed through a variety of methods; however, they are either (i) infeasible for a large-scale learner corpus study or (ii) designed to measure vocabulary breadth, rather than depth. This paper presents the preliminary results of an ongoing work to utilize contextualized word embeddings (CWEs) obtained from a large pre-trained language model to measure the depth of L2 speakers' vocabulary knowledge, operationalized as how similar L2 speakers' use of a given word is to that of L1 speakers'. We find that (i) the mean distance between L1 CWEs and L2 CWEs of a given word tends to decrease as the proficiency level becomes higher, and that (ii) while words that have similar CWEs in the L1 corpus and L2 corpus tend to reveal interesting properties about the word use, words that have dissimilar CWEs in the two corpora often suffer from domain effects.

1 Introduction

Characterizing learner language has been a major task in second language acquisition (SLA) literature. Various aspects of texts produced by second language (L2) English speakers have been shown to deviate from first language (L1) English speakers, such as syntactic (Pienemann, 1998) and morphological aspects (Goldschneider and DeKeyser, 2001). Among these, deviation in word use is particularly difficult to characterize as the "native-likeness" of word use is not as clear-cut as that of syntactic or morphological knowledge, where the correct and incorrect use is rather clearly defined. Hence, a number of methods to measure L2 speakers' word use have been proposed, and they are roughly categorized as capturing either the breadth (how *many*) or depth (how *well*) of vocabulary knowledge (Wesche and Paribakht, 1996). While a number of automatic measurements for vocabulary breadth have been proposed (e.g., Lu, 2012), measurements for vocabulary depth largely remain infeasible for a large-scale learner corpus study. As such, we propose a new approach to measure vocabulary depth by leveraging the word embeddings obtained from a large language model.

In fact, the idea of using word embeddings to compare word use across different populations is not new; for example, using this approach, Del Tredici and Fernández (2017) investigated semantic variation across different communities of practice, and Hamilton et al. (2016) studied diachronic semantic change. Since this approach is applicable to any comparative analysis as long as it involves multiple populations that speak the same language, the current study aims to extend this approach to measure the depth of vocabulary knowledge, operationalized as how similar L2 speakers' use of a given word is to that of L1 speakers' (i.e., a comparative analysis of L1 and L2 Englishes).

In the subsequent sections, we will first briefly review existing approaches to measure learners' word use in SLA literature (§2.1) and show how methods from distributional semantics can be employed to tackle this problem (§2.2). We then describe the data, model, and experiments (§3), followed by the results (§4) and discussion (§5), including implications and limitations, as well as future directions.

2 Relevant work

2.1 Vocabulary acquisition

Vocabulary acquisition garners a considerable attention in SLA literature, and various operationalizations and measurements have been proposed. For example, within the widely used proficiency measurement framework of complexity, fluency, and accuracy (CAF; Skehan et al., 1998), lexical complexity is measured by several indices, such as type-token ratio and lexical sophistication of L2 writing (Norris and Ortega, 2009). The former represents the (absence of) repetition in vocabulary,

Tatsuya Aoyama. Comparing Native and Learner Englishes Using a Large Pre-trained Language Model. *Proceedings of the 11th Workshop on Natural Language Processing for Computer Assisted Language Learning (NLP4CALL 2022).* Linköping Electronic Conference Proceedings 190: 1–9.

and the latter captures the use of low-frequency lexical items.

Other approaches suggest the importance of breadth-depth distinction: the former represents how many vocabulary items a learner knows, and the latter represents how well a learner knows a certain vocabulary item (Nation, 2001). Multiple choice questions are among the most common measures of vocabulary breadth, whereas a variety of tests are used to measure vocabulary depth, such as completing idiomatic expressions, filling in the blank using collocation knowledge, and writing down synonyms of a given vocabulary item (Milton, 2009).

Some approaches (e.g., type-token ratio, vocabulary sophistication) can be applied to written texts automatically (e.g., Lu, 2012) and hence scalable to a large-scale learner corpus study; however, they are not capable of measuring anything beyond vocabulary breadth (i.e., how *many* words) or how advanced those known words are. Other approaches (e.g., idiom, collocation, or synonym) are better proxies for measuring vocabulary depth, yet the reliance on the carefully crafted tests and the need for learners to take them make these approaches expensive. Hence, we argue for the use of methods from distributional semantics to obtain a richer representation of word usage, rather than relying on the *counts* of word use in a given text.

2.2 Distributional semantics

The idea that the meaning of a given word is captured in the distribution of the word (i.e, co-occurring words) in a given corpus is called distributional hypothesis (Harris, 1954). Building on this hypothesis, Salton (1971) proposed vector space model, where a word can be represented as a point in high-dimensional vector space based on the count of neighboring words. This count-based vector space model has spawned a number of studies that investigate its linguistic implications (Erk, 2012).

Replacing this count-based approach, Mikolov et al. (2013a) proposed a prediction-based approach called word2vec, enabling a given word to be represented as a low-dimensional dense vector, instead of the traditional term-to-term sparse vector. Subsequent studies find that surprising amount of linguistic information is captured in this dense representation. For example, Mikolov et al. (2013b) find that word vectors can be added and subtracted to derive another word vector. An often-cited example is that the vector for *Queen* can be approximated by $King - Man + Woman$.

Both count-based and prediction-based approaches described above generate type-based word vectors, meaning that each word type receives a single word vector. The advent of language models capable of taking contexts into consideration, such as ELMo (Peters et al., 2018), enables each *word token*, rather than *word type*, to receive a separate word vector, often referred to as contextualized word embeddings (CWEs). Of such language models, BERT (Devlin et al., 2019) is perhaps the most widely used and extensively studied (see Rogers et al. 2020 for an overview of the studies that investigate BERT's internal representation).

While much work has been devoted to applying word embeddings to downstream NLP tasks, and their usefulness has been widely recognized (e.g., Devlin et al., 2019; Liu et al., 2019), others utilized them for more theoretical investigations, such as semantic variation across communities of practice (Del Tredici and Fernández, 2017), diachronic semantic shift (Del Tredici et al., 2019; Hamilton et al., 2016), and variation in semantic frames across different languages (Sikos and Padó, 2018). Most, if not all, studies of the latter kind (theoretical investigation) adopt type-based word embeddings; hence, this study is arguably the first of its kind to apply CWEs to perform a comparative analysis of language use by multiple populations (see §3.2).

In light of all this, we ask the following two questions:

1. Do CWEs capture the depth of L2 speakers' vocabulary knowledge? In other words, can we infer how well L2 speakers know a given vocabulary item by comparing its CWE from that of L1 speakers'(§4.1)?
2. How does word use differ across the two populations (L1 and L2 speakers), and what are the words that diverge the most/least? (§4.2)?

3 Method

3.1 Data

Since few large-scale learner corpora are readily available, a learner corpus was selected first to ensure that an appropriate native English corpus could be selected based on the nature of the chosen learner corpus. For learner corpus, we use the EF-Cambridge Open Language Database (EFCAMDAT; Huang et al., 2017; Geertzen et al., 2013), a collection of essay assignments written by non-native English speakers of various first languages. EFCAMDAT contains more than 83,000,000 word tokens in the essays written by more than 170,000 learners of English, and each essay is accompanied by metadata, including the proficiency level that ranges from 1 to 16.[1] For this study, only the essays written by Japanese learners of English are used, amounting to 1,602,328 words from 21,374 essays written by 3,441 learners.

For native English corpus, we use the Louvain Corpus of Native English Essays (LOCNESS; Granger, 2014). LOCNESS is a corpus of argumentative and literary essays written by university students in the U.S. and in the U.K. To make the speaker profile homogeneous and to ensure the comparability of the texts to EFCAMDAT, only the argumentative essays written by university students in the U.S. were included in this study. This resulted in 176 essays and 149,574 words in total.

Note that the selected subcorpus from EFCAMDAT has the mean length of 74.96 words per essay, whereas the LOCNESS counterpart has the mean length of 849.85 words per essay. This is partly due to the fact that EFCAMDAT consists of essays written by learners of varying proficiency levels, and the ones written by lower proficiency learners are much shorter. Although the two corpora are not perfectly comparable, they share the same genre (i.e., essay assignment) and are considered at least minimally appropriate for the purpose of this study. Implications and limitations of the difference between the two corpora will be further discussed in §5.2.

3.2 Model

To obtain CWEs, we used `flair` implementation of BERT (Akbik et al., 2019). BERT has rarely been, if ever, used to perform a comparative analysis of language use by multiple populations, and most studies of this kind use type-based word embeddings, as discussed in §2.2. Although a similar approach could have been taken in this study as well, BERT was preferred for a few reasons.

First, language models like BERT are pre-trained on a large amount of data; therefore, we can obtain a CWE that represents the meaning of the word *given the context* by simply feeding a word with its context (e.g., sentence) to the model. Training a language model from scratch, as is the case with word2vec, often requires a large amount of data, and this is an important advantage in favor of BERT given the limited amount of accessible L2 English texts.

Second, BERT consists of 12 (`bert-base`) or 24 (`bert-large`) layers, and a number of studies have suggested that each layer encodes different linguistic information, such as surface, syntactic, and semantic information (e.g., Tenney et al., 2019; Jawahar et al., 2019). With these insights about BERT's internal structure, different aspects of word use could potentially be elucidated by analyzing CWEs obtained from each of the BERT's internal layers. We will leave this to future studies (see §5.2) and focus on the CWEs obtained from the final layer in this paper.

Lastly, BERT's attention mechanism (Vaswani et al., 2017) allows the model to learn how much attention to pay for each word (i.e. how much to *weigh* each word) in a given context. Therefore, CWEs obtained from BERT is, in a sense, a weighted sum of all the words' embeddings in a given context. This may allow us to capture the difference in word use more fully, compared to models that only use its k neighboring words, where k is a hyperparameter, during its training phase (e.g., word2vec).

3.3 Experiment

To answer the two research questions, we need to define what it means to *compare* the word use between two populations. Here, we base our comparative analyses on the two centroids of a given word, one for each population. More specifically, the following steps were taken to obtain CWEs for each of the native and learner corpora described in §3.1.

1. Create a vocabulary list of 1,000 most frequent lexical items.
2. Obtain CWEs for each occurrence of each lexical item in the vocabulary list created in 1.
3. Calculate the centroid of the embeddings for each lexical item.

In 1, we only use the top 1,000 frequent words to ensure that the centroids obtained in 3 is a reliable representation of the word usage by the population (i.e., L1 or L2). For 2, an entire sentence was fed into BERT (Devlin et al., 2019) to obtain a CWE of each occurrence of a given word. Once the above steps are completed for each of the corpora,

[1] Full details available at: `https://corpus.mml.cam.ac.uk/faq/EFCamDat-Intro_release2.pdf`

the similarity score between the two centroids was calculated for each lexical item that appears in both of the two vocabulary lists. For example, if a word *argument* appears 15 and 30 times and in native and learner corpus, respectively, and qualifies as the 1,000 most frequent items in both corpora, the centroid of those 15 CWEs of *argument* from the native corpus and the centroid of those 30 CWEs of *argument* from the learner corpus will be compared using Euclidean distance. Since we are interested in the difference (or similarity) in the word use between the two corpora, rather than among the individuals, we calculate the ratio of inter-corpus distance to intra-corpus average distance. Formally, we define the metrics as following:

$$Score = \frac{Dist_{inter-corpus}}{Dist_{intra-corpus}} \quad (1)$$

$Dist_{\text{inter-corpus}}$ is a simple Euclidean distance between the two centroids. $Dist_{\text{intra-corpus}}$ is an average distance of each CWE from the centroid of a given word w in a given corpus c:

$$\frac{\sum_{c\in\{L1,L2\}} \sum_{i=1}^{N_{w,c}} |Centroid_{w,c} - \vec{w_{i,c}}|}{\sum_{c\in\{L1,L2\}} N_{w,c}}, \quad (2)$$

where $N_{w,c}$ represents the total number of occurrences of the word w in a given corpus c.

For research question 1, hypothesizing that the depths of L2 learners' vocabulary knowledge increase as they become more proficient in their L2, we would expect the distance score to decrease (i.e., L2 CWEs become more similar to L1 CWEs) for learners with higher proficiency levels. In order to show this, the experimental steps are slightly modified: instead of using the aggregate L2 corpus, we treat each proficiency level as a separate population; hence, the steps defined above were repeated 16 times, once per proficiency level. Each of these sub corpora will be referred to as L2-{level} (e.g., L2-6 for the level 6 sub-corpus taken from the L2 corpus).

For research question 2, no such modifications were necessary, as we are interested in investigating how the word use diverges between the two populations, as well as what words show most/least divergences.

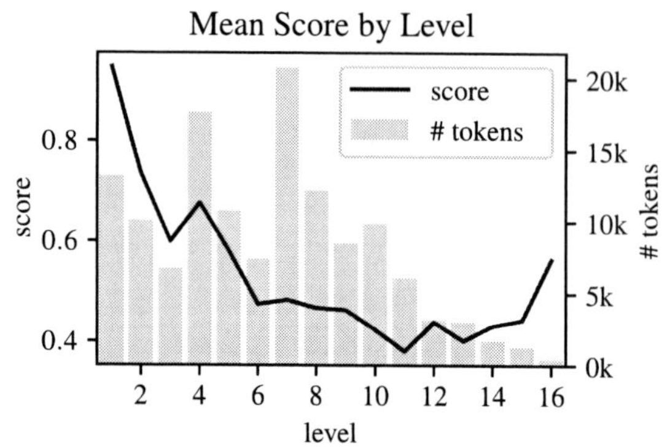

Figure 1: Mean Score by Proficiency Level

4 Results

4.1 Research question 1

A total of 100 words were found to be among the top 1,000 frequent words in all of the corpora (i.e., L1 corpus and 16 proficiency-based L2 sub-corpora). To quantify the (dis)similarities in word use between L1 corpus and each of the 16 L2 sub-corpora, we calculate the distance score defined in eq. (1) for each of these common 100 word types, and take their mean weighted by the number of tokens per word type for each of the 16 comparisons (i.e. L1 vs L2-1, L1 vs L2-2, ..., L1 vs L2-16). The results are summarized in figure 1, where the line plot represents the mean distance score, and the bar graph represents the total number of occurrences of the 100 common words per proficiency level.

We can observe an overall decreasing tendency, with the trend being particularly pronounced at levels from 1 to 11. This seems to validate the use of CWEs to measure the depth of vocabulary knowledge, hypothesizing that the depth grows (i.e. distance score should decrease) as the proficiency level becomes higher.

However, the slight increase in the mean distance score towards the highest proficiency levels is worth noting. Although a further investigation is necessary to explain this result, a few possibilities are considered here. First, as the bar graph suggests, the start of the increase in the mean distance score at level 12 coincides with the decrease in the sample size. That is to say, the number of tokens at levels 12 to 16 are substantially smaller than those at levels 1 to 11. Hence, this may be the result of small sample sizes, and the result may have been different with larger sample sizes for higher proficiency learners. Another possibility is that,

Word	Score	D_{Inter}	D_{Intra}	# (L1)	# (L2)	Word	Score	D_{Inter}	D_{Intra}	# (L1)	# (L2)
men	0.21	1.51	7.31	147	351	basketball	4.80	18.60	3.87	17	251
women	0.22	1.35	6.04	320	484	expensive	3.43	16.57	4.83	16	596
since	0.23	2.32	10.16	101	479	communication	3.04	15.42	5.08	14	214
time	0.24	2.12	8.87	288	3039	enjoy	2.73	16.29	5.97	18	831
things	0.24	1.80	7.44	111	666	concern	2.10	8.45	4.02	20	429
according	0.24	2.36	9.84	55	125	wild	1.72	8.10	4.71	37	182
one	0.26	2.55	9.97	595	2798	florida	1.65	6.37	3.85	49	128
less	0.26	1.98	7.75	82	254	name	1.33	7.62	5.72	24	2446
say	0.26	2.09	7.91	108	384	actually	1.25	11.35	9.11	38	300
even	0.27	2.83	10.64	213	594	contact	1.24	7.63	6.17	19	464

Table 1: Top 10 similar words (left) and top 10 dissimilar words (right)

because essay topics vary across proficiency levels, it may simply be the case that the topics at higher proficiency levels happened to be different from the topics L1 essays are written on. Alternatively, and more interestingly, if this U-shaped curve is truly capturing the relationship between the depth of vocabulary knowledge and proficiency level, we may have to revise our hypothesis that the distance score will monotonically decrease as a function of proficiency level. We will return to this point in §5.1.

4.2 Research question 2

A total of 465 words were found to be among the top 1,000 frequent words in both corpora. Of these 465 words, the most similar and dissimilar words were identified based on the distance score defined in eq. (1), and the results are summarized in table 1.

4.2.1 Words with smaller distances

For the 10 most similar words (left), the score ranges from 0.21 to 0.27, meaning that the distance between the L1 centroid and the L2 centroid was about 4-5 times smaller than the average distance between the centroid and each of the word token *within* the corpus. The 2 most similar words, *men* and *women*, are perhaps due to the similar essay topics coincidentally present in the two corpora. A naive comparison of the 10 most frequent words that appear in the same sentence as the word *men* show that *women*, *equal*, *society*, and *children* often co-occur with *men* in L1 corpus, while *women*, *work*, and *equal* are the common neighboring words in L2 corpus. This large overlap suggests that *men* and *women* both occur in the context of an essay prompt about gender equality in both corpora.

More interestingly, other words in table 1 include generic words that could appear in a variety of contexts, such as *since*, *according*, *even*, and *things*.

Word	# (L1)	Word	# (L2)
would	22	though	69
people	21	people	53
one	16	work	29
though	15	one	29
may	14	many	25
time	14	think	25
make	10	get	24
could	10	like	22
many	9	time	22
use	9	go	22

Table 2: Top 10 Co-occurring words with *even* in L1 corpus (left) and in L2 corpus (right)

Since the context in which these words appear is likely to be affected by the domain of the text, it is reasonable to expect these words to have high inter-corpus distances; however, they all have relatively small inter-corpus distance. For example, the 10 most frequently co-occurring items of the word *even* in each of the two corpora are summarized in table 2. In both corpora, *though*, *many*, and *people* seem to co-occur frequently with the word *even*. A possible interpretation is that, in argumentative essays, both L1 and L2 English speakers use *even* as a way to express concession or contrast (as in *even though*), and that the conceding or contrasting proposition, which is secondary to the main proposition, tends to be general.

In a similar vein, *things* frequently co-occur with *people*, *money*, *life*, and *time* in L1 corpus, and with *people*, *time*, and *life* in L2 corpus. This overlapping in the co-occurring words seems to suggest that L1 and L2 English speakers both use the word *things* as a way to describe general facts or truths about the world, pertaining to people, money, and time. This may be due to the genre of the L1 and L2 texts–because they both contain argumentative es-

Word	# (L1)	Word	# (L2)
many	10	like	16
prayer	7	'm	13
would	6	however	11
people	4	people	10
religion	4	work	9
society	3	know	7
public	3	show	5
students	3	much	5
recite	3	really	5
times	3	person	5

Table 3: Top 10 Co-occurring words with *actually* in L1 corpus (left) and in L2 corpus (right)

says,[2] these general statements may be used to set the scene before introducing the main arguments.

4.2.2 Words with larger distances

Of the 10 most dissimilar words (right), *basketball* had the highest score of 4.80, meaning that the distance between the two centroids was almost 5 times larger than the average distance within each of the corpora. The co-occurring words in the L1 corpus, such as *respect*, *men's*, *women*, *coach*, and *colleges* suggest that L1 English speakers tend to use *basketball* in the context of collegiate athletics. In the L2 corpus, on the other hand, the frequent co-occurring words, such as *afternoon*, *every*, *games*, and *computer* seem to suggest that the word is used in the context of hobbies or daily routines. This may not be so much of a difference in the word use as a difference in the domain, since EFCAMDAT contains non-argumentative essay assignments, such as describing routines.

Table 3 lists the top 10 co-occurring words of another dissimilar word *actually* in L1 corpus (left) and in L2 corpus (right). Apart from the effect of domain difference similar to above observation on *basketball*, table 3 reveals interesting ways in which its usage differs between the two population.

First, it is worth noting the contrast between *even* and *actually*. That is to say, although both of them are adverb and carry less "content" compared to more strongly content words, such as verbs and nouns, *even* is robust to the domain difference, whereas *actually* is not. This may be explained by their use in discourse. On the one hand, *actually* is commonly used to introduce a piece of information expected to be surprising to the audience, and the proposition is often specific to the topic or domain of the text. *Even*, on the other hand, can be used to mark concession or contrast (as in *even though*) as discussed above, and the subordinate clause introduced by *even* tends to be a general statement to which the main clause (often the main proposition) is antithetical.

Second, in L2 corpus, *however* is frequently used in combination with *actually*. A manual inspection of these 11 sentences where *actually* and *however* co-occurred shows that these two words occur within the same clause in 4 of these 11 sentences, meaning that they are used to modify the same proposition as shown in an example below:

(1) However, actually it's still difficult for women to continue their work after they get married and have children. *(writing id = 1064583)*

Notably, L1 corpus contains only 1 co-occurrence of *actually* and *however*, and it is not within the same clause. This difference may reasonably be attributed to the difference in the size of the two corpora; however, it may be the case that the meaning of *however* is construed slightly differently by the two populations. However, whether this is a difference in meaning (e.g., *actually* containing contrastive meaning or not) or a mere collocation knowledge (e.g., *actually* and *however* are simply not used together conventionally) remains inconclusive.

5 Discussion

5.1 Implication

This paper argued for the use of CWEs obtained from a large pre-trained language model to analyze the word use of L1 and L2 speakers of English and presented the preliminary results. We found that (i) the mean distance between L1 CWEs and L2 CWEs of a given word tended to decrease as a function of proficiency level, and that (ii) while similar uses of a given word by the two population are due to either a domain effect (e.g., *men* and *women*) or a particular function the word plays in the discourse (e.g., *things* and *even*), dissimilar uses of a word, on the other hand, were mostly the result of domain differences (e.g., *basketball*).

For (i), an exception to the overall decreasing trend was observed at levels 12 to 16, where the mean distance score slightly increased. This may be due to methodological reasons, such as imbal-

[2] Texts in EFCAMDAT are all essay assignments, but they include non-argumentative ones as well.

anced sample sizes and essay topics (see §4.1). Alternatively, U-shaped curve may actually be representative of the true relationship between the depth of vocabulary knowledge and proficiency level, rather than caused by some methodological limitations. This phenomenon, where a certain aspect of linguistic knowledge appears to *regress* in the process of L2 learning, is referred to as *back-sliding* or *regression* (Selinker, 1972;Selinker and Lamendella, 1981; Lantolf and Aljaafreh, 1995). If this was the case, it may be an oversimplification to operationalize the depth of vocabulary knowledge as how similar an L2 learner's use of a given word is to that of L1 speakers'. Although this point remains inconclusive in our preliminary results, it is an important question to address in the future research.

5.2 Limitations and future directions

Although this study contributes to the existing body of literature by arguing for the use of CWEs obtained from a large pre-trained language model to investigate L1 and L2 Englishes, some limitations and future directions were identified.

First, as has been mentioned in §3.1, the mean sentence length of the selected L2 subcorpus is much shorter (74.96 words) than that of the L1 corpus (849.85). Since longer essays may contain more anaphoric expressions such as pronouns, it may affect the contexts in which words occur. However, since low proficiency L2 speakers tend to write shorter sentences, it is challenging to balance the mean sentence length across the two populations.

Second, we opted for BERT as a way to obtain CWEs because of its use of the entire sentence to contextualize the word embeddings. However, this might have amplified the domain effect (i.e., differences in topic, prompt). Hence, using a model that leverages more immediately neighboring words (by adjusting the hyperparamter of n-gram size), such as word2vec (Mikolov et al., 2013a), separately for each of the two corpora may enable a more domain-agnostic comparison of the word use. In fact, Sikos and Padó (2018) used English and German corpora of different domains to train separate frame embeddings using word2vec, yet the results yielded meaningful comparisons and implications. However, training a model from scratch is not an viable option for the data used in this study, since some sub-copora, especially the ones with a higher proficiency, had substantially smaller sample sizes.

Third, BERT's layers have been shown to encode distinct linguistic information (Rogers et al., 2020). For example, middle layers encode syntactic information (Hewitt and Manning, 2019), whereas higher (closer to the final) layers encode more abstract semantic information (Jawahar et al., 2019; Tenney et al., 2019). Although this study used the outputs from the final layer, future studies could obtain different insights by obtaining outputs from each of the 12 layers.

Lastly, once the above limitations are resolved and more meaningful differences in word use between L1 and L2 Englishes can be reliably obtained, it may be promising to investigate the embedding space in multilingual BERT (Devlin et al., 2019). For example, hypothesizing that the different word use is the result of L1 transfer, the deviation of the centroid vector may be in the direction of the vector of an equivalent word in the learners' L1 (e.g., Japanese speakers' use of an English word *love* may be slightly shifted towards its Japanese counterpart *ai*, compared to native English speakers' use of the same word).

Acknowledgements

We thank the two anonymous reviewers for their insightful and constructive feedback.

References

Alan Akbik, Tanja Bergmann, Duncan Blythe, Kashif Rasul, Stefan Schweter, and Roland Vollgraf. 2019. FLAIR: An easy-to-use framework for state-of-the-art NLP. In *NAACL 2019, 2019 Annual Conference of the North American Chapter of the Association for Computational Linguistics (Demonstrations)*, pages 54–59.

Marco Del Tredici and Raquel Fernández. 2017. Semantic variation in online communities of practice. In *IWCS 2017 - 12th International Conference on Computational Semantics - Long papers*.

Marco Del Tredici, Raquel Fernández, and Gemma Boleda. 2019. Short-term meaning shift: A distributional exploration. In *Proceedings of the 2019 Conference of the North American Chapter of the Association for Computational Linguistics: Human Language Technologies, Volume 1 (Long and Short Papers)*, pages 2069–2075, Minneapolis, Minnesota. Association for Computational Linguistics.

Jacob Devlin, Ming-Wei Chang, Kenton Lee, and Kristina Toutanova. 2019. BERT: Pre-training of deep bidirectional transformers for language understanding. In *Proceedings of the 2019 Conference of the North American Chapter of the Association for*

Computational Linguistics: Human Language Technologies, Volume 1 (Long and Short Papers), pages 4171–4186, Minneapolis, Minnesota. Association for Computational Linguistics.

Katrin Erk. 2012. Vector space models of word meaning and phrase meaning: A survey. *Language and Linguistics Compass*, 6(10):635–653.

Jeroen Geertzen, Theodora Alexopoulou, Anna Korhonen, et al. 2013. Automatic linguistic annotation of large scale l2 databases: The ef-cambridge open language database (efcamdat). In *Proceedings of the 31st Second Language Research Forum. Somerville, MA: Cascadilla Proceedings Project*, pages 240–254. Citeseer.

Jennifer M Goldschneider and Robert M DeKeyser. 2001. Explaining the "natural order of l2 morpheme acquisition" in english: A meta-analysis of multiple determinants. *Language learning*, 51(1):1–50.

Sylviane Granger. 2014. The computer learner corpus: a versatile new source of data for sla research. In *Learner English on computer*, pages 3–18. Routledge.

William L. Hamilton, Jure Leskovec, and Dan Jurafsky. 2016. Diachronic word embeddings reveal statistical laws of semantic change. In *Proceedings of the 54th Annual Meeting of the Association for Computational Linguistics (Volume 1: Long Papers)*, pages 1489–1501, Berlin, Germany. Association for Computational Linguistics.

Zellig S Harris. 1954. Distributional structure. *Word*, 10(2-3):146–162.

John Hewitt and Christopher D. Manning. 2019. A structural probe for finding syntax in word representations. In *Proceedings of the 2019 Conference of the North American Chapter of the Association for Computational Linguistics: Human Language Technologies, Volume 1 (Long and Short Papers)*, pages 4129–4138, Minneapolis, Minnesota. Association for Computational Linguistics.

Yan Huang, Jeroen Geertzen, Rachel Baker, Anna Korhonen, Theodora Alexopoulou, and EF Education First. 2017. The ef cambridge open language database (efcamdat): Information for users.

Ganesh Jawahar, Benoît Sagot, and Djamé Seddah. 2019. What does BERT learn about the structure of language? In *Proceedings of the 57th Annual Meeting of the Association for Computational Linguistics*, pages 3651–3657, Florence, Italy. Association for Computational Linguistics.

James P Lantolf and Ali Aljaafreh. 1995. Second language learning in the zone of proximal development: A revolutionary experience. *International Journal of Educational Research*, 23(7):619–632.

Nelson F. Liu, Matt Gardner, Yonatan Belinkov, Matthew E. Peters, and Noah A. Smith. 2019. Linguistic knowledge and transferability of contextual representations. In *Proceedings of the 2019 Conference of the North American Chapter of the Association for Computational Linguistics: Human Language Technologies, Volume 1 (Long and Short Papers)*, pages 1073–1094, Minneapolis, Minnesota. Association for Computational Linguistics.

Xiaofei Lu. 2012. The relationship of lexical richness to the quality of esl learners' oral narratives. *The Modern Language Journal*, 96(2):190–208.

Tomas Mikolov, Kai Chen, Greg Corrado, and Jeffrey Dean. 2013a. Efficient estimation of word representations in vector space.

Tomas Mikolov, Wen-tau Yih, and Geoffrey Zweig. 2013b. Linguistic regularities in continuous space word representations. In *Proceedings of the 2013 Conference of the North American Chapter of the Association for Computational Linguistics: Human Language Technologies*, pages 746–751, Atlanta, Georgia. Association for Computational Linguistics.

James Milton. 2009. Measuring second language vocabulary acquisition. In *Measuring Second Language Vocabulary Acquisition*. Multilingual Matters.

Ian SP Nation. 2001. *Learning vocabulary in another language*. Cambridge university press.

John M Norris and Lourdes Ortega. 2009. Towards an organic approach to investigating caf in instructed sla: The case of complexity. *Applied linguistics*, 30(4):555–578.

Matthew E. Peters, Mark Neumann, Mohit Iyyer, Matt Gardner, Christopher Clark, Kenton Lee, and Luke Zettlemoyer. 2018. Deep contextualized word representations. In *Proceedings of the 2018 Conference of the North American Chapter of the Association for Computational Linguistics: Human Language Technologies, Volume 1 (Long Papers)*, pages 2227–2237, New Orleans, Louisiana. Association for Computational Linguistics.

Manfred Pienemann. 1998. *Language processing and second language development: Processability theory*, volume 15. John Benjamins Publishing.

Anna Rogers, Olga Kovaleva, and Anna Rumshisky. 2020. A primer in BERTology: What we know about how BERT works. *Transactions of the Association for Computational Linguistics*, 8:842–866.

G Salton. 1971. The smart system. *Retrieval Results and Future Plans*, 260.

Larry Selinker. 1972. Interlanguage. *International Review of Applied Linguistics in Language Teaching*, 10(1-4):209–231.

Larry Selinker and John T Lamendella. 1981. Updating the interlanguage hypothesis. *Studies in Second Language Acquisition*, 3(2):201–220.

Jennifer Sikos and Sebastian Padó. 2018. Using embeddings to compare FrameNet frames across languages. In *Proceedings of the First Workshop on Linguistic Resources for Natural Language Processing*, pages 91–101, Santa Fe, New Mexico, USA. Association for Computational Linguistics.

Peter Skehan et al. 1998. *A cognitive approach to language learning*. Oxford University Press.

Ian Tenney, Dipanjan Das, and Ellie Pavlick. 2019. BERT rediscovers the classical NLP pipeline. In *Proceedings of the 57th Annual Meeting of the Association for Computational Linguistics*, pages 4593–4601, Florence, Italy. Association for Computational Linguistics.

Ashish Vaswani, Noam Shazeer, Niki Parmar, Jakob Uszkoreit, Llion Jones, Aidan N. Gomez, Lukasz Kaiser, and Illia Polosukhin. 2017. Attention is all you need.

Marjorie Wesche and T Sima Paribakht. 1996. Assessing second language vocabulary knowledge: Depth versus breadth. *Canadian Modern Language Review*, 53(1):13–40.

The instructional effectiveness of automatically generated exercises for learning French grammatical gender: preliminary results

Stephen Bodnar
Department of Linguistics, University of Tübingen, Germany
stephen.bodnar@uni-tuebingen.de

Abstract

Research into Automatic Exercise Generation (AEG) contributes new tools aimed at reducing the barrier to creating practice material, but few have been deployed in actual instruction with real learners. The present study extends previous work by employing AEG technology in instruction with L2 learners to evaluate its pedagogical effectiveness. Thirty-two second language learners of French were assigned to either a treatment condition, who practised with generated exercises, or a control condition that did no extra work. Both groups completed pre-, post-, and delayed post-tests. Participants in the treatment condition also completed questionnaires that elicited data on their in-practice emotions and the situations in which they arose. Our preliminary results suggest that AEG-based instruction can be pedagogically effective and support positive learning experiences, help to identify aspects of the instruction that could be improved, and suggest that a peer review mechanism could have an important role in future CALL platforms that use generated exercises.

1 Introduction

Despite the success of artificial intelligence in many aspects of our daily lives, sightings of Intelligent Computer Assisted Language Learning (ICALL) systems outside of the research lab remain rare. One barrier to their more wide-spread adoption is that equipping these systems with enough exercises for sustained practice is costly, requires a special skill set, and is beyond the scope of many projects. Fortunately, a growing body of research is investigating technology for Automatic Exercise Generation (AEG), which employs language technologies and linguistic resources to automatically generate practice materials.

The present study extends work in AEG by exploring the feasibility of using generated exercises with real learners. The learning context is an e-learning tool we have developed called COLLIE. While previous work tends to focus on English, COLLIE targets French grammatical gender, a linguistic target that learners find difficult (Lyster and Izquierdo, 2009). COLLIE scaffolds learning of gender-predictive noun suffixes with nine exercise types, including three spoken exercises, all of which can be generated automatically from arbitrary French texts, and an instruction sequence adapted from an effective human-led intervention.

We evaluated COLLIE by recruiting 32 French L2 learners from three North American universities. Half of the participants were assigned to a control condition, while another half completed an automated version of the instructional treatment in Lyster and Izquierdo's (2009) study adapted to online self-study and featuring only automatically generated exercises. In this paper we report on our findings showing positive learning outcomes from pre-test to delayed-posttest, suggesting that AEG can provide an effective context for learning a challenging element of French grammar. Self-reports from learners who practised with COLLIE report largely positive emotional experiences, and responses to open item questionnaires pinpoint sources of frustration, related to speech recognition and the instructional format, with the majority of negative experiences not attributable to the use of AEG.

2 Background

Research on tools aimed at reducing the burden of creating learning materials for ICALL systems has taken place since at least the early 2000s (e.g., Heift and Toole, 2002) and since then its value has continued to be recognised (e.g., Presson et al., 2013). Studies in the area aim at developing computational methods, often based on underlying natural language processing technology but not always (e.g., Malafeev, 2014), for automatically creating L2 practice exercises of different types.

An important aspect of research into AEG is

Stephen Bodnar. The instructional effectiveness of automatically generated exercises for learning French grammatical gender: preliminary results. *Proceedings of the 11th Workshop on Natural Language Processing for Computer Assisted Language Learning (NLP4CALL 2022)*. Linköping Electronic Conference Proceedings 190: 10–22.

evaluation. In our experience, the evaluations in the literature can be grouped into three main concerns:

- evaluations of the technology underlying the exercise generation (e.g., Heift and Toole, 2002; Chalvin et al., 2013; Freitas et al., 2013; Aldabe et al., 2006; Beinborn, 2016; Colin, 2020; Ferreira and Pereira Jr., 2018; Malafeev, 2015; Perez-Beltrachini et al., 2012; Zilio et al., 2018; Baptista et al., 2016; Zanetti et al., 2021);

- human expert judgments of exercise quality along different dimensions (e.g., Chinkina and Meurers, 2017; Chinkina et al., 2020; Burstein and Marcu, 2005; Antonsen et al., 2013; Chalvin et al., 2013; Pilán et al., 2017; Pilán, 2016; Slavuj and Prskalo, 2021; Malafeev, 2014; Freitas et al., 2013); and

- reports from actual tool use by students (e.g., Chinkina et al., 2020; Malafeev, 2014; Antonsen and Argese, 2018; Antonsen et al., 2013; see also Galvan et al., 2016) or instructors (Toole and Heift, 2002; Burstein and Marcu, 2005; Antonsen and Argese, 2018).

Most evaluations fall into the first two categories, and while the third type is certainly related to our interest in the readiness of AEG for deploying to real learning situations, none of the studies investigate the instructional effectiveness of generated exercises.

A crucial step in evaluating AEG is establishing that new algorithms can deliver real value to L2 language instructors and learners. To this end, the present study explores the extent to which practice with automatically generated exercises delivers effective L2 learning. In this context, it is clearly important to study how learners' proficiency on target linguistic features changes as a result of practice. Alongside L2 proficiency, learners' affective (i.e., emotion-related) experiences in the practice activities are also important to consider because of the potential for different emotional experiences to influence learning outcomes. The pathways between emotions and L2 proficiency development are theorised to be dynamic and bidirectional (Shao et al., 2020), and to interact with personal goals as well as the environment (Dörnyei, 2009), and so are very complex, but evidence for the important role of emotions in SLA is emerging: Teimouri et al. (2019) in their meta-analysis of SLA research on anxiety found strong support for a negative relationship between anxiety and L2 achievement, suggesting that feelings of "tension, apprehension, nervousness, and worry" (p. 2, as cited in Spielberger, 1983) hinder L2 learning at a macro level. In a longitudinal study of classroom learning, Saito et al. (2018) found evidence for the facilitating effects of positive emotions on practice behaviour and L2 development.

In the context of self-study CALL practice using AEG, anxiety is perhaps less likely to play an important role, but due to the uncertain readiness of the emerging technology, other negative emotions such as confusion, frustration or boredom could hinder learning. Similarly, in-practice feelings of enjoyment, interest, curiosity, or confidence could "facilitate holistic thinking and creative problem solving, broaden the scope of attention and cognition, ... and enhance intrinsic motivation and long-term efforts" (Shao et al., 2020, p. 8). Thus, affective experiences play an important role in L2 instruction and so are a valuable dimension of evaluating instructional effectiveness. For these reasons, in the present study we target the following two research questions:

- To what extent can instruction based on automatically generated practice exercises improve learners' L2 grammatical accuracy?

- To what extent does AEG-based instruction support positive learning experiences?

3 The present study

The study proceeded in three phases. In the design phase we searched the SLA literature for an instructional approach to provide a solid pedagogical basis for the to-be-generated exercises that at the same time appeared technically feasible to automate. The approach we identified is a practice sequence developed by Lyster (2016, 2018) with three types of activities: *noticing activities* expose learners to written and spoken language carefully chosen to draw their attention to L2 features that are difficult to learn; *awareness activities* stimulate learners to reflect on the patterns they see in the language; *output activities* prompt learners to test their hypotheses by producing written and spoken language and receiving feedback. A successful intervention study in the SLA literature

(Lyster and Izquierdo, 2009) provided a concrete example of the practice sequence and its exercises. The intervention guided learners to notice and use noun suffixes in French that predict grammatical gender (e.g., most nouns ending in *-ette* tend to be feminine), and we adopted it as a reference for the technology we would develop. In what follows, we refer to this study as the *original intervention*.

In the development phase, we developed the technology to automatically generate the 9 different exercises used in the original intervention. One or two could not be used because they were technically too challenging, and we replaced those with similar ones that were technically feasible. This included an exercise generation pipeline using NLP, various linguistic resources, and a learner model (see Section 4.1). To be able to collect data on the effectiveness of the exercises with real learners, we also developed user interfaces for the exercises, a Learning Management System (LMS) for researchers to carry out experiments, and a number of research instruments (see Section 4.2).

In the evaluation phase we arranged a new intervention modelled closely after the original intervention we identified in the design stage. Keeping our planned evaluation similar to the original intervention had two advantages: 1) we could be confident our instructional treatment had validity, and 2) the human-led study could serve as a gold standard against which we could compare learning outcomes of a second intervention that used automatically generated exercises (see Malafeev, 2014 and Chinkina et al., 2020, who use a similar approach of comparing ratings of exercises to a human gold standard).

4 Materials and Methods

4.1 Exercise generation pipeline

Among the existing methods for exercise generation (see Perez-Beltrachini et al., 2012 for a discussion of different methods), our approach has the most in common with the systems developed by Heift and Toole (2002) and Heck and Meurers (2022) as our pipeline relies on NLP tools to handle arbitrary documents as input (as opposed to being based on static corpora, e.g. Pilán et al., 2017, or automatically generated language, e.g. Perez-Beltrachini et al., 2012; Verweij, 2020). Our approach differs from (Heift and Toole, 2002) because the pipeline requires another NLP component, namely a dependency parser, and unlike the work by Heck and Meurers (2022), our pipeline does not accept HTML but is limited to plain text, as preserving the original look and feel of the document was not an important requirement to realise the instructional approach we selected.

The pipeline can be divided into two stages, an intake stage, and a generation stage (see Figure 1).

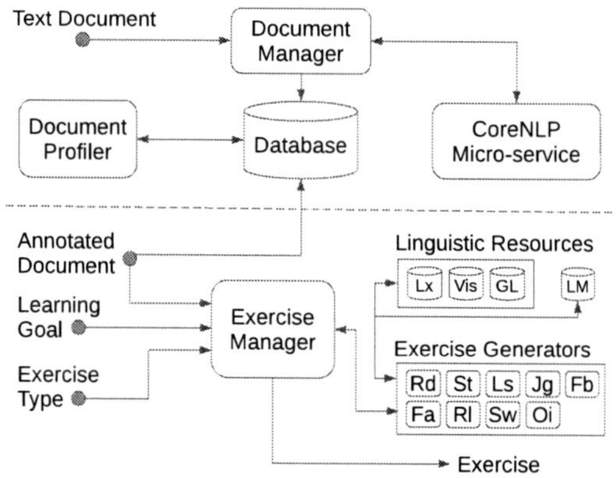

Figure 1: The exercise generation pipeline consists of an intake stage (top) and a generation stage (bottom). The system supports generating nine exercise types for practising French grammatical gender: Reading / Noticing (Rd); Sorting (St); Listing (Ls); Judging (Jg); Fill-in-the-Blanks targeting determiners (Fb) and determiners and adjectives (Fa); Riddles (Rl); Say the Word that Fits (Sw); and Object Identification (Oi). During generation the system makes use of three linguistic resources, Lexique (Lx); a database of readily visualisable words (Vis); and GLAWI (GL), as well as a Learner Model (LM).

In the intake stage, the pipeline stands ready for processing. Documents can be submitted to a Document Manager component by instructors or researchers through a web authoring tool; alternatively, larger numbers of documents can be batch processed using a script utility. Once received, the document is parsed into a structured data representation with Part of Speech tags and Dependency Parsing annotations. These annotations are obtained automatically using the Stanford CoreNLP toolkit (Manning et al., 2014), which we have implemented as a remote micro-service. Following parsing, the document and its corresponding parsed data structure is saved to a database for later retrieval. Immediately after being stored, a Document Profiler component analyses the document annotations to search for instances of language that are suitable for a given learning goal; for each supported learning goal, matching instances are counted, and the results of this document intake are also saved to the database as a cached profile to support efficient ranking of documents according to a learning goal of interest, or to discover which learning goals are supported by a particular document.

For the generation stage, we implement on-the-fly exercise generation. This means that after documents are fully processed no exercises are generated immediately. Instead, the system waits until there is a request from a user. Requests specify three arguments, 1) a document, 2) a learning goal and 3) an exercise type. These arguments are received by an Exercise Manager component, which orchestrates the generation of the exercise. First, the manager looks in the database to see if an exercise for this triplet has already been generated, and if found it is returned. If not, the manager searches in its registry of exercise generators. Exercise Generators in the system are specialized components that know how to build exactly one exercise type for exactly one learning goal. At pipeline initialisation time, the system searches through its codebase and registers all components implementing an Exercise Transformer interface. Then, when a request to generate an exercise arrives, the Exercise Manager searches this registry to see if it has a suitable generator and if so, delegates the exercise generation request.

Exercise generators all have in common that they iterate over the lines of a document to perform checks on each line for pedagogical relevance. These checks involve searching for dependency parse relations as well as additional linguistic criteria. Each line is processed differently depending on the results of the checks: if the generator determines that a line contains an instance of the learning goal (e.g., French grammatical gender), the line is transformed to a data structure with a format dictated by the particular exercise type being generated (e.g., a fill-in-the-blank). Otherwise, the generator either includes the raw text as is for meaningful context, as with the Reading exercise generator, or discards the line, as in the Riddle exercise. Depending on the exercise, generators employ additional linguistic resources for different purposes:

- Checking for adherence to predicted grammatical gender: When a generator encounters a target word with a gender-predictive suffix (e.g., words ending in *-ette* are nearly always feminine), it must verify that the gender predicted by the suffix is indeed the word's actual gender (there can be exceptions, such as *squelette* "skeleton" which has masculine grammatical gender). The pipeline integrates a Lexique database (New et al., 2004) to look up the gender of words with predictive suffixes and avoid words that are exceptions.

- Identification of readily visualisable words: In the case of Object Identification exercises, the generator must determine if a word with a gender-predictive suffix can be easily depicted in an image. For this, we developed an in-house resource that distinguishes between words that can be visualised easily (e.g., *une éruption* "an eruption") or with difficulty (*e.g., une abstraction "an abstraction"*). The resource draws on three English-language databases in psycholinguistics containing ratings for words related to their ease of visualisation (Wilson, 1988; Brysbaert et al., 2013; Scott et al., 2018). In these partially overlapping databases, each word has a score related to how readily it can be visualised. As an approximation we first automatically translated headwords to French and then combined available ratings from the different databases by taking their mean. Finally, we set a threshold by experimenting with different values and choosing the lowest value that did not return unsuitable words. [1]

- Clue creation for Riddle exercises: Our approach to clue creation is straightforward. We integrate a linguistic resource called GLAWI (Hathout and Sajous, 2016), which is a lexical database containing definitions (among other information) derived from Wiktionnaire. The riddle generator obtains clues for a target word by loading the relevant definitions from GLAWI. Because the target word can sometimes appear in the returned definitions, in a second step we replace all occurrences of the target with underscore characters to ensure the riddle is not too easy.[2]

[1] We also manually reviewed the images to mark content that was inappropriate for an educational context (e.g., nudity, violence) but a detailed presentation of this is beyond the scope of this paper.

[2] For a more creative approach to clue generation for those working with English as a target language, see Galvan et al., 2016

- Selecting previously unseen words: an additional resource used by some generators is the system's Learner Model. The learner model tracks which nouns a learner has seen and how often. For example, in Reading exercises, when a target word appears on the page, the word's appearance is logged and registered with the learner model. This data is then an important resource during the generation of the Judgment exercise, which aims to help the learner generalise their knowledge from words they have already seen to words with the same gender predictive suffixes that they have not yet encountered.

Currently the exercise pipeline supports generation for French grammatical gender with nine exercises (see Figures 2 - 4 below for examples), and support for more languages is planned for the future (e.g., grammatical gender for Dutch and German). The pipeline is implemented in Java, and is designed to be modular so that it can be integrated into any back-end web application based on the Java virtual machine.

4.2 COLLIE e-learning platform

To support our evaluation of AEG, we developed a web-based e-learning platform that learners could use and into which the exercise pipeline described above could be embedded. The platform we have developed is called COLLIE, an abbreviation of *Counter-balanced Language Learning & Instruction made Easier*. The name and platform draws inspiration from Lyster's (2007) approach to balancing meaning-focused classroom learning, which can fall short of pushing learners to become fully accurate speakers, with accuracy-focused practice where they are pushed to notice L2 features that are difficult to learn, reflect on and apply patterns in the L2, and practice producing written and spoken language. The vision for COLLIE is to make it easier for teachers to supplement their classroom-based activities, which are usually about communicating, with accuracy-focused exercises that students can practice on their own time, using content related to their classroom activities.

In its current implementation, COLLIE supports written and spoken practice with immediate feedback. Scaffolded feedback is feasible because of the system's closed exercise design and narrow focus on grammatical gender, though expanding to support other learning goals or more open exercises would require a more sophisticated feedback mechanism (c.f. Rudzewitz et al., 2018). To support feedback in spoken exercises, we rely on a commercial Automatic Speech Recognition (ASR) service provided by Google Cloud (Google Cloud, nd) for transcribing recordings before they are processed by the system's feedback module. The recognition model used by the system is for European French (language tag 'fr-FR'), and we use a mechanism offered by the service to provide a set of hints consisting of all possible combinations of French singular definite and indefinite determiners and a target noun (e.g. *le squelette* | *la squelette* | *un squelette* | *une squelette*). This setting helps to guide the ASR towards transcriptions that are most likely for a given practice item.

As a web application, COLLIE consists of a back-end web server based on the Grails framework and a front-end set of user interfaces that communicate using HTTP requests. The front-end interface generates requests, which are received at specific URL endpoints by the back-end for processing by different application modules. The modules are implemented in Java and Groovy as object-oriented classes and deliver core functionalities from the AEG and LMS domains related to entities such as Document, Exercise, User, LogEvent, SpeechRecording and so on. All modules have accompanying unit tests to support refactoring.

Results from back-end processing are serialised to JSON and returned to the front-end for rendering. All user interfaces for the platform are implemented using the React.js single page web application framework. User interface elements are modular and paremeterised into reusable components (e.g., a VoiceRecorder for audio recording).

4.3 Instruments

To measure changes in French grammatical accuracy, we adopted three proficiency tests used in the original intervention, two oral production measures and a binary-choice test. As annotations for the oral production recordings are not yet complete, in this paper we present the binary-choice test results as a preliminary indicator of instructional effectiveness. Participants completed the test on the COLLIE platform. They viewed 80 different items featuring words with gender-predictive suffixes one at a time (see Figure 5).

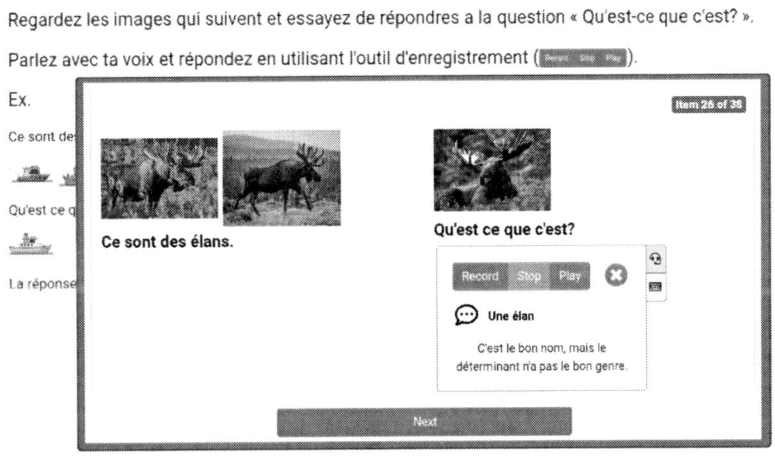

Figure 2: In the *Object Identification* exercise, learners must name the object they see on the right while using the correct determiner. This is a spoken exercise, where student's answers are first transcribed using speech recognition, and then evaluated for correctness.

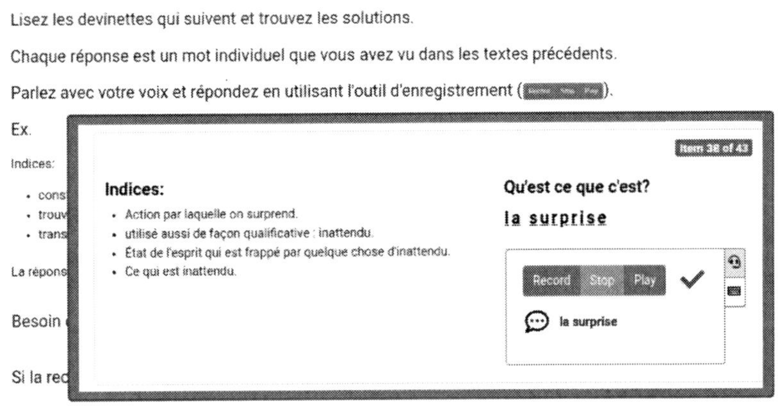

Figure 3: In *Riddle* exercises, clues appear on the left in bullet points, which learners must read to guess the determiner and noun on the right (in blanks). Clues are selected automatically, and because their helpfulness can vary, there is a hint button that if pressed reveals approximately half of the letters for the noun.

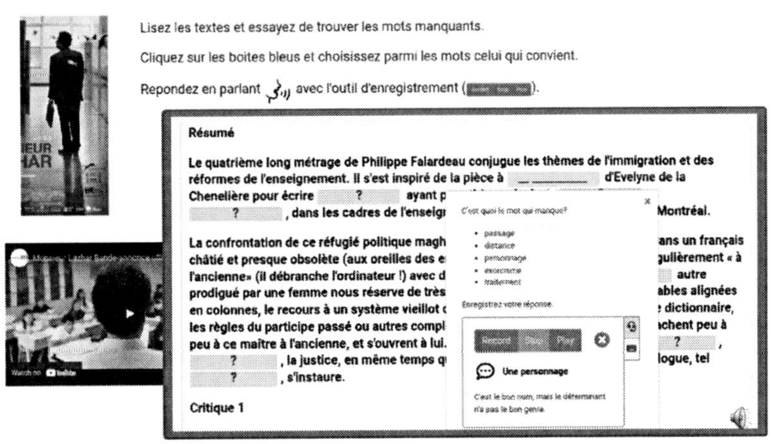

Figure 4: The *Say the Word that Fits* exercise asks students to fill blanks in a document by speaking the correct determiner and noun combination. In the cases where speech recognition does not work accurately, which can be the case sometimes for some participants, there is a keyboard icon they can press to type their answer.

Presented with each word were buttons they could click to choose between a masculine and feminine determiner. Participants received instructions and completed a short practice test before starting the actual test.

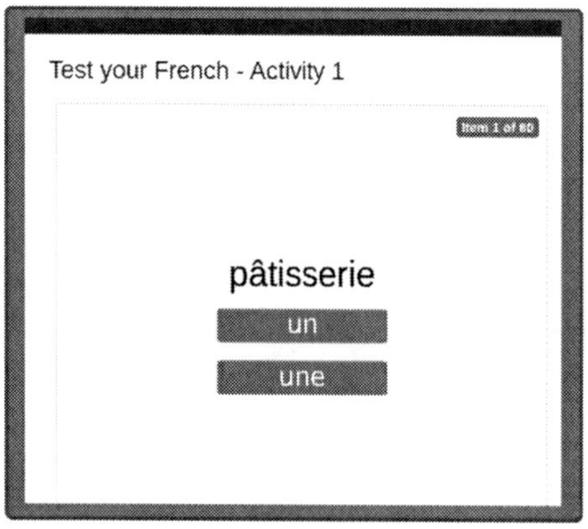

Figure 5: An example item from the binary-choice test.

Along with the proficiency measures, we also employed a questionnaire to measure affective experiences related to the practice exercises. The instrument we selected is based on the well-known Achievement Emotions Questionnaire (Pekrun et al., 2002) which is now gaining attention in SLA research (e.g., Shao et al., 2019). In our adapted version of the questionnaire (see Figure 6), participants reported how frequently they felt an emotion (Diener et al., 2009) in response to the following prompt:

> Please think about what you have been doing and experiencing during today's grammar exercises. Then report how often you experienced each of the following feelings, using the scale below. For each item, select a number from 1 to 5, and indicate that number with a mouse-click.

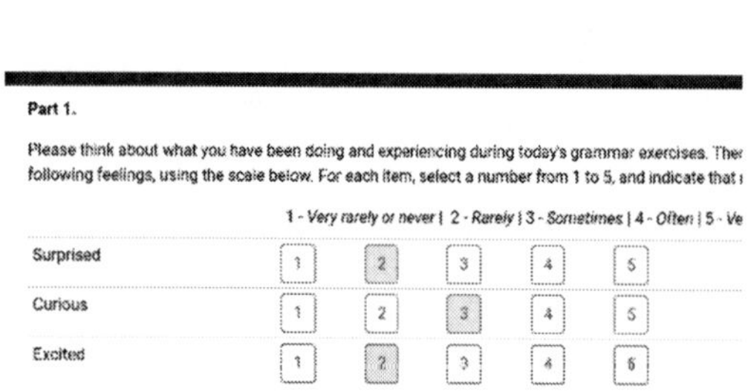

Figure 6: A close-up of the questionnaire used to elicit data on participants' emotions during practice.

The questionnaire included 7 positive valence emotions and 7 negative valence emotions, where *valence* refers to whether an emotion is positive, like feeling interested or curious, or negative, like feeling bored or confused. Participants responded using a 5-point scale, from very rarely (1), to rarely (2), to sometimes (3), to often (4), or very often and always (5).

Along with these quantitative items, the questionnaire also included open-ended items to prompt learners to describe in their own words the situations in which they felt the emotions they reported.

4.4 Data collection

For the evaluation of COLLIE and its AEG technology, we arranged an intervention closely modelled after the original intervention by Lyster and Izquierdo (2009). In Fall of 2021 we recruited 32 participants from three North American universities. The participants were intermediate-level learners of French and were actively attending a French course at the time.

The entire data collection took place over 9 weeks (see Figure 7). At week 1 participants completed the pretest. Immediately following the pretest they were assigned to a treatment or control condition. The mechanism used for assignment was an anticlustering algorithm available in R (Papenberg and Klau, 2021) which distributed participants between the two conditions based on their pretest scores in order to ensure the two conditions were balanced at the outset. Over the next three weeks participants in the treatment condition completed three practice sessions, once per week, and following practice an exit survey on approximately the fourth week. Both groups completed a post-test on the sixth week of the study, and a delayed post-test on the ninth and final week.

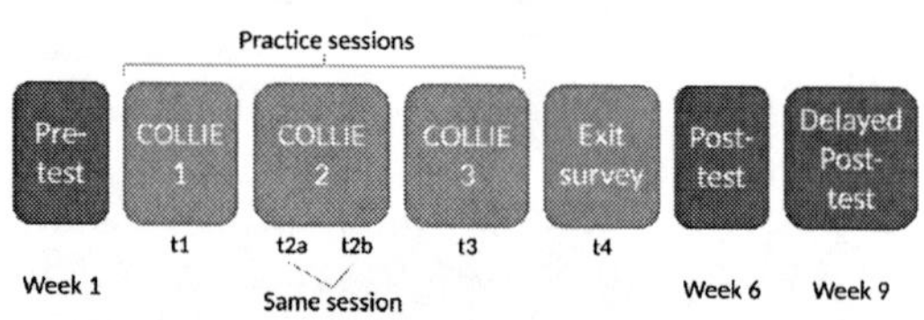

Figure 7: Data collection took place over 9 weeks.

The L2 instruction offered by COLLIE was online self-study and proceeded as follows. Each week participants received an invitation to register for a time slot to practice. Each time participants logged in, they were shown a home screen with a simple list of tasks for them to complete in the session. Tasks appeared as links that participants could click to launch a practice exercise. After participants completed a task, they were returned to their home screen and the completed task appeared with a line through it to indicate it had been completed and to help build a sense of progress. As participants worked on the exercises, their work was automatically stored and saved on the back-end so that in the event of a break or accidental page refresh their work was preserved. At the end of each session participants completed the learning experience questionnaire, after which a message appeared informing them they have completed their session and that they could safely log out.

Participants completed the learning experience questionnaire on five occasions: once at the end of session 1 (t1), two times in session 2 (t2a and t2b), as this was a longer session and we wanted to check the emotions halfway through the session and again at the end of the session; and again at the end in session 3 (t3). Finally, we also included the emotion questionnaire in the exit survey approximately 1 week after practice (t4), to see what kind of emotional experiences the participants would report after having not practised for some time.

4.5 Analysis

In our analysis of learning outcomes, we have the independent variable *condition* (either treatment or control) and the dependent variable *score*, which in this preliminary analysis is the raw score from the binary-choice tests. Participants completed pre-, post- and delayed post-tests. To investigate how test scores changed over time, our analysis compares scores for the two groups using a two-way repeated measures ANOVA with a 2 (*condition*: treatment or control) x 3 (*test*: pre, post or delayed post) design.

For our analysis of participants' learning experiences we take a slightly different approach. Rather than look at the frequency of the individual 14 emotions sampled by the questionnaire, we adopt a more coarse-grained view that compares the frequency of positive versus negative emotions. The independent variable is *valence* (either positive or negative), and the dependent variable is the self-reported *frequency*. Treatment condition participants completed the questionnaire five times, yielding a two-way repeated measures ANOVA with a 2 (*valence*: positive or negative) x 5 (*time*: t1, t2a, t2b, t3, t4) design.

The aim with eliciting information about particular learning situations was to gain insight into what the context or cause was for the emotions participants reported. We reviewed the open item responses and coded them with short one or two-word labels, for example *system error* or *exercise repetitiveness*. We then went over the labels and distinguished between situations resulting from the use of AEG technology and other causes. In the present study we focus on situations related to negative emotions, to detect any negative effects of using generated exercises.

5 Results

5.1 Learning gains

Our analysis of learning outcomes returned a main effect for test, $F(1.78, 53.42) = 10.82$, $MSE = 19.20$, $p < .001$, $\hat{\eta}_p^2 = .265$, suggesting that the scores change from pretest to delayed posttest. There was no main effect of condition, $F(1, 30) = 3.60$, $MSE = 270.04$, $p = .068$, $\hat{\eta}_p^2 = .107$. Also returned is a test by condition effect, $F(1.78, 53.42) = 14.38$, $MSE = 19.20$, $p < .001$, $\hat{\eta}_p^2 = .324$.

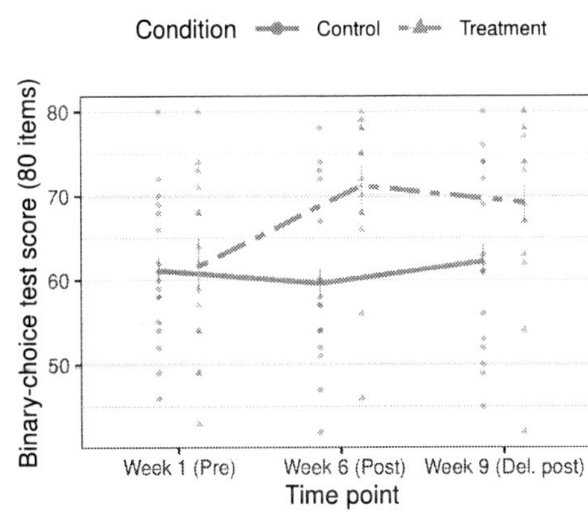

Figure 8: Participant binary-choice test scores on French grammatical gender at Week 1 (pre-test), Week 6 (post-test) and Week 9 (delayed post-test). The treatment group improves with time, while control group remains stable.

Post-hoc analysis of the test by condition effect (Sidak) points to important changes for the treatment group, returning a significant difference between pretest (M = 61.7) and posttest (M = 71.2), and no difference between posttest and delayed posttest (*M* = 69.2). This suggests the intervention helped the treatment group improve, and that this improvement had not faded three weeks later. For the control group, there were no significant differences, and their scores remained equivalent from pretest (*M* = 61.1) to posttest (*M* = 59.6) to delayed posttest (*M* = 62.2), suggesting that the control group remained stable. Together, these findings point to the pedagogical effectiveness of practising with the system.

5.2 Learning experience

Analysis of learning experience returned a main effect of valence, $F(1, 14) = 20.66$, $MSE = 2.14$, $p < .001$, $\hat{\eta}^2_p = .596$, suggesting that positive emotions were experienced more frequently than negative ones. There was no main effect for time, $F(3.17, 44.43) = 2.18$, $MSE = 0.16$, $p = .101$, $\hat{\eta}^2_p = .134$. We also observed a valence by time effect, $F(3.13, 43.85) = 15.94$, $MSE = 0.17$, $p < .001$, $\hat{\eta}^2_p = .532$, suggesting that positive and negative emotions had frequencies that changed differently in the practice sessions.

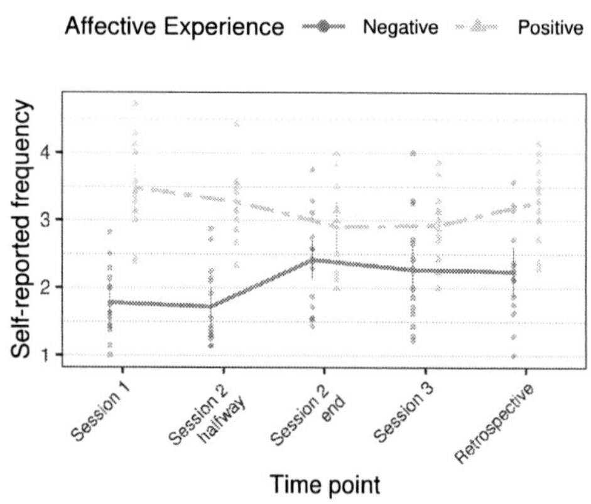

Figure 9: Self-reported frequency of positive vs. negative experiences over four weeks. Positive emotions (in green) follow a U-shape curve, while for negative emotions (in blue) there is a modest increase.

Post-hoc analysis indicates that positive emotions follow a U-shape curve; they start high (*M* = 3.49), but then drop significantly at the end of session 2 (*M* = 2.9) and do not change significantly in session 3, (*M* = 2.92). During this period positive and negative emotions occur equally frequently. At time point 4 there is again a significant increase (*M* = 3.27), when students had had a break from practice and were looking back. For the negative emotions, there is a modest but significant increase from the start to the end of the second session (*M* = 1.4 vs. *M* = 2.8).

5.3 Learning situations

In total we observed 169 instances of situations described in the open questionnaire data that were related to negative emotions, from which 37 unique categories emerged. Table 1 presents a subset of the most frequently occurring situations associated with negative emotions during practice, together with less common situations that are interesting because they can be attributed to the use of AEG technology for creating the practice materials.

From the entries in the table, we see that there are some clear links between negative emotions and certain situations. Participants reported feeling frustrated, discouraged or confused when the ASR failed to accurately transcribe their speech. Apparently the length of the exercises was sometimes too long, and this resulted in participants feeling bored or frustrated. In some cases participants appeared to have difficulty with learning the gender-predictive suffix patterns, despite the special instructional sequence, and this led to frustration and confusion.

Interestingly, there appear to have been relatively few situations directly related to the use of AEG technology, but from a pedagogical point of view those that we observed seem important and worth sharing here. First, a number of participants reported being unable to answer an item correctly even when they tried all possible answers. This occurred in a *Say the Word that Fits* exercise (see Figure 4), where the exercise generation pipeline created an item that had no target answer. The problem seems to have occurred due to a dependency parsing error that incorrectly assigned a determiner relation to the text *un peu* (a little). This caused the system to then look up the gender of *peu* in Lexique which failed and then resulted in no target answer being specified for the item. When students came across this and tried all possible combinations of determiner and noun without managing to have their answer accepted by the system they understandably reported feeling frustrated or confused.

A second AEG-related error occurred in the generation of Object Identification exercises (see Figure 2) in which participants reported being con-

Situation	Example	% Responses (169)	Related emotions (desc)	Related to AEG
Inaccurate speech recognition	"it took a really long time for the computer to recognize my voice on certain exercises"	13.6	frustration, discouragement, confusion	No
Length of exercises	"the exercises feel too long"	13.6	boredom, frustration	No
Learning challenges	"I was frustrated because I couldn't exactly figure out the pattern"	8.9	frustration, confusion	No
Unanswerable questions	"even when I copy pasted the answer in, it would not accept it"	8.9	frustration, confusion	Yes
System errors	"when I put un or une , it said something's not right"	7.7	frustration, confusion, discouragement	No
Repetitive exercises	"There was no variation in the format"	7.1	boredom	No
Unsuitable images	"some of the images which were meant to display singular [objects] showed multiple"	0.6	frustration	Yes
Inappropriate riddle clues	"definitions for the devinettes are sometimes very unhelpful ... and sometimes downright offensive"	0.6	frustration	Yes

Table 1: Example situations from open-items, showing negative emotions only.

fused by some of the images that appeared. To elicit the singular form of a target noun with its determiner the exercise requires that the right-most image shows a single instance of an object. The images used in this exercise were automatically downloaded and it appears in some cases the right-most image actually contained multiple instances. This led to confusion about whether the system expected an answer in singular or plural form.

A final issue occurred during the generation of a Riddle exercise (see Figure 3). As described above, clues for the riddles were created automatically by retrieving definitions from a lexical database called GLAWI (Hathout and Sajous, 2016), with content derived from Wiktionnaire. During the creation of a riddle for the target *une baleine* (a whale), the system regrettably included a colloquial and offensive definition from the database, which a small number of participants rightfully found unpleasant and frustrating.

6 Discussion

Tools that help to quickly author practice material for ICALL systems have the potential to help increase their impact in L2 instruction. Research into technology for AEG has demonstrated the feasibility of generating a variety of exercise types, and human experts tend to judge the output of these tools favourably, yet there has so far been relatively little research evaluating the effectiveness of L2 instruction with generated exercises. The present study aimed to address this gap by developing an exercise generation pipeline and e-learning platform targeting French grammatical gender with pedagogy informed by SLA research. Our evaluation of the platform investigated two dimensions of instructional effectiveness: 1) learning outcomes and 2) affective learning experiences. With regard to learning, our preliminary analysis of the binary-choice test scores showed that participants who completed the instruction improved significantly in comparison to a control group, suggesting that AEG can be an effective instructional tool. In the original intervention, Lyster and Izquierdo (2009) found that scores on two oral proficiency measures followed the same pattern as the binary-choice data. Currently we are working on completing annotations of the speech recordings from our own oral production measures, but we are optimistic that an analysis of the data will also show improvements and provide additional evidence for the effectiveness of practice with AEG.

Our analysis of participants' in-practice affective experiences indicates that positive emotions were experienced more frequently than negative ones, which is an encouraging finding. At the same time, we found that the frequency of positive and negative experiences changed over time, with positive emotions following a U-shaped curve in which they occurred less frequently in later sessions. These findings appear to indicate that the instruction delivered by COLLIE is on the right track but also that there is still room for improvement.

In this regard, the descriptions that participants provided of situations in which they experienced negative emotions are an important source of information for improving the instruction. It is somehow encouraging to find that the majority of negative experiences seem to result from situations unrelated to the use of AEG technology, being attributable instead to issues with the instructional format, such as repetitive or overly long exercises, which can be addressed relatively easily. Improving the accuracy of the speech recognition is also an important issue which can potentially be addressed by using an ASR engine trained on non-native speech (van Doremalen, 2014), though this is a much larger undertaking.

Although we observed relatively few negative experiences directly attributable to AEG, the three types of situations that did occur clearly will have a negative impact on learning and should be addressed. The issue with the inappropriate riddle clue is particularly concerning because it left at least one individual feeling uncomfortable for the rest of the practice session.

In the present study, only the images used in the generation of Object Identification exercises were reviewed to ensure their appropriateness for instruction, but the issue above suggests that human review of automatically generated content has a more important role in AEG than we initially anticipated, and which without assessing affective dimensions of learning might have gone undetected.

A recommendation, based on the study here, is for future work looking at exercise generation in the context of a CALL platform to consider exploring the idea of a peer review mechanism that encourages users to share the exercises they generate and to review each other's exercises. One can imagine a learning platform that shows the number of reviews for generated exercises, and possibly makes use of badges to clearly mark exercises that have been vetted by the community, to avoid some of the negative experiences that we saw here.

7 Conclusions and Future work

In conclusion, this study suggests that it is feasible to use automatic exercise generation to more easily create L2 practice exercises that are pedagogically effective and support positive learning experiences. At the same time, the affective data suggest that there is room for improvements to the instruction, and that a peer review mechanism could be an important feature of future CALL systems with AEG pipelines, to ensure more positive learning experiences.

In order to draw stronger conclusions about the efficacy of AEG, there are some limitations that need to be addressed. First, the current findings are based on just one proficiency measure, the binary-choice test. However, during the data collection we also gathered data from two oral production measures that, once annotated, could provide additional support. A second point would be to recruit additional annotators to analyse and label the open-item questionnaire data for a more robust qualitative analysis. Third, an interesting point to follow up on would be to compare the learning outcomes of the present study with those found in the original human-led intervention (Lyster and Izquierdo, 2009).

Finally, the present study focused on a single aspect of learning a foreign language, grammatical gender, over a relatively short time (three practice sessions). To obtain more support for the instructional effectiveness of AEG-based instruction in general, it would be interesting to carry out an evaluation with a system that supports a variety of linguistic targets, such as the system developed by Heck and Meurers (2022), over a longer period of time and with more participants.

Acknowledgements

Parts of this study were presented at the 2022 EUROCALL conference. I am grateful to two anonymous NLP4CALL reviewers for their helpful comments. I would like to thank Roy Lyster, who was my postdoctoral supervisor for this project, as well as the instructors who helped with recruiting participants. I would also like to thank Detmar Meurers for his support of my continuation of this project. This research was made possible by a grant from the *Fonds de recherche du Québec – Société et culture* (258852).

References

Aldabe, I., de Lacalle, M. L., Maritxalar, M., Martinez, E., and Uria, L. (2006). ArikIturri: An Automatic Question Generator Based on Corpora and NLP Techniques. In Ikeda, M., Ashley, K. D., and Chan, T.-W., editors, *Intelligent Tutoring Systems*, volume 4053 of *Lecture Notes in Computer Science*, pages 584–594. Springer.

Antonsen, L. and Argese, C. (2018). Using authentic texts for grammar exercises for a minority language. In *Linköping Electronic Conference Proceedings*, page 152.

Antonsen, L., Johnson, R., Trosterud, T., and Uibo, H. (2013). Generating Modular Grammar Exercises with Finite-State Transducers. In *Proceedings of the second workshop on NLP for computer-assisted language learning at NODALIDA*.

Baptista, J., Lourenco, S., and Mamede, N. J. (2016). Automatic generation of exercises on passive transformation in Portuguese. In *2016 IEEE Congress on Evolutionary Computation (CEC)*, pages 4965–4972.

Beinborn, L. M. (2016). *Predicting and Manipulating the Difficulty of Text-Completion Exercises for Language Learning*. PhD thesis, Technische Universität Darmstadt.

Brysbaert, M., Warriner, A. B., and Kuperman, V. (2013). Concreteness ratings for 40 thousand generally known English word lemmas. *Behavior Research Methods*, 46(3):904–911.

Burstein, J. and Marcu, D. (2005). Translation exercise assistant: automated generation of translation exercises for native-Arabic speakers learning English. In *HLT-Demo '05: Proceedings of HLT/EMNLP on Interactive Demonstrations*, page 16–17.

Chalvin, A., Eensoo, E., and Stuck, F. (2013). Mining a parallel corpus for automatic generation of Estonian grammar exercises. In *Third biennial conference on electronic lexicography (eLex 2013) "Electronic lexicography in the 21st century: thinking outside the paper"*, pages 280–295, Tallinn, Estonia.

Chinkina, M. and Meurers, D. (2017). Question Generation for Language Learning: From ensuring texts are read to supporting learning. In *Proceedings of the 12th Workshop on Innovative Use of NLP for Building Educational Applications*, pages 334–344, Copenhagen, Denmark. Association for Computational Linguistics.

Chinkina, M., Ruiz, S., and Meurers, D. (2020). Crowdsourcing evaluation of the quality of automatically generated questions for supporting computer-assisted language teaching. *ReCALL*, 32(2):145–161.

Colin, É. (2020). *Traitement automatique des langues et génération automatique d'exercices de grammaire*. Theses, Université de Lorraine.

Diener, E., Sandvik, E., and Pavot, W. (2009). *Assessing Well-Being. Social Indicators Research Series*, chapter Happiness is the Frequency, Not the Intensity, of Positive Versus Negative Affect, pages 213–231. Springer, Dordrecht.

Dörnyei, Z. (2009). The L2 Motivational Self System. In Dornyei, Z. and Ushioda, E., editors, *Motivation, Language Identity and the L2 Self*, pages 9–42. Multilingual Matters.

Ferreira, K. and Pereira Jr., A. R. (2018). Verb Tense Classification And Automatic Exercise Generation. In *Proceedings of the 24th Brazilian Symposium on Multimedia and the Web*, WebMedia '18, page 105–108, New York, NY, USA. Association for Computing Machinery.

Freitas, T., Baptista, J., and Mamede, N. J. (2013). Syntactic REAP.PT: Exercises on Clitic Pronouning. In *Proceedings of the 2nd International Symposium on Languages, Applications and Technologies (SLATE 2013)*, Porto, Portugal.

Galvan, P., Francisco, V., Hervás, R., and Méndez, G. (2016). Riddle Generation using Word Associations. In *Proceedings of the Tenth International Conference on Language Resources and Evaluation LREC 2016, Portorož, Slovenia*.

Google Cloud (n.d.). Google Cloud - Speech-to-Text. https://cloud.google.com/speech-to-text. Retrieved 10 October 2022.

Hathout, N. and Sajous, F. (2016). Wiktionnaire's Wikicode GLAWIfied: a Workable French Machine-Readable Dictionary. In *Proceedings of the Tenth International Conference on Language Resources and Evaluation (LREC 2016)*, Portorož, Slovenia.

Heck, T. and Meurers, D. (2022). Parametrizable exercise generation from authentic texts: Effectively targeting the language means on the curriculum. In *Proceedings of the 17th Workshop on Innovative Use of NLP for Building Educational Applications (BEA 2022)*, pages 154–166, Seattle, Washington. Association for Computational Linguistics.

Heift, T. and Toole, J. (2002). Task Generator: A Portable System for Generating Learning Tasks for Intelligent Language Tutoring Systems. In Barker, P. and Rebelsky, S., editors, *Proceedings of ED-MEDIA 2002–World Conference on Educational Multimedia, Hypermedia & Telecommunications*, pages p. 1972–1977. Denver, Colorado, USA.

Lyster, R. (2007). *Learning and teaching languages through content: A counterbalanced approach*. Amsterdam: John Benjamins.

Lyster, R. (2016). *Vers une approche intégrée en immersion*. Montréal : Les Éditions CEC.

Lyster, R. (2018). *Content-based language teaching*. New York: Routledge.

Lyster, R. and Izquierdo, J. (2009). Prompts Versus Recasts in Dyadic Interaction. *Language Learning*, 59(2):453–498.

Malafeev, A. (2014). Language Exercise Generation: Emulating Cambridge Open Cloze. *Int. J. Concept. Struct. Smart Appl.*, 2(2):20–35.

Malafeev, A. (2015). Exercise Maker: Automatic Language Exercise Generation. In *Computational Linguistics and Intellectual Technologies. Papers from the Annual International Conference "Dialogue"*, volume 14 of *21*, pages 441–452, Moscow.

Manning, C. D., Surdeanu, M., Bauer, J., Finkel, J., Bethard, S. J., and McClosky, D. (2014). The Stanford CoreNLP natural language processing toolkit. In *Association for Computational Linguistics (ACL) System Demonstrations*, pages 55–60.

New, B., Pallier, C., Brysbaert, M., and Ferrand, L. (2004). Lexique 2 : A new French lexical database. *Behavior Research Methods, Instruments, &amp Computers*, 36(3):516–524.

Papenberg, M. and Klau, G. W. (2021). Using anticlustering to partition data sets into equivalent parts. *Psychological Methods*, 26(2):161–174.

Pekrun, R., Goetz, T., Titz, W., and Perry, R. (2002). Academic Emotions in Students' Self-Regulated Learning and Achievement: A Program of Qualitative and Quantitative Research. *Educational Psychologist*, 37(2):91–105.

Perez-Beltrachini, L., Gardent, C., and Kruszewski, G. (2012). Generating Grammar Exercises. In *NAACL-HLT 7th Workshop on Innovative Use of NLP for Building Educational Applications*, Montreal, Canada.

Pilán, I. (2016). Detecting Context Dependence in Exercise Item Candidates Selected from Corpora. In *Proceedings of the 11th Workshop on Innovative Use of NLP for Building Educational Applications*, pages 151–161, San Diego, CA. Association for Computational Linguistics.

Pilán, I., Volodina, E., and Borin, L. (2017). Candidate sentence selection for language learning exercises: from a comprehensive framework to an empirical evaluation. *Traitement Automatique des Langues (TAL)*, 57(3):67–91.

Presson, N., Davy, C., and MacWhinney, B. (2013). *Innovative Research and Practices in Second Language Acquisition and Bilingualism*, chapter Experimentalized CALL for adult second language learners., pages 139–164. John Benjamins Publishing Company.

Rudzewitz, B., Ziai, R., De Kuthy, K., Möller, V., Nuxoll, F., and Meurers, D. (2018). Generating Feedback for English Foreign Language Exercises. In *Proceedings of the Thirteenth Workshop on Innovative Use of NLP for Building Educational Applications*, pages 127–136, New Orleans, Louisiana.

Saito, K., Dewaele, J.-M., Abe, M., and In'nami, Y. (2018). Motivation, Emotion, Learning Experience, and Second Language Comprehensibility Development in Classroom Settings: A Cross-Sectional and Longitudinal Study. *Language Learning*, 68(3):709–743.

Scott, G. G., Keitel, A., Becirspahic, M., Yao, B., and Sereno, S. C. (2018). The Glasgow Norms: Ratings of 5, 500 words on nine scales. *Behavior Research Methods*, 51(3):1258–1270.

Shao, K., Nicholson, L. J., Kutuk, G., and Lei, F. (2020). Emotions and Instructed Language Learning: Proposing a Second Language Emotions and Positive Psychology Model. *Frontiers in Psychology*, 11.

Shao, K., Pekrun, R., and Nicholson, L. J. (2019). Emotions in classroom language learning: What can we learn from achievement emotion research? *System*, 86:102121.

Slavuj, V. and Prskalo, L. N.and Bakaric, M. B. (2021). Automatic generation of language exercises based on a universal methodology: An analysis of possibilities. *Bulletin of the Transilvania University of Brasov. Series IV: Philology and Cultural Studies*, 16(43)(2):29–48.

Teimouri, Y., Goetze, J., and Plonsky, L. (2019). Second language anxiety and achievement: A meta-analysis. *Studies in Second Language Acquisition*, 41(2):363–387.

Toole, J. and Heift, T. (2002). The Tutor Assistant: An Authoring Tool for an Intelligent Language Tutoring System. *Computer Assisted Language Learning*, 15:373–386.

van Doremalen, J. (2014). *Developing automatic speech recognition-enabled language learning applications: from theory to practice*. PhD thesis, Radboud Universiteit Nijmegen.

Verweij, R. (2020). Automated Exercise Generation in Mobile Language Learning. Online: `https://digitalcommons.bard.edu/senproj_s2020/297/`.

Wilson, M. (1988). MRC psycholinguistic database: Machine-usable dictionary, version 2.00. *Behavior Research Methods, Instruments, &amp Computers*, 20(1):6–10.

Zanetti, A., Volodina, E., and Graën, J. (2021). Automatic Generation of Exercises for Second Language Learning from Parallel Corpus Data. *International Journal of TESOL Studies (2021)*, 3(2):55–70.

Zilio, L., Wilkens, R., and Fairon, C. (2018). SMILLE for Portuguese: Annotation and Analysis of Grammatical Structures in a Pedagogical Context. In *International Conference on Computational Processing of the Portuguese Language*.

The Teacher-Student Chatroom Corpus version 2: more lessons, new annotation, automatic detection of sequence shifts

Andrew Caines[1] **Helen Yannakoudakis**[2] **Helen Allen**[3]
Pascual Pérez-Paredes[4] **Bill Byrne**[5] **Paula Buttery**[1]

[1] ALTA Institute & Computer Laboratory, University of Cambridge, U.K.
{andrew.caines|paula.buttery}@cl.cam.ac.uk
[2] Department of Informatics, King's College London, U.K.
helen.yannakoudakis@kcl.ac.uk
[3] Cambridge University Press & Assessment, University of Cambridge, U.K.
helen.allen@cambridge.org
[4] Departamento de Filología Inglesa, Universidad de Murcia, Spain
pfp23@cam.ac.uk
[5] Department of Engineering, University of Cambridge, U.K.
bill.byrne@eng.cam.ac.uk

Abstract

The first version of the Teacher-Student Chatroom Corpus (TSCC) was released in 2020 and contained 102 chatroom dialogues between 2 teachers and 8 learners of English, amounting to 13.5K conversational turns and 133K word tokens. In this second version of the corpus, we release an additional 158 chatroom dialogues, amounting to an extra 27.9K conversational turns and 230K word tokens. In total there are now 260 chatroom lessons, 41.4K conversational turns and 363K word tokens, involving 2 teachers and 13 students with seven different first languages. The content of the lessons was, as before, guided by the teacher, and the proficiency level of the learners is judged to range from B1 to C2 on the CEFR scale. Annotation of the dialogues continued with conversational analysis of sequence types, pedagogical focus, and correction of grammatical errors. In addition, we have annotated fifty of the dialogues using the Self-Evaluation of Teacher Talk framework which is intended for self-reflection on interactional aspects of language teaching. Finally, we conducted machine learning experiments to automatically detect shifts in discourse sequences from turn to turn, using modern transfer learning methods with large pre-trained language models. The TSCC v2 is freely available for research use.

1 Introduction & Related Work

Caines et al. (2020) introduced the Teacher-Student Chatroom Corpus (TSCC), a collection of 102 online English lessons between 2 teachers and 8 students containing 13.5K conversational turns and 133K word tokens, with the students adjudged to be writing at the CEFR levels of B1, B2 and C1. The lessons contained in the TSCC were anonymised, annotated with grammatical error corrections and discourse analyses, and made freely available to other researchers[1]. The motivation was to collate a dataset with which to study one-to-one interaction and language teaching, to investigate the linguistic skills involved in online chat at different levels of English proficiency, and potentially in the long-term to gather training data for developing a tutoring dialogue manager or chatbot.

In this paper, we report on further development of the corpus into a second version of the TSCC, with new lessons, annotations in the same style as those carried out before, and new annotations within a pre-defined pedagogical framework which we present below. The TSCC 2.0 includes an additional 158 lessons from new and existing students, amounting to 27.9K conversational turns and 230K word tokens. In total the 2nd version of the corpus features 2 teachers and 13 students, 41.4K conversational turns and 362.9K word tokens. The range of student CEFR levels found in the TSCC now includes C2 as well as B1 to C1.

[1] Visit forms.gle/pKc48WMhnySC8zDk9 to review the licence and submit a data request.

Andrew Caines, Helen Yannakoudakis, Helen Allen, Pascual Pérez-Paredes, Bill Byrne and Paula Buttery. The Teacher-Student Chatroom Corpus version 2: more lessons, new annotation, automatic detection of sequence shifts. *Proceedings of the 11th Workshop on Natural Language Processing for Computer Assisted Language Learning (NLP4CALL 2022)*. Linköping Electronic Conference Proceedings 190: 23–35.

Turn	Role	Anonymised	Corrected	Resp.to	Sequence
1	T	Hi there ⟨STUDENT⟩, all OK?	Hi there ⟨STUDENT⟩, all OK?		opening
2	S	Hi ⟨TEACHER⟩, how are you?	Hi ⟨TEACHER⟩, how are you?		
3	S	I did the exercise this morning	I did *some* exercise this morning		
4	S	I have done, I guess	I have done, I guess		repair
5	T	did is fine especially if you're focusing on the action itself	did is fine especially if you're focusing on the action itself		scaffolding
6	T	tell me about your exercise if you like!	tell me about your exercise if you like!	3	topic.dev

Table 1: Example of numbered, anonymised and annotated turns in the TSCC (where role T=teacher, S=student, and 'resp.to' means 'responding to'); the student is here chatting about physical exercise. From Caines et al. (2020).

The new lessons, like those in the first release of the corpus, have been annotated for various discourse and classroom properties. These include the 'threading' of conversational turns so that non-sequential responses are connected with their appropriate conversational threads; the delineation of major and minor sequences in the discourse, as well as the labelling of their types; the identification of the pedagogical focus of sequences where applicable, along with any resources referred to; correction of grammatical errors by the student, and an assessment of student CEFR level for each lesson. The corpus and annotation are described in more detail in section 2.

In addition, fifty of the original lessons have been annotated using the Self-Evaluation of Teacher Talk framework (SETT) (Walsh, 2006, 2013), a schema designed for 'reflective practice' by language teachers for the purpose of their continuing professional development (Walsh, 2006). We annotated both teacher and student turns with aspects from SETT which we could identify. This gives us another way of considering the data collected, from a pedagogical and discourse-based perspective, and in section 3 we present the procedure for SETT annotation and the analyses we conducted.

We also describe initial experiments attempting to automatically detect when new discourse sequences are initiated in the lesson transcripts. This involved a 'transfer learning' approach, fine-tuning a large language model pre-trained with transformers on our specific machine learning task (Ruder et al., 2019). We cast the task as one of identifying when a turn in a chat lesson is followed by a new discourse sequence. As such, we are modelling the data collected so far in terms of discourse management by both teachers and students.

Finally in sections 5 and 6, we review the work which has already been done with the first version of the corpus, and we outline our future plans to further expand the corpus, improve our automated lesson manager, and develop teacher and student lesson feedback for self-development purposes for those taking part in the chatroom conversations.

2 Corpus description

The design and collection of data for the original TSCC was described in full in Caines et al. (2020), and we give a brief recap here. Participants arranged to hold one-to-one English language lessons in an online and private chatroom. The lessons were about one hour each, and the structure and content of each lesson was determined by the teachers. The students were recruited by the teachers themselves or through social media, and were located in several different countries around the world. An excerpt from the corpus is shown in Table 1, with selected annotation labels to illustrate the type of data available.

Transcriptions of the lessons were prepared for inclusion in the corpus through several annotation stages: firstly, they were anonymised by replacing any personal names with placeholders such as

	Version 1	Version 2
Lessons	102	260
Conv.turns	13,552	41,484
Words	132,895	362,440

Table 2: Comparative statistics for versions 1 and 2 of the TSCC.

CEFR	Version 1	Version 2
B1	36	36
B2	37	143
C1	29	29
C2	0	52

Table 3: Number of lessons by student CEFR level in versions 1 and 2 of the TSCC.

⟨TEACHER⟩ and ⟨STUDENT⟩. Next, grammatical errors by the student were identified and corrected in a minimal fashion. Then, various linguistic and pedagogical features were marked up, including any non-sequential conversation threads (where a participant responded to a turn which was not the other participant's previous one), the start of new sequence types within the dialogue, the identification of the skill(s) focused on within that sequence, along with the use of any resources both internal and external to the chatroom.

The timeline of the lessons ranges from November 2019, through the onset of the COVID-19 pandemic to June 2021. We are open to collecting new data, and so the corpus may continue to grow, but this version of the TSCC comes from that twenty-month period.

2.1 New lessons

New data has been collected for the TSCC in the form of 158 new lessons. Now the corpus involves 2 teachers and 13 students, amounting to 41K conversational turns and 362K whitespace-delimited words (Table 2). The bulk of additional data was assessed by an expert to be at CEFR levels B2 and C2 (Table 3). The students' first languages are: Italian, Japanese, Mandarin Chinese, Russian, Spanish, Thai and Ukrainian. Table 4 shows how contributions to chatroom conversations compare for teachers and students.

2.2 Sequence, focus & resource types

Sequence types represent major or minor shifts in conversational sequences – sections of interaction with a particular purpose, whether that purpose is

	Teachers	Students
Conv.turns	22,130	19,342
Words	238,324	124,090
Words/turn	10.8	6.4

Table 4: Comparing teacher and student contributions in version 2 of the TSCC.

social or educational or a mixture of both. Borrowing key concepts from the CONVERSATION ANALYSIS approach (Sacks et al., 1974), we seek out groups of turns which together represent the building blocks of the chat transcript: teaching actions which build the structure of the lessons.

Teaching focus records which skill or skills were being targeted within a given sequence. **Use of resource** indicates whether any materials or stimuli external to the lesson are referred to

Compared to the original corpus, we have amended the annotation schema in various ways. First, some quality checks led to corrections to labels which were misspelled or in the wrong field. Second, we added new sequence types based on our work with the corpus over a longer time period. Now there is a 'non-English' sequence type, which might occur when the teacher and student switch to a different language (the learner's L1, for instance) either to explore or clarify a concept, or check and discover new vocabulary in English. And there is 'free practice', which relates to the learner being encouraged to make use of target content more freely than they would in a controlled exercise. In addition, it seemed sensible to move 'admin' of the lesson into the set of sequence types, rather than the set of sequence foci/focuses as it was in the original corpus.

We made minor modifications to the set of sequence foci, such that the skills 'writing', 'speaking', 'listening' and 'reading' are added, while the previously existing 'typo' is subsumed by the new 'writing' focus type. 'Exam practice' is renamed 'exam prep' – as in, exam *preparation* – because we found that not only were the teachers setting practice drills for the students but they were also discussing preparation strategies.

Finally, we note that many types of teaching resource emerged through collection of new data: the original list was open-ended, and has been extended in a bottom-up fashion.

In the Appendix, the full list of annotation types and their descriptions are copied from Caines et al. (2020) along with the amendments described above.

3 SETT annotation

The Self-Evaluation of Teacher Talk framework (SETT) was designed for reflective practice by language teachers (Walsh, 2006). This means that it was intended for teachers to review recordings of their lessons, indicate the modes and 'interactures' they were engaged in with their class as the lesson progressed, and reflected on these practices for continuing self-improvement. The focus of reflection is on the interaction between teacher and students, in order to develop 'classroom interactional competence' (Walsh, 2013), and as such the framework is useful and relevant to our own analysis and quest for deeper understanding of the conversations in the TSCC. It was designed for use by teachers but the generic interaction-based aspects of SETT are still applicable to students as well, even if the teacher-driven management aspects are not.

Within the SETT framework, a **mode** is a 'classroom micro-context' and an **interacture** is an 'interactional feature'. Thus, classroom interaction is framed as a series of interactions and micro-contexts, where discourse is co-constructed by teachers and students, and the resulting conversations support and enable student learning (Walsh, 2013). SETT is a way for teachers to reflect on these interactions, in the scenario where their lessons have been recorded, and notice where learning opportunities and a 'space for learning' are created (Walsh and Li, 2012). This is in line with proposals for interactive and engaging learning environments in state school classrooms, which may equally be applied to a language school scenario (Alexander, 2008; Mercer, 2019).

3.1 SETT modes

There are four modes in the SETT framework. These are listed and defined below:

- **Managerial**: to transmit information, refer learners to materials, introduce/conclude an activity, or change from one mode of learning to another;
- **Classroom context**: to enable learners to express themselves clearly, establish a context, and promote oral fluency;
- **Materials**: to provide language practice around a piece of material, to elicit responses in relation to the material, check and display answers, clarify if needed;
- **Skills & systems**: to enable learners to produce correct forms, manipulate target language, to provide corrective feedback, and display correct answers*.

* For reasons explained below in section 3.3 we reduced these four modes to three for our annotation exercise, merging 'skills & systems' with 'materials'.

3.2 SETT interactures

We use the following nine original SETT interactures, and based on our initial experience annotating lesson transcriptions, we augmented these with an additional three interactures which are marked in italics below:

- **Confirmation check (CC)**: the teacher confirms that they have understood the learner's utterance, or vice versa;
- **Display question (DQ)**: a question to which the teacher knows the answer;
- **Direct repair (DR)**: the teacher corrects an error quickly and directly;
- ***Enquiry (EN)***: the learner asks a language question.
- **Extended teacher/learner turn (ExtT)**: a turn containing either more than one substantial main clause, many relative clauses, at least one long relative clause, or a combination of such clauses;
- **Form-focused feedback (FBF)**: the teacher gives explicit feedback on the words or form used by the learner, rather than the perceived intended meaning of their utterance;
- ***Instruction (IN)***: the teacher gives direct instructions;
- **Referential question (RQ)**: a genuine question to which the teacher does not know the answer, which typically encourages extended learner turns;

- **Scaffolding:Extension (S:E)**: the teacher does not accept a learner's first answer, implicitly or explicitly encouraging more output;

- **Scaffolding:Modelling (S:M)**: the teacher provides an example of the target language feature for the learner;

- ***Scaffolding:Presentation (S:P)***: the teacher explains a language point;

- **Seeking clarification (SC)**: the teacher asks a student to clarify something the student has said, or vice versa;

It is apparent that SETT is mainly teacher-focused but does have some capacity for application to student turns: the scaffolding, repair, instruction, question, and feedback interactures are almost certain to be applied to teacher turns, but the clarification, confirmation and extended turn interactures could be on either side, and enquiry is intended for student turns.

3.3 SETT annotation in the TSCC

For this new version of the corpus, we selected 50 lessons for annotation of modes and interactures, in order to investigate the types of teacher-student dialogues and pedagogical observations we could make in our dataset. Based on initial attempts to make annotation decisions in practice, we adapted the existing SETT labels so that the modes were reduced from 4 to 3 different types, and 3 new interactures were appended to 9 of the originals. In terms of modes, we found that it was difficult in practice to distinguish between 'materials' and 'skills & systems', since both relate to affording the opportunity for students to display what they know and to provide feedback accordingly. Therefore these two modes were merged into one for practical purposes.

As an exploratory exercise, we annotated the first 50 lessons in the corpus, for SETT modes and interactures on both the teacher and student side. One annotator carried out the work, based on clear guidelines – in future, it would be beneficial to collect multiple annotations for the same transcriptions, and to cover more lessons from the corpus. Here we report on the results of this initial annotation exercise, finding overall that the distribution of modes and interactures between teachers and students is broadly as expected on the basis of their definitions.

Mode	Teacher	Student
classroom context	18.2	26.2
managerial	42.1	27.1
materials/skills	30.1	41.1
multi-modes	9.6	5.6

Table 5: Proportion of SETT modes for teachers and students in a sample of 50 lessons from the TSCC (%).

Firstly it is worth noting that the proportion of turns between teacher and student is approximately even in the transcriptions as a whole (at a ratio of 53:47 respectively). Nevertheless, three times as many modes are set by the teacher as by the student. This is to be expected because the modes relate to lesson management and pedagogical acts. Table 5 shows how the three modes are distributed for teachers and students. For teachers, most of the modes they set are managerial, whereas the students mostly set modes for materials or skills practice. A small number of turns involved multiple modes at once.

Then in terms of interactures, we found that there were four times as many identifiable interactures by teachers as there were by students. On the one hand this fits with the fact that SETT was developed with teachers in mind, and on the other hand indicates that more of the interactional moves in a one-to-one lesson are made by the teacher, as might be expected. Specifically, instruction, feedback, repair, questions and scaffolding tended to be on the teacher side, whereas enquiry tended to be on the student side. Both teachers and students used extended turns, confirmation checks and sought clarification.

Figure 1 shows how student and teacher interactures differ both in magnitude (the teacher bars tend to reach higher on the y-axis) and type (the distribution of bars on the x-axis is quite different). In future work, we intend to analyse how modes and interactures relate to each other, since they were not devised as independent variables but ones which interplay and depend on each other to some extent. The SETT framework sets out some expected mode-interacture correspondences, and this is something that warrants investigation in our own dataset. The annotation of 50 lessons within the SETT framework is included in this second release of the corpus.

4 Classification experiments

As well as attempting to understand how teacher-student chatroom interactions progress during and across lessons, we can also attempt to apply machine learning techniques to predict features of the data. It is potentially useful to be able to predict when to introduce new sequences, and as such we report on experiments which detect and classify sequence shifts within chatroom transcripts. It is common practice in modern NLP to apply transfer learning methods whereby large language models pre-trained with transformers are 'fine-tuned' to a given task and dataset (Ruder et al., 2019). The BERT model is the best-known example of this, but there are many derivatives and alternative models (Devlin et al., 2019; Rogers et al., 2020).

We apply the transfer learning approach to our problem of classifying sequence shifts in the chatroom transcripts. Using our corpus of chatroom lessons, the classifier is trained to learn when new discourse sequences begin. Given a turn t_i from the corpus, the machine learning task is to predict whether a new discourse sequence begins in the next turn t_{i+1} or not.

4.1 Data preparation

The lesson transcripts in the TSCC need to be prepared for the machine learning task: the reshaped dataset is included with the new corpus release. We cast the text classification task as a binary one of *new sequence detection* – that is, does a new sequence begin after the current turn, or not? The initial input string is therefore turn t_i and the corresponding label comes from t_{i+1} as a 0 or 1.

To exemplify, consider the imagined turns below between teacher (T) and student (S):

turn		label
1	T: Does that all make sense?	0
2	S: yes, understood.	0
3	T: Good, time for some revision!	1
4	S: ok	0

If we consider turn 1 here, then the input string is 'does that all make sense?' and its corresponding label comes from turn 2; i.e. 0. With turn 2 on the other hand, the input string is 'yes, understood.', and the label is 1 because turn 3 marks the start of a new discourse sequence relating to revision.

Moreover, we experiment with longer inputs by using the special separator token `[SEP]` available in the BERT-ish vocabulary[2]. Thus, two text strings may be passed to a BERT-ish model, with `[SEP]` between them, and we use this to include the preceding turn t_{t-i} when learning to detect sequence shifts. This takes advantage of the long inputs which large pre-trained models can handle (usually 512 tokens[3]) and models an intuition that the preceding turn is useful context when determining whether a new discourse sequence is needed.

To exemplify these longer input strings, we return to the imagined turns between teacher and student. Looking at turn 2, the input string becomes a concatenation of turn 1, the `[SEP]` token, and turn 2 (lower-cased) –

> does that all make sense? `[SEP]` yes, understood.

– and the label is 1. For comparison, the input string for turn 3 is –

> yes, understood. `[SEP]` good, time for some revision!

– and the label is 0, because turn 4 does not involve a new discourse sequence.

In subsequent variations, we experiment by prefixing the current turn t_i with the *two* previous turns, to incorporate more of the preceding context, and we introduce two new special tokens `[t]` and `[s]` at the start of each turn, to indicate whether it is the teacher's or student's turn. The intuition here is that, since teachers and students play different roles in the discourse, it may be useful to signal which one is chatting when.

4.2 Implementation

We opt to work with the DistilBERT compressed language model rather than a larger language model, because it brings energy savings without compromising greatly on performance (Sanh et al., 2019). In addition, a model which is faster for inference would be beneficial in CALL applications where users do not want to be kept waiting overly long. We use the `transformers` Python library from HuggingFace (Wolf et al., 2020), obtaining the pre-trained model and tokenizer for

[2]The `[SEP]` token exists because one of the original training tasks for BERT was next sentence classification – this can be used to tackle question answering challenges, by concatenating the question and answer with `[SEP]` in between (Devlin et al., 2019).

[3]Note that tokens in the context of transformer language models are 'subword tokens' automatically derived from training corpora via byte-pair encoding or an algorithm such as WordPiece (Gage, 1994; Schuster and Nakajima, 2012).

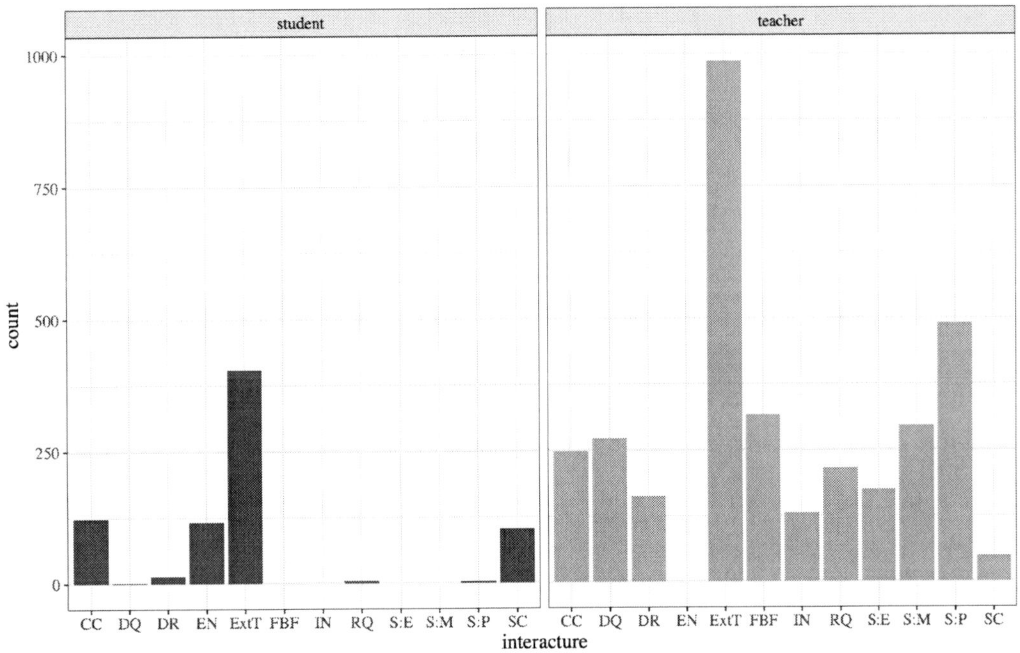

Figure 1: Frequency of interactures by students and teachers in a sample of 50 lessons from the TSCC.

DistilBERT 'base' (smaller than 'large') uncased (the vocabulary is all in lowercase).

We prepare the turns from the 260 chatroom lessons in our corpus in the formats described above. Each data instance is a turn prefixed with 0, 1 or 2 preceding turns. We randomly split these instances into an 80:20 train-test split. The majority of chat turns are not succeeded by a new sequence. Therefore we have a class imbalance whereby approximately 30% of turns bear a positive label, the remainder are negative. To address this issue, we weight the positive instances three times more than the negative ones in the loss function.

To fine-tune DistilBERT on our classification task, we use the built-in `transformers` trainer on 2 GPU for 2 epochs per experiment, with the default batch size of 8, AdamW optimizer (Loshchilov and Hutter, 2019), initial learning rate of 5e-05 and linear learning rate scheduler.

Our evaluation measures are precision (true positives over true positives and false positives) and recall (true positives over true positives and false negatives). We also report the F_1 scores which are the harmonic mean of precision and recall.

For comparison, we implement two probabilistic baselines based on statistical information in the training data. The first is based on the proportion of new sequences over all the turns in the training set (**overall prob**) – 0.288 – using that probability as a weight in randomly predicting whether a turn is followed by a new discourse sequence or not.

The second baseline uses information from the training data as to the number of turns between new discourse sequences (**sequence length prob**). For each turn in the training data we record the sequence length (in turns) at that point. Thus we can say how many times we have observed a sequence of length l and how many times we see a sequence one turn longer ($l + 1$). The probability of a new sequence given a sequence of length l is thus the count of sequences of that length (c_l) divided by the sum of c_l and the count of times we see a sequence one longer than l (c_{l+1}). This is a way of stating how probable we think it is that a sequence will stop at length l:

$$p_{new.seq} = \frac{c_l}{c_l + c_{l+1}} \tag{1}$$

Then for each turn in the test set, a prediction of 0 or 1 for a new sequence is generated using $(1 - p_{new.seq})$ and $p_{new.seq}$ as sample weights respectively. We also impose an upper bound on the length of a sequence, given the longest seen in the

Expt	P	R	F_1
Overall prob†	.291	.290	.291
Sequence length prob†	.288	.584	.386
Current turn t_i	.377	.433	.403
+ role tokens	.382	.455	.415
+ 1 previous turn	**.398**	**.636**	**.489**
+ role tokens	.391	.454	.420
+ 2 previous turns	.393	.515	.445
+ role tokens	.395	.447	.420

Table 6: Text classification experiments to automatically detect new discourse sequences in the following turn t_{i+1}: precision, recall, and F_1-measure. † indicates the mean of 100 runs. Best performance in bold.

training data: 32 turns. We run both baselines one hundred times each and report average results in Table 6.

4.3 Results

As shown in Table 6, we find that the best performing model is the one trained on the current turn t_i concatenated with the previous one t_{i-1}, mainly due to much better recall than the other experiment settings. This way of preparing the data outperforms the basic case of only passing the current turn as input to the model, as well as the additional context available from two previous turns. Prefixing each turn with the special teacher and student tokens `[t]` and `[s]` only helped in the basic case of having only turn t_i as input: it did not help when one or two preceding turns were included.

All models outperform the probabilistic baselines, suggesting that a machine learning approach is a good direction for future work. It may be that a hybrid approach involving heuristics, additional features and transfer learning will bring further advances, as discussed below.

4.4 Discussion

There are other variations that could be tried to improve the performance of our models. Among these are pre-trained language models which are larger than DistilBERT, albeit with greater environmental impact (Strubell et al., 2019), or which can take longer inputs (e.g. Big Bird or Longformer (Zaheer et al., 2020; Beltagy et al., 2020)). Different hyperparameters might be trialled, along with different ways of representing the text such as additional features or encodings with the input strings. It might be helpful, for instance, to include grammatical error detection as a pre-processing task, since it may be that certain errors are associated with new sequences such as scaffolding, elicitation or presentation. A temporal feature might help determine when to shift topics or call on management sequences such as homework and lesson closure.

Furthermore, the task could be reformulated as teacher-centric: for CALL, it may only be necessary to model the teacher's shift in discourse sequences rather than both teacher and student shifts as we have done here. This would fit with the perspective of the teacher as manager (Legutke and Thomas, 1991). In future, models could be trained to only predict the teacher side of the discourse and to steer the lesson in an adaptive, orderly and meaningful way.

In addition, human evaluation would be beneficial because our notion of 'ground truth' here is based on a series of teacher-student dyads and the discourses they built on specific occasions, and the judgements of the annotators who identified sequence shifts and sequence types in the lesson transcriptions. Aside from the lesson beginning with an opening sequence and ending with a closing sequence, there is in reality no absolute *truth* as to when new sequences are required. Each lesson could have been constructed in a myriad different ways and still be perfectly good. Therefore, evaluation via precision and recall is a decent indicator, but does not tell the whole story. It may be that we can train a new sequence classifier on such data as the TSCC, but that the best measures of performance will be derived from human-computer interaction.

Beyond the detection of new sequences, it may also be useful to automatically predict which sequence type comes next. So far we have approached the problem as binary classification, but the annotation exists in the TSCC to train a multi-class classifier identifying the types listed in the appendix – a much more challenging proposition. However, decisions would need to be made whether to separate the major and minor sequence types into separate machine learning tasks, or to tackle them both at the same time. Also, many sequences are multi-label in the sense that there can be more than one sequence type associated with a given turn. This makes the machine learning task harder, and has implications for how the data should be prepared and the models evaluated.

5 Related work

Caines et al. (2020) featured a review of other work related to the TSCC, and we refer the interested reader to that section of the paper rather than repeat it here. In the intervening period others have cited the original TSCC paper, and we wish to highlight some of those new publications[4].

A similar dataset has been produced by Yuan et al. (2022) – ErAConD, an Error Annotated Conversational Dialog Dataset – which is intended for research into grammatical error correction in English chat conversations. ErAConD features 186 conversations between crowdworkers and the BlenderBot dialogue system (Roller et al., 2020). Some distinguishing features are that the conversations are between human and machine rather than human-to-human, and the error annotation has been carried out in a manner similar to Náplava et al. (2022). Like the TSCC, ErAConD is available for research use[5].

There has been other research using the Blender chatbot, along with GPT-3 (Brown et al., 2020), to construct AI teachers (Tack and Piech, 2022), using the student turns in the first version of the TSCC and the mathematics Uptake dataset (Demszky et al., 2021) to generate and evaluate chatbot responses. Tack & Piech found that the models performed well on conversational uptake (how well the response expanded on the student input) – especially Blender – but still have some way to go in terms of realism, comprehension and helpfulness. In addition, Tyen et al. (2022) seek to automatically adapt Blender outputs for different levels of English proficiency using a variety of different methods and English language resources. The prompt the adapted models to 'self-chat' and find that a re-ranking approach works best, after evaluating the level of the chats with human examiners.

Filighera et al. (2022) focus on improved feedback systems for language learners, giving short answer feedback to explain scores for German and English exercises. Nguyen et al. (2022) give an assessment of the state-of-the-art for educational technologies and how well they handle code-switching, pointing to future directions and opportunities for research. In this second version of the TSCC, the turns which feature words from languages other than English are labelled as 'non-English' sequences. This does not mean that the turns are entirely in another language – though they may be – but rather that there is at least some non-English present in the turn. It may be fruitful to identify whether those turns tend to be explanatory (the teacher drawing on another language to build knowledge of English) or naturalistic conversational code-switching.

Jain et al. (2022) present EDICA (Educational Domain Infused Conversational Agent), a virtual agent for language teaching. They fine-tune the GPT-2 language model (Radford et al., 2019) on the CIMA dataset of Italian tutoring dialogues collected from crowdworkers role-playing student and tutor roles (Stasaski et al., 2020). CIMA is enriched with conceptual information about the exercises and the actions taken by the students. This kind of meta-information is an approach we could consider for future work with the TSCC.

Two new corpora have been created: the first a corpus of online lessons in Russian as a foreign language (RuTOC; (Lebedeva et al., 2022)), and the second a corpus of Korean task-oriented dialogue data (Seung-Kwon et al., 2022). Notably, the latter states that the aim is to collaborate with human teachers, not replace them; a sentiment we echo.

6 Conclusions & future work

In this paper we have described the second version of the Teacher-Student Chatroom Corpus. The new version adds another 158 hour-long chatroom transcripts to the 102 lessons in version 1 of the corpus. Two teachers and thirteen students are involved, representing seven L1s, and ranging from CEFR proficiency level B1 to C2. The new transcripts have been annotated in the same way as those in the first version, and a subset of 50 transcripts have been annotated for SETT modes and interactures.

We presented some initial experiments to automatically detect new discourse sequences. We showed that a fine-tuned DistilBERT model could outperform probabilistic baselines in detecting new sequences, based on a concatenation of the preceding and current turn. There remains room for improvement through further experimentation and feature-engineering, as well as alternative evaluation methods where we move from the idea of a single ground truth to human ratings of tim-

[4]Citing papers were obtained from Google Scholar (accessed 11 October 2022).

[5]See `https://github.com/yuanxun-yx/eracond`

ing and appropriateness. In these machine learning experiments we are working towards discourse modelling in pedagogic scenarios; in future, such models could be applied to online tutoring applications where we wish to guide the lesson from sequence to sequence.

Other future plans include further expansion of the corpus, and work to develop teacher feedback systems to aid in teacher training and professional development.

Acknowledgments

This paper reports on research supported by Cambridge University Press & Assessment, University of Cambridge. Additional funding was provided by the Cambridge Language Sciences Research Incubator Fund and the Isaac Newton Trust. We thank Helena Edmondson, Rowan Amber Jones, Olga Cherrington, and Professors Michael McCarthy & Steve Walsh for their help and contributions to this work. We are grateful to the teachers, students and annotators without whose enthusiastic participation this corpus would not have been feasible. We also thank audience members at the Teaching and Language Corpora Conference (TaLC) 2022, and the anonymous NLP4CALL reviewers for their feedback.

References

Robin Alexander. 2008. *Towards Dialogic Teaching: Rethinking Classroom Talk (4th edn).* York: Dialogos.

Iz Beltagy, Matthew E. Peters, and Arman Cohan. 2020. Longformer: The long-document Transformer. *arXiv*.

Tom Brown, Benjamin Mann, Nick Ryder, Melanie Subbiah, Jared D Kaplan, Prafulla Dhariwal, Arvind Neelakantan, Pranav Shyam, Girish Sastry, Amanda Askell, Sandhini Agarwal, Ariel Herbert-Voss, Gretchen Krueger, Tom Henighan, Rewon Child, Aditya Ramesh, Daniel Ziegler, Jeffrey Wu, Clemens Winter, Chris Hesse, Mark Chen, Eric Sigler, Mateusz Litwin, Scott Gray, Benjamin Chess, Jack Clark, Christopher Berner, Sam McCandlish, Alec Radford, Ilya Sutskever, and Dario Amodei. 2020. Language models are few-shot learners. In *Advances in Neural Information Processing Systems*.

Andrew Caines, Helen Yannakoudakis, Helena Edmondson, Helen Allen, Pascual Pérez-Paredes, Bill Byrne, and Paula Buttery. 2020. The teacher-student chatroom corpus. In *Proceedings of Natural Language Processing for Computer-Assisted Language Learning (NLP4CALL)*.

Dorottya Demszky, Jing Liu, Zid Mancenido, Julie Cohen, Heather Hill, Dan Jurafsky, and Tatsunori Hashimoto. 2021. Measuring conversational uptake: A case study on student-teacher interactions. In *Proceedings of the 59th Annual Meeting of the Association for Computational Linguistics and the 11th International Joint Conference on Natural Language Processing (Volume 1: Long Papers)*.

Jacob Devlin, Ming-Wei Chang, Kenton Lee, and Kristina Toutanova. 2019. BERT: Pre-training of deep bidirectional transformers for language understanding. In *Proceedings of the 2019 Conference of the North American Chapter of the Association for Computational Linguistics: Human Language Technologies, Volume 1 (Long and Short Papers)*.

Anna Filighera, Siddharth Parihar, Tim Steuer, Tobias Meuser, and Sebastian Ochs. 2022. Your answer is incorrect... would you like to know why? introducing a bilingual short answer feedback dataset. In *Proceedings of the 60th Annual Meeting of the Association for Computational Linguistics (Volume 1: Long Papers)*.

Philip Gage. 1994. A new algorithm for data compression. *C Users Journal*, 12(2):23–38.

Raghav Jain, Tulika Saha, Souhitya Chakraborty, and Sriparna Saha. 2022. Domain infused conversational response generation for tutoring based virtual agent. In *Proceedings of the International Joint Conference on Neural Networks (IJCNN)*.

Maria Yu Lebedeva, Antonina N Laposhina, Natalia A Alksnit, and Tatyana V Lyashenko. 2022. RuTOC: A corpus of online lessons in Russian as a foreign language. *Philological Class*, 27.

Michael Legutke and Howard Thomas. 1991. *Process and Experience in the Language Classroom.* London: Routledge.

Ilya Loshchilov and Frank Hutter. 2019. Decoupled weight decay regularization. In *Proceedings of the International Conference on Learning Representations (ICLR)*.

Neil Mercer. 2019. *Language and the Joint Creation of Knowledge: the selected works of Neil Mercer.* Abingdon: Routledge.

Jakub Náplava, Milan Straka, Jana Straková, and Alexandr Rosen. 2022. Czech grammar error correction with a large and diverse corpus. *Transactions of the Association for Computational Linguistics*, 10.

Li Nguyen, Zheng Yuan, and Graham Seed. 2022. Building educational technologies for code-switching: Current practices, difficulties and future directions. *Languages*, 7(3).

Alec Radford, Jeff Wu, Rewon Child, David Luan, Dario Amodei, and Ilya Sutskever. 2019. Language models are unsupervised multitask learners.

Anna Rogers, Olga Kovaleva, and Anna Rumshisky. 2020. A primer in BERTology: What we know about how BERT works. *Transactions of the Association for Computational Linguistics*, 8:842–866.

Stephen Roller, Emily Dinan, Naman Goyal, Da Ju, Mary Williamson, Yinhan Liu, Jing Xu, Myle Ott, Kurt Shuster, Eric M. Smith, Y-Lan Boureau, and Jason Weston. 2020. Recipes for building an open-domain chatbot. *arXiv*, 2004.13637.

Sebastian Ruder, Matthew E. Peters, Swabha Swayamdipta, and Thomas Wolf. 2019. Transfer learning in Natural Language Processing. In *Proceedings of the 2019 Conference of the North American Chapter of the Association for Computational Linguistics: Tutorials*, pages 15–18.

Harvey Sacks, Emanuel Schegloff, and Gail Jefferson. 1974. A simplest systematics for the organization of turn-taking for conversation. *Language*, 50:696–735.

Victor Sanh, Lysandre Debut, Julien Chaumond, and Thomas Wolf. 2019. DistilBERT, a distilled version of BERT: smaller, faster, cheaper and lighter. In *Proceedings of the 5th Workshop on Energy Efficient Machine Learning and Cognitive Computing*.

Mike Schuster and Kaisuke Nakajima. 2012. Japanese and Korean voice search. In *2012 IEEE International Conference on Acoustics, Speech and Signal Processing (ICASSP)*, pages 5149–5152. IEEE.

Choi Seung-Kwon, Lee Yo-Han, and Kwon Oh-Wook. 2022. A study on task-oriented dialogue data of a dialogue system for foreign language tutoring: Focusing on Korean dialogue data. *Foreign Languages Education*, 29(1):105–124.

Katherine Stasaski, Kimberly Kao, and Marti A. Hearst. 2020. CIMA: A large open access dialogue dataset for tutoring. In *Proceedings of the Fifteenth Workshop on Innovative Use of NLP for Building Educational Applications*.

Emma Strubell, Ananya Ganesh, and Andrew McCallum. 2019. Energy and policy considerations for deep learning in NLP. In *Proceedings of the 57th Annual Meeting of the Association for Computational Linguistics*.

Anaïs Tack and Chris Piech. 2022. The AI Teacher test: Measuring the pedagogical ability of Blender and GPT-3 in educational dialogues. In *Proceedings of the 15th International Conference on Educational Data Mining (EDM)*.

Gladys Tyen, Mark Brenchley, Andrew Caines, and Paula Buttery. 2022. Towards an open-domain chatbot for language practice. In *Proceedings of the 17th Workshop on Innovative Use of NLP for Building Educational Applications (BEA 2022)*.

Steve Walsh. 2006. *Investigating Classroom Discourse*. London: Routledge.

Steve Walsh. 2013. *Classroom Discourse and Teacher Development*. Edinburgh: Edinburgh University Press.

Steve Walsh and Li Li. 2012. Conversations as space for learning. *International Journal of Applied Linguistics*, 23:247–266.

Thomas Wolf, Lysandre Debut, Victor Sanh, Julien Chaumond, Clement Delangue, Anthony Moi, Pierric Cistac, Tim Rault, Remi Louf, Morgan Funtowicz, Joe Davison, Sam Shleifer, Patrick von Platen, Clara Ma, Yacine Jernite, Julien Plu, Canwen Xu, Teven Le Scao, Sylvain Gugger, Mariama Drame, Quentin Lhoest, and Alexander Rush. 2020. Transformers: State-of-the-art natural language processing. In *Proceedings of the 2020 Conference on Empirical Methods in Natural Language Processing: System Demonstrations*.

Xun Yuan, Derek Pham, Sam Davidson, and Zhou Yu. 2022. ErAConD: Error annotated conversational dialog dataset for grammatical error correction. In *Proceedings of the 2022 Conference of the North American Chapter of the Association for Computational Linguistics: Human Language Technologies*.

Manzil Zaheer, Guru Guruganesh, Avinava Dubey, Joshua Ainslie, Chris Alberti, Santiago Ontanon, Philip Pham, Anirudh Ravula, Qifan Wang, Li Yang, and Amr Ahmed. 2020. Big Bird: Transformers for longer sequences. In *Proceedings of the 34th Conference on Neural Information Processing Systems (NeurIPS)*.

Appendix: annotation types in TSCC 2.0

In this section we provide a full list of sequence types and teaching foci. We also give a list of resources encountered so far, but note that this is an open-ended class, because the labels are data-driven and the possibilities are endless (though slow-growing). For the most part, the labels and their definitions are copied over from the original TSCC paper (Caines et al., 2020), with some amendments as described in section 2.

Sequence types: We indicate major and minor shifts in conversational sequences – sections of interaction with a particular purpose. We define a number of sequence types listed and described below, firstly the major and then the minor types, or 'sub-sequences':

- Opening – greetings at the start of a conversation; may also be found mid-transcript, if for example the conversation was interrupted and conversation needs to recommence.
- Topic ___ – relates to the topic of conversation (minor labels complete this sequence type).
- Exercise – signalling the start of a constrained language exercise (*e.g.* 'please look at textbook page 50', 'let's look at the graph', *etc*); can be controlled or freer practice (*e.g.* gap-filling versus prompted re-use).
- Redirection – managing the conversation flow to switch from one topic or task to another.
- Disruption – interruption to the flow of conversation for some reason; for example because of loss of internet connectivity, telephone call, a cat stepping across the keyboard, and so on...
- Homework – the setting of homework for the next lesson, usually near the end of the present lesson.
- Closing – appropriate linguistic exchange to signal the end of a conversation.
- Admin – lesson management, such as 'please check your email' or 'see page 75' (*compared to version 1: moved from 'teaching focus'*).
- Free practice – ... (*new in version 2*).
- Non-English – ... (*new in version 2*).

  Below we list our minor sequence types, which complement the major sequence types:

  - Topic opening – starting a new topic: will usually be a new sequence.
  - Topic development – developing the current topic: will usually be a new sub-sequence.
  - Topic closure – a sub-sequence which brings the current topic to a close.
  - Presentation – (usually the teacher) presenting or explaining a linguistic skill or knowledge component.
  - Eliciting – (usually the teacher) continuing to seek out a particular response or realisation by the student.
  - Scaffolding – (usually the teacher) giving helpful support to the student.
  - Enquiry – asking for information about a specific skill or knowledge component.
  - Repair – correction of a previous linguistic sequence, usually in a previous turn, but could be within a turn; could be correction of self or other.
  - Clarification – making a previous turn clearer for the other person, as opposed to 'repair' which involves correction of mistakes.
  - Reference – reference to an external source, for instance recommending a textbook or website as a useful resource.
  - Recap – (usually the teacher) summarising a take-home message from the preceding turns.
  - Revision – (usually the teacher) revisiting a topic or task from a previous lesson.

Teaching focus: Here we note what type of knowledge is being targeted in the new conversation sequence or sub-sequence. Note that these do not accompany every sequence type – they are only used where applicable.

- Grammatical resource – appropriate use of grammar.
- Lexical resource – appropriate and varied use of vocabulary.
- Meaning – what words and phrases mean (in specific contexts).
- Discourse management – how to be coherent and cohesive, refer to given information and

introduce new information appropriately, signal discourse shifts, disagreement, and so on.

- Register – information about use of language which is appropriate for the setting, such as levels of formality, use of slang or profanity, or intercultural issues.
- Task achievement – responding to the prompt in a manner which fully meets requirements.
- Interactive communication – how to structure a conversation, take turns, acknowledge each other's contributions, and establish common ground (*does not yet feature in the corpus*).
- World knowledge – issues which relate to external knowledge, which might be linguistic (*e.g.* cultural or pragmatic subtleties) or not (they might simply be relevant to the current topic and task).
- Meta knowledge – discussion about the type of knowledge required for learning and assessment; for instance, 'there's been a shift to focus on X in teaching in recent years'.
- Content – a repair sequence which involves a correction in meaning; for instance, Turn 1: Yes, that's fine. Turn 2: Oh wait, no, it's not correct.
- Writing - a focus on writing skills and orthographic issues such as spelling, grammar, punctuation (*new in version 2, and subsumes 'typo' from version 1*).
- Speaking - a focus on speaking skills (*new in version 2*).
- Listening - a focus on listening skills (*new in version 2*).
- Reading - a focus on reading skills (*new in version 2*).
- Exam prep – specific drills to prepare for examination scenarios, as well as discussions around exam strategy (*updated label and definition for version 2*).

Use of resource: At times the teacher refers the student to materials in support of learning. The resources encountered so far are, `book`, `chat`, `dictionary`, `movie`, `sample paper`, `social media account`, `student's writing`, `textbook`, `video`, `website`.

Swedish MuClaGED:
A new dataset for Grammatical Error Detection in Swedish

Judit Casademont Moner
University of Gothenburg / Sweden
guscasaju@student.gu.se

Elena Volodina
University of Gothenburg / Sweden
elena.volodina@svenska.gu.se

Abstract

This paper introduces the Swedish MuClaGED[1] dataset, a new dataset specifically built for the task of Multi-Class Grammatical Error Detection (GED). The dataset has been produced as a part of the *multilingual Computational SLA*[2] shared task initiative[3]. In this paper we elaborate on the generation process and the design choices made to obtain Swedish MuClaGED. We also show initial baseline results for the performance on the dataset in a task of Grammatical Error Detection and Classification on the sentence level, which have been obtained through (Bi)LSTM ((Bidirectional) Long-Short Term Memory) methods.

1 Introduction

Due to high migration of people around the globe, learning a language of a new country of residence is increasingly important, and educational applications such as grammar checkers and other evaluation tools suitable for language learners are increasingly in demand. Grammatical Error Correction (GEC) (e.g. Omelianchuk et al., 2020; Bryant et al., 2019) and Grammatical Error Detection (GED) (e.g. Yuan et al., 2021; Daudaravicius et al., 2016) are two well-established fields in NLP that focus on techniques to support development of language users' writing skills, where errors are flagged (detection) and suggestions for corrections are generated (correction) - often in synchronous mode, i.e. as the user writes (e.g. Ranalli and Yamashita, 2022).[4] However, correction of errors without explaining reasons behind corrections does not necessarily lead to effective learning, and we argue therefore that GED **and** subsequent classification of errors by an error type constitute a critical first step for generation of meaningful corrective feedback.

Within Second Language Acquisition (SLA), *corrective feedback* can be defined as the teacher's identification of an error and subsequent attempt(s) to inform the learner about it in some way (Chaudron, 1988). The research in the field has moved from an earlier position where corrective feedback was considered unhelpful for language learning (Krashen, 1981) to the current understanding that corrective feedback can indeed be important and sometimes even crucial for adult learners to advance in the second/foreign language (Van Beuningen et al., 2012; Lyster et al., 2013). Research on the topic is based on the firm assumption that corrective feedback is necessary for second language learners. And recent studies have focused on the quality of automatic error detection and classification, as well as the best ways of providing feedback - among others, on the timing of said feedback (i.e. synchronous versus asynchronous) and on its effects on the cognitive process, e.g. Ranalli and Yamashita (2022).

In view of that, the Computational SLA team has considered **error detection and classification**, as the main focus for a shared task, which we argue should be given more attention.

1.1 MuClaGED task in a nutshell

The task has been defined as a *multi-lingual multi-class grammatical error detection in low-resource contexts*. One of the important principles is that the data should be *authentic language learner data*. Many current grammar checkers have been trained on texts produced by native speakers (L1) or on the language produced by advanced non-native speakers in highly academic texts, such as in the case of the Helping Our Own (HOO) shared

[1]MuClaGED = Multi-Class Grammatical Error Detection

[2]SLA = Second Language Acquisition

[3]Note that this version of the dataset is preliminary. The final guidelines for the dataset and the task may change as a result of the current experiments and further work on the definition of the task and datasets. However, the current dataset will be made available as such for the community one the shared task is over.

[4]Interrelation of the two fields is well-captured by Google Ngrams, even though we realize that the corpus is decisive for this type of generalizations: https://tinyurl.com/bddadpus

Judit Casademont Moner and Elena Volodina. Swedish MuClaGED: A new dataset for Grammatical Error Detection in Swedish. *Proceedings of the 11th Workshop on Natural Language Processing for Computer Assisted Language Learning (NLP4CALL 2022)*. Linköping Electronic Conference Proceedings 190: 36–45.

task (Dale and Kilgarriff, 2011). Intuitively, these systems are not as well suited for Intelligent Computer-Assisted Language Learning (ICALL) or Automatic Writing Evaluation (AWE) systems. Indeed, Leacock et al. (2014) have convincingly shown that foreign language learners' error correction and feedback will benefit from models trained on real L2 students' texts. Hence the importance of using *authentic language learner data*.

Another principle is the *focus on low-represented languages*. Both GEC and GED have been mainly researched on the basis of English data. Therefore, shared tasks on other, less-represented languages are needed to stimulate further research. However, unlike English, many other languages have smaller datasets of error-annotated L2 data compared to English. Therefore, the Computational SLA team has initiated a multi-lingual task where several language datasets, potentially small ones, should be unified in format and annotation for the shared task with a possibility to augment data, and/or use datasets from several languages through domain adaptation, transfer learning, and other modern techniques. Swedish, as one of the less-represented languages, is a part of this task, alongside Czech, Italian, German and English.

The teams will have sentence-scrambled authentic learner data with the task to develop methods for the following:

(1) binary classification on a sentence level (correct – incorrect)

(2) binary classification on a token level (correct – incorrect)

(3) error classification on a sentence level (5-class taxonomy)

(4) error classification on a token level (5-class taxonomy)

The results will be evaluated using recall, precision, accuracy and F-scores per the target language, and teams will have a possibility to use additional data in addition to the one provided by the organizers.

In other words, the goal of the shared task is to use L2 learners' texts to develop models capable of not only detecting grammatical errors (i.e. a binary classification between correct and incorrect), but also of multi-class error detection, that is, classifying detected errors into five main categories (Punctuation, Orthographic, Lexical, Morphological and Syntactic). The five categories have been defined broadly, so that all languages could convert their tagsets to produce comparable annotations.

The task is aimed at promoting a few languages which have not been in much focus for GED or GEC, and where appropriately annotated datasets are available, even if modest in size. Therefore the size of the datasets is limited to 10,000 sentences, imitating the low-resource context even where more data is available. The latter does not, however, apply to Swedish since error-annotated Swedish data contains only approximately 8,500 sentences from learner essays (including correct ones).

This will be the first time that original L2 learner data for Swedish will be used in a shared task focusing on GED. The main focus of this article is to present the generation process of the Swedish GED dataset necessary for the MuClaGED shared task according to specifications agreed on between the task organizers. In Section 3 we describe the resulting dataset. Additionally, we present an initial experiment on the resulting dataset to explore and evaluate its functionality in the task of Grammatical Error Detection and Classification on the sentence level (task (3) above) and to present the first baseline for the task (Section 4).

2 Related work

2.1 Grammatical Error Detection and Classification

Grammatical Error Detection (GED) is a challenging task in NLP which has gained considerable attention in the recent years. It is generally agreed on that, in the modern digital world, people tend to rely on a number of tools to learn new languages and improve their writing skills (Madi and Al-Khalifa, 2018a), as well as to assess their work (Rei and Yannakoudakis, 2016). The need for these tools exists in all languages, even in languages with a notable research focus such as English, but especially in low-resource languages that are not researched as much, such as the case of L2 Swedish.

GED is the task of detecting grammatical errors in a written text (Yuan et al., 2021). It can be performed on the token level or on the sentence level. Traditionally, GED has been treated as a binary sequence labelling task where, for each token or sentence, a label of either 'correct' or 'incorrect' is assigned (Rei and Yannakoudakis, 2016).

The task of GED can be extended into Grammatical Error Classification, where each of the errors needs to be labeled as belonging to one of the pre-established types. This task is also referred to as multi-class detection (Yuan et al., 2021).

2.2 Approaches to GED and GEC

Over time, various attempts have been made to address the task of detecting grammatical errors in written text. As presented by Madi and Al-Khalifa (2018a), the main approaches that have been used to perform GED and GEC are rule-based, syntax-based and machine learning. Additionally, lately some techniques have explored the use of transformer-based models (Bryant et al., 2019).

One popular approach to tackle the task is using deep learning models, such as Neural Networks (NN) or Recurrent Neural Networks (RNN), as it does not require manually writing rules nor any other kind of feature engineering, as the model features are learned automatically. The methods in this area that have proven to be more effective in detecting and correcting grammatical errors are RNNs, such as Long Short-Term Memory (LSTM) (Madi and Al-Khalifa, 2018b).

With the recent arrival of transformers in the field of NLP, transformer-based models have been explored as a new method to perform GED and GEC tasks. A recent example is that of Yuan et al. (2021), who have shown that transformer-based language models for multi-class GED for downstream GEC output considerably detailed results when detecting and classifying errors in written English. In their work, Yuan et al. (2021) prove that simply finetuning ELECTRA yields new state of the art results in multi-class error detection.

There is also the possibility of combining more than one of the aforementioned methods. Such is the case of Bell et al. (2019), who have used a bidirectional LSTM (Bi-LSTM) with contextual word embeddings from transformers (namely ELMo, BERT and Flair embeddings) to detect grammatical errors.

2.3 Data required for GED

Obtaining useful data for the tasks of GED and GEC can be challenging, especially when the desired approaches are statistical or machine learning methods, which require large quantities of labeled data. Written error data to perform GED and GEC for educational purposes can be obtained from two different types of sources: original learner data, namely texts written by L2 students, and synthetic data, which has been automatically generated. Whereas manually annotated human-made errors are representative and can therefore be useful to detect new errors, obtaining large datasets containing this kind of annotated data is expensive. And synthetic datasets are by some considered to deviate from the natural distribution of human-made errors (Yasunaga et al., 2021). Finding the perfect method to obtain high quality representative error data is still an ongoing and demanding challenge, and currently some datasets are formed by a combination of data sources (Leacock et al., 2014).

Labeled error datasets can be annotated on the sentence level or on the token level, although the latter is notably more common, habitually containing a diverse taxonomy of error types. Such is the case of the Cambridge Learner Corpus First Certificate in English (CLC FCE) dataset by Yannakoudakis et al. (2011), with 77 error types. Another case is the data structure mentioned in the work by Bryant et al. (2017), where they present a taxonomy of 25 error types distributed amongst three edit operation categories, 'Unnecessary' (U), 'Missing' (M) and 'Replacement' (R).

Original learner data appears to be the most logical source for the creation of datasets that are used to train models to create systems and tools intended for L2 students. To accurately perform GEC or GED on student-produced text, it is key to use data with a similar language use to that of the text we want to detect errors in (Leacock et al., 2014). Current corpora available to the public and for general use are usually extracted from formal and correct sources such as news sites or encyclopedias. The written texts' language style found in these corpora is usually different from the one used by students in their essays or other language learning tasks. This means that it is possible that a language model trained on encyclopedic text will not perform accurately GED on L2 students' texts. Therefore, we consider the use of original learner data the right choice for the task at hand.

3 Constructing MuClaGED

3.1 Original learner data

The source of the data used to craft the Swedish MuClaGED dataset is the SweLL (Swedish

Learner Language) gold corpus (Volodina et al., 2019). SweLL is an infrastructure with several linguistic datasets, one of which is SweLL-gold, a collection of 502 essays (7,807 sentences in the source) written by learners of Swedish as a second language. The texts have been manually corrected and annotated by a team of researchers lead by Språkbanken, a research unit and a part of the Nationella Språkbanken (the National Language Bank of Sweden), with the purpose to set the foundations of the research on Second Language Acquisition (SLA) on the Swedish language (Rudebeck and Sundberg, 2021).

The 502 texts in SweLL-gold have been written by adult (16+) second language learners of Swedish who are undergoing a formal education in Swedish as a Second Language, such as university, upper education courses or Swedish For Immigrants (SFI), or taking official examinations to test their knowledge of the language (TISUS or CEFR-based).

The learner texts have undergone a certain amount of manipulation, that includes transcription (from hand-written originals), pseudonymization (to ensure the writers' privacy) and normalization (i.e. rewriting to correct version), and they are accompanied with demographic information of the writers and their performance in the form of metadata. The metadata includes, among others: age range, approximate level (one of "Avancerad", "Fortsättning" or "Nybörjare"[5] levels), course subject, date, education level, essay id, gender, grading scale and native language(s) of the learner. Not all parameters are provided for all the essays, and only a few are kept in MuClaGED.

The SweLL-gold correction taxonomy consists of 29 error correction tags, which can be grouped into the following six subgroups: Punctuation, Orthographic, Lexical, Morphological, Syntactical and Other. For this work, we consider the first five categories, namely POLMS. Furthermore, the Other category represents comments and tags for unintelligible words in other languages, corrections that cannot be included in any of the established categories and pseudonymization notes. Further information can be found in the annotation guidelines (Rudebeck and Sundberg, 2021).

[5] Advanced", "Continuing" (standing for "Intermediate") and "Beginner".

3.2 From SweLL-gold to MuClaGED

In this project, we transform the existing original learner data in Swedish, the SweLL-gold dataset (Volodina et al., 2019), into the CoNLL-like format agreed on by the Computational SLA team to build Swedish MuClaGED, exemplified in Fig. 2.

The format specifications go as follows. The established taxonomy contains five error categories, to be distributed into three correction operation types, represented in columns. These error categories are the top error tags used in Volodina et al. (2019), namely POLMS (**P**unctuation, **O**rthographic, **L**exical, **M**orphologic and **S**yntactic). The three error edit operation columns are inspired by the work by Bryant et al. (2017) but renamed slightly differently as ADR, standing for **A**ddition, **D**eletion and **R**eplacement.

In practical terms it means that, for example, if a sentence contains a misspelled word, the edit operations would be 'R' – replacement, and the error type be 'O' – orthographic. The 'O' code will be filled into the column 'R' for that particular token. If the same word is involved in some other error types, e.g. morphological agreement, a code 'M' – morphological error – will be added into the same column 'R'.

Additions are attached to the token after, where the additional necessary token (or tokens) should be added to render the sentence grammatically correct. For this purpose, a dummy token ('@') is added as the last position of the sentence, to store the information in case a token needs to be added at the end of the sentence. As it can be seen in the example in Figure 2, each sentence in the dataset is formed of

(1) four comment-lines containing (i) the original sentence ('text'), (ii) the corrected version of the sentence ('corrected_text'), (iii) sentence id ('sent_id') and (iv) the metadata with level, first language ('L1') and the data split (80% is'Train', 10% is 'Dev', and 10% is 'Test'); during the development period we kept essay ids for potential need to double-check with the full essays. For the shared task essay ids are unnecessary and will be removed.

(2) one line per token with the token index, the word itself and the three edit operation columns (Addition, Deletion, Replacement). The columns are filled with corresponding error type(s) that have undergone that particular editing operation.

To complete the format transformation of the

```
# text = Vi fortfarande behöver vårt bibliotek ! @
# corrected_text = Vi behöver fortfarande vårt bibliotek ! @
# sent id = 86
# metadata = Approximate level = Nybörjare, L1 = Berberspråk, Marockansk arabiska, Split = Train
1       Vi              _       _       _
2       fortfarande     _       _       ['S']
3       behöver         _       _       _
4       vårt            _       _       _
5       bibliotek       _       _       _
6       !               _       _       _
7       @               _       _       _
```

Figure 1: Sentence example of the dataset with a word order error. The columns, in order, are: token id, token, addition errors, deletion errors, replacement errors. Translation: 'We still need our library!'

```
# text = Jag kunde inte forbi med de så var ensama . @
# corrected_text = Jag kunde inte lämna dem så de var ensamma . @
# sent id = 114
# metadata = Approximate level = Fortsättning, L1 = Oromo, Split = Train
1       Jag     _       _       _
2       kunde   _       _       _
3       inte    _       _       _
4       forbi   _       _       ['L', 'S']
5       med     _       ['S']   _
6       de      _       _       ['M']
7       så      _       _       _
8       dem     _       _       ['M']
9       var     _       _       _
10      ensama  _       _       ['O']
11      .       _       _       _
12      @       _       _       _
```

Figure 2: Sentence example of the dataset. The columns, in order, are: token id, token, addition errors, deletion errors, replacement errors. Translation: 'I couldn't leave them so they were alone.'

dataset, a few steps have to be carried out. These steps involve creating a sentence-level alignment, simplifying the error tags and distributing them according to the ADR error correction operations, dividing the essays into sentences, and finally obtaining POS (Part of Speech) information and gathering metadata.

The first step to obtain Swedish MuClaGED from SweLL-gold is to reach a sentence level alignment between the original text ('source') and its corrected version ('target'). The goal of this step is to distribute the error labels into the proper error correction operation type, represented in the ADR columns, specifically the additions and the deletions. When aligning the original text and the corrected text, we obtain 3 possible situations: one-to-one matches, where one token in the source corresponds to one token in the target; one-to-zero (no matches), where a token or more in the source cannot be matched to the target, or vice-versa, zero-to-one; and matches on different number of tokens (many-to-one, one-to-many and many-to-many). In the last situation, the difference in the number of tokens is taken into account to determine whether it indicates an addition or a deletion.

The error label distribution amongst the three ADR error correction operations is determined by either a strict manually-established limitation based on the linguistic analysis of the pattern of each error type, or by an automatic distribution decided by the token-level extension of the error tag. Each error type tag has been looked into to observe its behaviour in the sentences, and it has been found that, whereas some error tags consistently behave in the same manner and only involve one of the three error edit operation types, other error tags could be placed in more than one category. The error label distribution, also referred to as 'label logic' is shown in Table 1.

Finally, the error tags are simplified so that we are left with only the five main categories (Lexical, Morphological, Orthographic, Punctuation and Syntactic) by removing the second part of the original tags. The 35 labels found in the SweLL

Operation types	Error labels
Addition (A)	'S-M', 'S-Msubj', 'P-M'
Deletion (D)	'S-R', 'P-R'
Replacement (R)	'O', 'O-Cap', 'O-Comp', 'L-Der', 'L-FL', 'L-Ref', 'L-W', 'M-Adj/adv', 'M-Case', 'M-F', 'M-Gend', 'M-Other', 'M-Verb', 'S-Adv', 'S-Comp', 'S-FinV', 'S-Type', 'P-Sent', 'P-W'
No fixed category	'M-Def', 'M-Num', 'S-Clause', 'S-Ext', 'S-WO', 'S-Other'

Table 1: Error label distribution by error operation column.

taxonomy (Volodina et al., 2019) are thus reduced to five categories according to the first head category of the SweLL tag (e.g., 'M-Verb', which represents Morphological errors involving verbs and auxiliaries, becomes simply 'M'). Error corrections spanning a group of tokens receive numbering starting from the second token. This is done by adding ':2' (and consecutively) to the error tag.

To make sure that the dataset can be shared with any team willing to participate in the shared task despite the GDPR restrictions, (1) metadata was restricted to two labels - levels of the course and mother tongues; and (2) essays were scrambled and sentences were ordered randomly to limit a possibility to reconstruct original essays.

3.3 The resulting dataset

The final Swedish MuClaGED dataset, based entirely on the SweLL-gold dataset (Volodina et al., 2019), is formed by a total of 8,553 sentences (155,415 tokens). These sentences are represented in a 'CoNLL-like' format, where each sentence is representas as follows: an initial comment-line with the full text, a second comment-line with the corrected text, a third comment-line with the sentence id and a fourth comment-line with metadata, containing the approximate level of the student, their native language or languages and the split the sentence belongs to (either train, test or dev splits, which represent 80%, 10% and 10% of the dataset respectively). The comment-lines are followed by one line for each individual token in the sentence. The token-level information consists of three error correction operation categories, namely ADR, standing for **A**ddition, **D**eletion and **R**eplacement.

In the dataset we can find the following error distribution by token (Table 2). One sentence might contain more than one error of the same type, and one token might be involved in more than one type of errors at once.

Error type	Number of tokens containing this error
Lexical	4,862
Morphological	7,957
Orthographic	4,360
Punctuation	2,888
Syntactical	7,422
Total count of errors	27,489
Error-free tokens	127,926

Table 2: Error distribution by token

Table 3 presents the error distribution on the sentence level, that is, it shows how many sentences contain at least one error for each of the types. This means that, even though one sentence might contain, for example, 3 grammatical errors of the type 'Syntactic', it is only counted once.

Error type	Number of sentences containing this error
Fully correct sentences	2,100
Lexical	3,146
Morphological	3,922
Orthographic	2,688
Punctuation	1,843
Syntactical	3,763

Table 3: Error distribution by sentence

Table 4 shows the error distribution by correction operation categories (Addition, Deletion or Replacement).

Column type	Number of errors
Addition (A)	6,120
Deletion (D)	2,394
Replacement (R)	20,058

Table 4: Error counts by column

4 Baseline experiments on MuClaGED

4.1 Methods

The experiment was carried out by using LSTMs and Bi-LSTMs on simple word embeddings, word embeddings combined with POS tags information and on Swedish BERT sentence embeddings (Rekathati, 2021).

LSTMs and Bi-LSTMs Long Short-Term Memory (LSTM) and their bidirectional counterpart (Bi-LSTM) are a type of artificial neural networks called Recurrent Neural Networks (RNN). An RNN makes use of sequential data to feed the output of a previous step to the current

```
# text = Tre barn har jag Jag tyckem min lägenhet . @
# corrected_text = Tre barn har jag. Jag tycker om min lägenhet . @
# sent id = 103
# metadata = Approximate level = Nybörjare, L1 = Arabiska, Kurdiska, Split = Test
1       Tre      _       _       _
2       barn     _       _       _
3       har      _       _       _
4       jag      _       _       _
5       Jag      ['P']   _       _
6       tyckem   _       _       ['O']
7       min      ['S']   _       _
8       lägenhet         ['S']   _       _
9       .        _       _       _
10      @        _       _       _
```

Figure 3: Sentence example with a missing punctuation error (on token 5). The columns, in order, are: token id, token, addition errors, deletion errors, replacement errors. Translation: 'I have three children I like my apartment.'

training step (Abiodun et al., 2019). They are notable for their memory, which allows the output from previous steps to influence the following step. Nonetheless, RNNs do not learn well from long sequences of data (Sarker, 2021). To overcome this limitation involving the gradients of the neural network surged LSTMs and Bi-LSTMs.

Bi-LSTMs have the same structure as the original LSTM, but the difference between the two is that Bi-LSTMs are formed by two hidden layers (two LSTMs) that take in the input from opposite directions (i.e., one does take the input starting from the beginning and the other does it starting from the end), inputting data from the past and the future and consequently taking into consideration the entire context of an element in a sequence (Sarker, 2021), instead of just the previous elements, which is what is done by simple LSTMs. Bi-LSTMs are a common choice of method in many tasks involving context, which are most NLP tasks.

Since Bi-LSTMs consider the whole context of a token in a sequence and grammatical errors can oftentimes be related to other elements in the sentence, it seemed natural for the purpose of performing GED to make use of this type of RNN. For experimentation purposes, both LSTMs and Bi-LSTMs were employed in this work.

The conscious choice was made to use LSTMs and Bi-LSTMs for this project instead of a transformer-based approach, which currently tends to yield the most promising results. We consider the main focus of this work to be the generation of a new dataset specifically designed for the task of grammatical error classification and not the obtainment of state-of-the-art results, as that will be the goal for the participants in the eventual shared task.

Swedish BERT sentence embeddings Bidirectional Encoder Representations from Transformers, commonly referred to as BERT, are large language representation models which provide pre-trained deep bidirectional representations for written text "by jointly conditioning on both left and right context in all layers" (Devlin et al., 2018). Through training, these models acquire substantial knowledge about how a language works by learning contextual relations amongst all words in a sequence of words and it produces rich feature representations (embeddings), both on the word level (the most frequently used for training models) and on the sentence level. BERT allows the building of models to perform a diverse amount of NLP tasks from its pre-trained word and sentence embeddings on a wide range of languages, including Swedish.

For this work, we decide to utilize sentence-level BERT embeddings instead of word-level ones due to the fact that incorrectly written words would be given split pre-trained embeddings by the model, which was trained on grammatically correct data. Therefore, the semantically meaningful sentence embeddings from KBLab's Swedish Sentence-BERT (Rekathati, 2021) are used.

4.2 MuClaGED classification experiment

A machine learning experiment was performed on the generated Swedish MuClaGED dataset, with the goal (i) to test the functionality of the generated dataset for a possible task in the field of GED, and (ii) to obtain tentative baseline results for the planned shared task, to compare the participants' scores against.

This task has the aim of detecting the existence of errors on the sentence level and classifying them according to the five aforementioned categories (Lexical, Morphological, Orthographic, Punctuation and Syntactical). This is done regardless of the error frequency in the sentence, as the goal is simply to detect the existence of some error of a certain type. For example, for an input sentence that contains two Orthographic (O) errors and three Syntactic (S) errors, the correct output for the model would be to predict the tags 'O' and 'S'. Therefore, we are not using the token-level information for this evaluation task, we are exclusively testing the capacity of the model to detect the presence of errors and to classify them into five categories.

To perform this task, two distinct word embedding methods have been utilized. In the first method, they were created from a simple mapping from words to real numbers through a 'nn.Embedding' layer, which generates a M x N matrix, where M is the number of words in the vocabulary and N is the size of each word vector. The second method utilized Swedish BERT sentence embeddings extracted using the pretrained Swedish sentence transformer (Rekathati, 2021). The models constructed are either Long Short-Term Memory (LSTM) or Bidirectional Long Short-Term Memory (Bi-LSTM) neural networks. The Bi-LSTM has the same structure as the LSTM, but the difference is that it adds one more LSTM layer, which looks at the input information in reverse.

4.3 Results of the experiments

The evaluation metrics chosen to test the performance of the models were the traditional main metrics employed in NLP, namely accuracy, precision, recall, F1-score and F0.5-score. These were performed on all error labels overall as well as individually to be able to find the best performing models for each of them. Additionally, the instances where the model would predict all five error tags correctly for one sentence were counted and averaged. However, for these initial baseline results, to decide on the best performing model, we consider mainly the F0.5-score, although other metrics such as accuracy, precision and recall will also be considered as evaluation metrics in the shared task.

The model predictions are of a decimal number between 0 and 1 for each of the error tags (in the shape of [Orthographic, Lexical, Morphological, Punctuation, Syntactic]) and, to determine the real binary score, it is rounded up or down to the closest full number. That is, a probability of ≥ 0.5 will be considered a 1 (standing for True, the existence of a tag of a certain type), and a probability of < 0.5 will be considered a 0 (standing for False, the non-existence of a tag of a certain type).

Table 5 shows the two best performing models for the two data representations used for the experiments: the original L2 data and the original L2 data with POS information added. Only the results for the Bi-LSTM models are shown because, in both cases, the results improved notably when using a Bi-LSTM compared to using an LSTM.

	L2 data BERT Bi-LSTM	L2 data with POS BERT Bi-LSTM
Lexical	0.54894179	0.44901065
Morphological	0.60539215	0.51724137
Orthographic	0.57565789	0.33475783
Punctuation	0.46072507	0.05263157
Syntactic	0.64680232	0.55408472

Table 5: Best performing models by error type.

5 Concluding remarks

We have presented Swedish MuClaGED, one of five language datasets for the shared task on multi-class error detection. The dataset was evaluated for the task and we have reported the baseline results.

The main limitation is the size of the dataset. It is apparent that the Swedish MuClaGED is of limited size (8,553 sentences coming from 502 student essays), especially considering that most tasks, not only in GED and NLP specifically but in the general field of machine learning, commonly require greater amounts of data to train models capable of producing satisfactory results. Therefore, there is the possibility that, for certain purposes, especially if the dataset is to be used on its own, the quantity of data present, of 8,553 sentences, might not suffice. However, as the goal of the Computational SLA shared task for which the MuClaGED dataset has been built is to offer the participants a dataset containing approximately 10,000 sentences of each participating language to construct a larger multilingual dataset, we consider its size to be rather appropriate.

A second possible inconvenience is the imbalance in the amount of error labels, namely the fact that the five possible errors are not found in the same frequency amongst the sentences forming the dataset. It is therefore likely that the models trained with this data will have a better performance on the most frequent error types (Syntactical and Morphological). Although, overall, the results in Table 5 show no remarkably large difference in performance, we consider it relevant to note that the error types that show the highest f0.5-scores correspond with the error types with more representation in the dataset, and vice versa.

Regarding the results of the experimentation on the task of Grammatical Error Detection and Classification on the sentence level, a first conclusion that can be drawn is that the models trained on Swedish BERT sentence-level embeddings yield significantly better general results. A possible reason for the better performance of models trained using pre-trained BERT embeddings could be the fact that Swedish BERT, like BERT in its other available languages, is trained on grammatically correct data. Therefore, it is likely that BERT captures enough grammatical knowledge that, when generating an embedding for a sentence containing grammatical errors, the error gets reflected and the model can detect and classify it with more ease.

Secondly, adding POS information to the automatically generated through the Embedding dimension word embeddings, counter-intuitively does not seem to provide relevant enough information for the models to yield better results. There is a possibility that the lower scores (relative to better performing models) were caused by the method of combining the tensors of the word embeddings with the tensors representing the POS tags, which was 'torch.add', an element-wise addition of tensors. Other ways of combining both representations for the model to learn from would need additional exploration.

The results on the task of error type detection on the sentence level show that the proposed format of the dataset and the approach chosen for the experiment are promising. Additionally, the structure design of Swedish MuClaGED offers the possibility of more in-depth experiments which could be explored in the future.

In this work, only LSTM and Bi-LSTM models were trained for both tasks. However, considering the improvement in performance when working with BERT sentence-level embeddings, one would consider the employement of pre-trained models (either BERT itself or other transformer-based models) for the task. Similarly, other type of word embeddings could be explored within the same LSTM and Bi-LSTM structure, such as FastText, for example.

Experiments with synthetic error datasets to complement MuClaGED have been initiated and shown very promising results (Casademont Moner, 2022). Synthetic data could have helped reach the necessary level of 10,000 sentences for the shared task and reduce the imbalance of underrepresented error types. However, this work is outside the scope of this article and the type of the data that the shared task requires.

Finally, the requirement on cross-language similarity/comparability of the datasets in the shared task (with regards to labels) might require additional changes and modifications to the presented dataset before the final version is adopted. The presented experiment and dataset are to be viewed as a proof-of-concept.

Acknowledgments

This work has been supported by a research grant from the Swedish Riksbankens Jubileumsfond *SweLL - research infrastructure for Swedish as a second language*, IN16-0464:1; by *Nationella språkbanken*, funded by the Swedish Research Council (2018-2024, contract 2017-00626) and their participating partner institutions; and by VINNOVA through its funding of *SwedishGlue: a benchmark suite for language models* (2020-02523).

References

Oludare Abiodun, Aman Jantan, Oludare Omolara, Kemi Dada, Abubakar Umar, Okafor Linus, Humaira Arshad, Abdullahi Aminu Kazaure, Usman Gana, and Muhammad Kiru. 2019. Comprehensive Review of Artificial Neural Network Applications to Pattern Recognition. *IEEE Access*, PP:1–1.

Samuel Bell, Helen Yannakoudakis, and Marek Rei. 2019. Context is Key: Grammatical Error Detection with Contextual Word Representations. *CoRR*, abs/1906.06593.

Christopher Bryant, Mariano Felice, Øistein E. Andersen, and Ted Briscoe. 2019. The BEA-2019 Shared Task on Grammatical Error Correction. In *Proceedings of the Fourteenth Workshop on Innovative*

Use of NLP for Building Educational Applications, pages 52–75, Florence, Italy. Association for Computational Linguistics.

Christopher Bryant, Mariano Felice, and Ted Briscoe. 2017. Automatic Annotation and Evaluation of Error Types for Grammatical Error Correction. In *Proceedings of the 55th Annual Meeting of the Association for Computational Linguistics (Volume 1: Long Papers)*, pages 793–805, Vancouver, Canada. Association for Computational Linguistics.

Judit Casademont Moner. 2022. Multi-Class Grammatical Error Detection: Data, Benchmarks and Evaluation Metrics for the First Shared Task on Swedish L2 Data. Master's thesis, University of Gothenburg.

Craig Chaudron. 1988. *Second Language Classrooms. Research on Teaching and Learning.* Cambridge University Press, New York.

Robert Dale and Adam Kilgarriff. 2011. Helping Our Own: The HOO 2011 Pilot Shared Task. In *Proceedings of the 13th European Workshop on Natural Language Generation*, pages 242–249, Nancy, France. Association for Computational Linguistics.

Vidas Daudaravicius, Rafael E. Banchs, Elena Volodina, and Courtney Napoles. 2016. A report on the automatic evaluation of scientific writing shared task. In *Proceedings of the 11th Workshop on Innovative Use of NLP for Building Educational Applications*, pages 53–62, San Diego, CA. Association for Computational Linguistics.

Jacob Devlin, Ming-Wei Chang, Kenton Lee, and Kristina Toutanova. 2018. BERT: Pre-training of Deep Bidirectional Transformers for Language ´Understanding. *CoRR*, abs/1810.04805.

Stephen Krashen. 1981. Second language acquisition. *Second Language Learning*, 3(7):19–39.

Claudia Leacock, Martin Chodorow, Michael Gamon, and Joel Tetreault. 2014. *Automated Grammatical Error Detection for Language Learners, Second Edition*, volume 7.

Roy Lyster, Kazuya Saito, and Masatoshi Sato. 2013. Oral corrective feedback in second language classrooms. *Language teaching*, 46(1):1–40.

Nora Madi and Hend S. Al-Khalifa. 2018a. A Proposed Arabic Grammatical Error Detection Tool Based on Deep Learning. *Procedia computer Science, volume 142, p. 352-355.*

Nora Madi and Hend Suliman Al-Khalifa. 2018b. Grammatical Error Checking Systems: A Review of Approaches and Emerging Directions. *2018 Thirteenth International Conference on Digital Information Management (ICDIM)*, pages 142–147.

Kostiantyn Omelianchuk, Vitaliy Atrasevych, Artem Chernodub, and Oleksandr Skurzhanskyi. 2020. Gector–grammatical error correction: tag, not rewrite. *arXiv preprint arXiv:2005.12592*.

Jim Ranalli and Taichi Yamashita. 2022. Automated written corrective feedback: Error-correction performance and timing of delivery. *Language Learning & Technology*, 26(1):1–25.

Marek Rei and Helen Yannakoudakis. 2016. Compositional Sequence Labeling Models for Error Detection in Learner Writing. In *Proceedings of the 54th Annual Meeting of the Association for Computational Linguistics (Volume 1: Long Papers)*, pages 1181–1191, Berlin, Germany. Association for Computational Linguistics.

Faton Rekathati. 2021. The KBLab Blog: Introducing a Swedish Sentence Transformer.

Lisa Rudebeck and Gunlög Sundberg. 2021. SweLL correction annotation guidelines. Technical report, GU-ISS Research report series, Department of Swedish, University of Gothenburg. http://hdl.handle.net/2077/69434.

Iqbal Sarker. 2021. Deep Learning: A Comprehensive Overview on Techniques, Taxonomy, Applications and Research Directions.

Catherine G Van Beuningen, Nivja H De Jong, and Folkert Kuiken. 2012. Evidence on the effectiveness of comprehensive error correction in second language writing. *Language learning*, 62(1):1–41.

Elena Volodina, Lena Granstedt, Arild Matsson, Beáta Megyesi, Ildikó Pilán, Julia Prentice, Dan Rosén, Lisa Rudebeck, Carl-Johan Schenström, Gunlög Sundberg, and Mats Wirén. 2019. The SweLL Language Learner Corpus: From Design to Annotation. *Northern European Journal of Language Technology.*

Helen Yannakoudakis, Ted Briscoe, and Ben Medlock. 2011. A New Dataset and Method for Automatically Grading ESOL Texts. In *Proceedings of the 49th Annual Meeting of the Association for Computational Linguistics: Human Language Technologies*, pages 180–189, Portland, Oregon, USA. Association for Computational Linguistics.

Zheng Yuan, Shiva Taslimipoor, Christopher Davis, and Christopher Bryant. 2021. Multi-Class Grammatical Error Detection for Correction: A Tale of Two Systems. In *Proceedings of the 2021 Conference on Empirical Methods in Natural Language Processing*, pages 8722–8736, Online and Punta Cana, Dominican Republic. Association for Computational Linguistics.

Interactive Word Sense Disambiguation in Foreign Language Learning

Jasper Degraeuwe
LT[3] / MULTIPLES
Ghent University
Belgium
Jasper.Degraeuwe@UGent.be

Patrick Goethals
LT[3] / MULTIPLES
Ghent University
Belgium
Patrick.Goethals@UGent.be

Abstract

"Word sense awareness" is a feature which is not yet implemented in most corpus query tools, Intelligent Computer-Assisted Language Learning (ICALL) environments or computer-readable didactic resources such as graded word lists (Alfter and Graën, 2019; Pilán et al., 2016; Tack et al., 2018). The present paper aims to contribute to filling this lacuna by presenting a word sense disambiguation (WSD) method for ICALL purposes. The method, which is targeted at Spanish as a foreign language (SFL), takes a few prototypical example sentences as input, converts these sentences into "sense vectors", and integrates part of the training data collection process into interactive vocabulary exercises. The evaluation of the method is based on a selection of 50 ambiguous items related to the domain of economics and compares different types of input data. With a top weighted F1 score of 0.8836, the present study shows that the currently available NLP tools, resources and methods provide all the necessary building blocks for developing a WSD method which can be integrated into interactive ICALL environments.

1 Introduction

Compared to single-meaning words, lexically ambiguous items (e.g. *empleo*: 'usage' / 'job') have shown to be more challenging to process and learn (Bensoussan and Laufer, 1984; Degani and Tokowicz, 2010). Nevertheless, the distinction of word senses has often been overlooked in the design of vocabulary learning curricula and graded word lists (Tack et al., 2018). Moreover, when foreign language teachers or textbook designers need a set of usage examples for each sense of an ambiguous word, they often have to manually gather or invent these example sentences. Or, if they are able to use corpus query tools, they have to rely on concordance searches which do not distinguish between word senses, as most of those tools only allow performing searches on word forms.

It is for these kinds of time-consuming tasks that the field of ICALL aims to offer solutions: by means of Natural Language Processing (NLP)-driven methodologies, ICALL studies seek to facilitate and/or (partially) automate the creation of language learning materials to be used in a CALL environment. To tackle the lexical ambiguity issue, the NLP technique of WSD can be applied (Kulkarni et al., 2008). Although performance levels have recently breached the "80% glass ceiling set by the inter-annotator agreement" (Bevilacqua et al., 2021), WSD is still an open problem (Blevins et al., 2021; Navigli, 2018), especially for languages other than English and for specific purposes such as ICALL. However, thanks to the recent advances within NLP, the tools and resources to successfully develop an ICALL-tailored WSD method do seem to be available. Therefore, with this study we aim to make a plea for integrating WSD in ICALL, presenting a straightforward method which can easily be implemented in existing ICALL environments.

The paper is structured as follows: Section 2 first of all zeroes in on the concepts of lexical ambiguity (as conceived in NLP) and WSD, and also provides a brief overview of the recent developments within ICALL. Next, in Section 3 we present our WSD method, which is aimed at Spanish as the target language (3.1), takes a few prototypical example sentences as input (3.2), leverages the ability of Transformer models to create contextualised "sense vectors" (3.3), and integrates part of the process of compiling training data into interactive vocabulary exercises for SFL students (3.4). The WSD method is applied to and evaluated on custom datasets (3.5), the results of which are discussed in Section 4. Finally, Section 5 includes a conclusion and discussion of the study, alongside some possible directions for future research.

Jasper Degraeuwe and Patrick Goethals. Interactive word sense disambiguation in foreign language learning. *Proceedings of the 11th Workshop on Natural Language Processing for Computer Assisted Language Learning (NLP4CALL 2022)*. Linköping Electronic Conference Proceedings 190: 46–54.

2 Related research

2.1 Lexical ambiguity in NLP

In the domain of (written) NLP, a lexically ambiguous item is usually defined as a lemma of a specific part of speech (POS) for which more than one sense can be distinguished. For reasons of feasibility and scalability, to determine which senses are included in the sense inventory (i.e. the lexicon in which ambiguous words are linked to their different senses), most computationally-focused studies on WSD rely on established resources such as (Euro)WordNet (Fellbaum, 1998) or BabelNet (Navigli and Ponzetto, 2012). However, the sense distinctions in these resources are often of a very fine-grained nature, which makes them sometimes even difficult for humans to distinguish (Loureiro et al., 2021) and, in many cases, unsuitable for real-life NLP applications (Hovy et al., 2013). Moreover, Kilgarriff (1997) argues that "there is no reason to expect a single set of word senses to be appropriate for different NLP applications", since "different corpora, and different purposes, will lead to different senses".

In other words, our specific ICALL setting requires a specific sense inventory, tailored to the needs of SFL learners (see Section 3.2). An example of an inventory with coarse-grained sense distinctions that are easily interpretable by humans is the CoarseWSD-20 dataset (Loureiro et al., 2021), which consists of a manual expert selection of twenty English nouns and their corresponding senses, and is based on Wikipedia as reference inventory and corpus. Degraeuwe et al. (2021) undertake a similar effort, but in this case to build a WSD system which distinguishes between sensory and non-sensory meanings of ambiguous items for the specific purpose of analysing the use of sensory language as a rhetoric technique in tourism discourse.

2.2 Word sense disambiguation

As formulated by Navigli (2009), WSD is "the ability to computationally determine which sense of a word is activated by its use in a particular context". Formally, this means that WSD aims to identify a mapping A from words to senses (i.e. to assign the appropriate sense(s) to all or some of the words in a text), such that $A(i) \subseteq SensesD(w_i)$, where $SensesD(w_i)$ is the set of senses encoded in a dictionary D (i.e. the sense inventory) for word w_i, and $A(i)$ is that subset of the senses (usually of length 1) of w_i which are appropriate in the context (Navigli, 2009). In the following example, a WSD system is expected to map *operación* in sentence (a) to the sense "operation", and in sentence (b) to the sense "surgery".

(a) La **operación** supuso la transferencia de cerca de 500 trabajadores. ('The operation entailed transferring around 500 workers.')

(b) La **operación** se ha efectuado por medio de un cateterismo. ('The surgery has been performed by means of a catheterisation.')

WSD can be conceived as a classification task, with the word senses as the classes, and an automatic classification method as the means to assign each occurrence of a word to one or more classes based on the evidence from the context and/or from external knowledge sources. In this regard, it should be highlighted that, contrary to other NLP classification tasks such as POS tagging and Named Entity Recognition (NER), in WSD there is no fixed number of predefined categories (classes), since the set of senses (classes) is different for each individual word. In other words, "WSD actually comprises n distinct classification tasks, where n is the size of the lexicon" (Navigli, 2009). As a result, building a WSD system usually constitutes an accumulative process.

2.3 WSD in ICALL

Driven by the recent advances in NLP, current ICALL applications which can be used for vocabulary learning purposes are doing more and more credit to the "Intelligent" part of their name. In the category of intelligent corpus consultation applications, the hybrid HitEx system for Swedish (Pilán et al., 2016) is a well-known example: it allows extracting context-independent example sentences of a given proficiency level from corpora by performing fine-grained and customisable queries. To this end, the system relies on computer-readable lexical-semantic resources and POS-tagged, lemmatised and parsed Swedish corpora, to which then a series of rule-based and machine learning-based selection criteria are applied. Next, for the category of exercise generation applications, different examples are to be found in the work of Graën, whose research explores the use of (multi)parallel corpora as input data for the automatic generation of (gamified) language learning

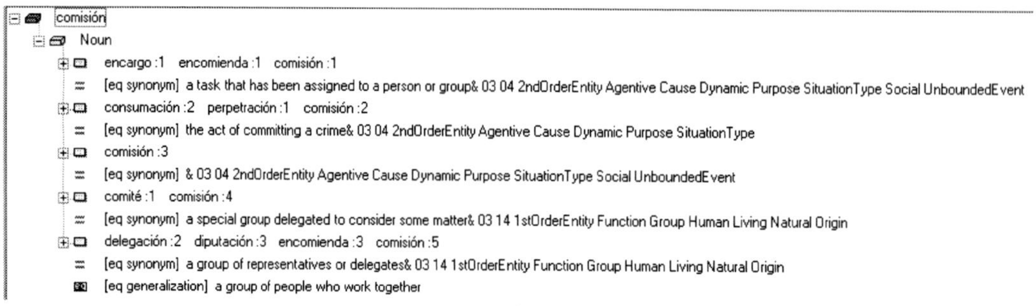

Figure 1: Spanish WordNet entry for *comisión*, in which two of its five "synsets" (synonym sets) refer to the sense "committee" with hardly any difference between them: the synset *[comité, comisión]* and the synset *[delegación, diputación, encomienda, comisión]*. Furthermore, despite being used very frequently, *comisión* as "intermediary fee" is not included amongst the senses.

exercises, ranging from training knowledge of particle verbs (Alfter and Graën, 2019) to reordering exercises (Zanetti et al., 2021).

However, although this kind of systems have proven to be a valuable complement to vocabulary learning activities in the classroom (Ruiz et al., 2021), using ICALL still comes with its limitations. Recognising lexically ambiguous items and distinguishing between their senses is one of those pending issues (Pilán et al., 2016), as the NLP-driven technique of WSD is rarely integrated in ICALL environments, in corpus query tools or in the development of computer-readable resources for didactic purposes (e.g. graded word lists).

3 Methodology

3.1 Setting

As mentioned in the introduction, one of the novel aspects of our WSD method is its embedding in an educational context. For this study, we take a B2+ level Spanish writing course at university as the target setting. As a part of the vocabulary learning module of the course, which specifically focuses on learning business vocabulary, the 35 enrolled students work with the ICALL environment of the Spanish Corpus Annotation Project (SCAP; scap.ugent.be; Goethals, 2018) and have to complete an online module on lexical ambiguity. It is in that module on lexical ambiguity that part of the training process of our WSD system is integrated (Section 3.4).

To arrive at a selection of target items the WSD method can be applied to and tested upon, all nouns in a 11M corpus containing newspaper articles on economics, are first ranked from highest to lowest keyness compared to a reference corpus (both corpora are available within the SCAP platform), with the keyness calculation being performed according to the Log Ratio formula (Hardie, 2014). Next, we ask an SFL expert to select the first 50 items (see Table 2) which have at least two relatively frequent meanings and fit within the business vocabulary scope of the B2+ writing course.

3.2 Sense inventory

Since using existing resources such as the Spanish WordNet and BabelNet would result in a too-fine grained and sometimes incomplete inventory (see Figure 1 for an example), we elaborate a custom sense inventory based on the senses included in the Spanish dictionary Clave. [1] Given its status as a general dictionary and its focus on "contemporarily used expressions and terms in daily life" (Fundación SM, 2021), Clave provides suitable input for building an SFL-focused sense inventory. To build the actual contents of the inventory, we ask an SFL expert to go over the Clave senses and, if deemed necessary, group related senses together into coarse-grained "main senses". In addition, the expert is instructed to eliminate all domain-specific Clave senses which are not related to the domain of economics (e.g. *matriz* as "matrix" in the domain of mathematics). Importantly, for most of its senses, the Clave dictionary provides a prototypical usage example, which will be used as the input data of our WSD methodology. If no example sentence is available for a given main sense (which is the case for 16.5% of the main senses), a usage example taken from one of the SCAP cor-

[1] Complete sense inventory available at https://github.com/JasperD-UGent/sense-inventory-economics-50.

Unseen sentence to be classified		
Eso sí, tendrás que aprobar también el examen de **ingreso**. ('Of course, you will have to pass the entrance exam.')		
Senses	**Labelled example sentences**	**Cosine similarity**
Sense 1 "entry"	Apoyaremos tu **ingreso** en la comisión. ('We will support your entry into the commission.')	.5591
	Hoy a las seis de la tarde es el **ingreso** del nuevo académico. ('Today at six in the afternoon the inauguration of the new academic takes place.')	**.5626**
Sense 2 "deposit"	El **ingreso** puedo realizarlo en cualquier sucursal. ('I can make the deposit in any branch.')	**.5026**
Sense 3 "income, revenue"	Este mes, los **ingresos** han sido menores porque ha habido menos ventas. ('This month, revenue has been lower because there have been fewer sales.')	**.3893**

Table 1: Authentic application example of the cosine similarity classifier, with the maintained cosine similarity values put in bold. The predicted output for the unseen sentence containing the ambiguous item *ingreso* is "entry", as the highest maintained value corresponds to this sense.

pora is manually added.

3.3 Sense vectors

Next, for each of the 50 target items, the prototypical example sentences included in the sense inventory are transformed into "sense vectors". To this end, we take the contextualised word embedding of the ambiguous item in the sentences with the help of the RoBERTa-BNE model (Gutiérrez-Fandiño et al., 2021). As a result, each main sense in the sense inventory is now represented by a set of n unique vectors, where n is the number of prototypical sentences linked to the main sense (see Figure 2 for an example). Usually, n is equal to 1, but if multiple Clave senses have been grouped together n can also be greater than 1. Finally, the sense vectors are used to predict the correct sense of ambiguous instances in new, unseen sentences. To perform this classification task, we use cosine similarity calculations, a measure closely related to distance metrics such as the Euclidean distance (which is used in k-NN classifiers), with the main difference being that instead of the distance between two vectors, it is the cosine of the angle between them which is measured. Cosine similarity calculations usually yield outcome values between 0 (no similarity) and 1 (complete similarity), and can be used to rank relative similarity levels (i.e. higher scores indicate a higher level of similarity).

In summary, given a new target sentence with an ambiguous word, the individual cosine similarity values between the vector of the ambiguous item in this target sentence and its sense vector(s) are computed. Next, only the highest cosine similarity value for each sense is maintained, after which the classifier assigns the target sentence to the sense with the highest maintained value (see Table 1 for an example).

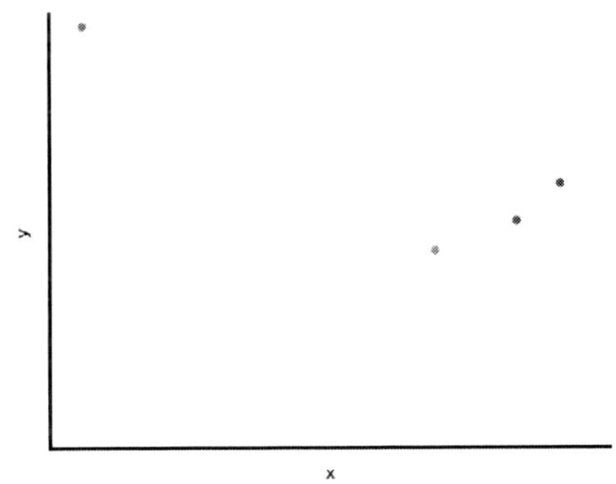

Figure 2: Authentic example of sense vectors visualised in a two-dimensional space, for the item *ingreso* (see Table 1 for the sentences used to create the vectors). The blue dots correspond to sense vectors of the sense "entry", the orange dot to "deposit", and the green one to "income, revenue".

3.4 Interactive exercises for training

As mentioned in Section 3.1, we use an online module on lexical ambiguity included in an SFL writing course at university to compile additional training data. To this end, for each of the 50 selected target items, a series of interactive exercises are elaborated in which the 35 SFL students enrolled in the course familiarise themselves with the linguistic phenomenon of lexical ambiguity and

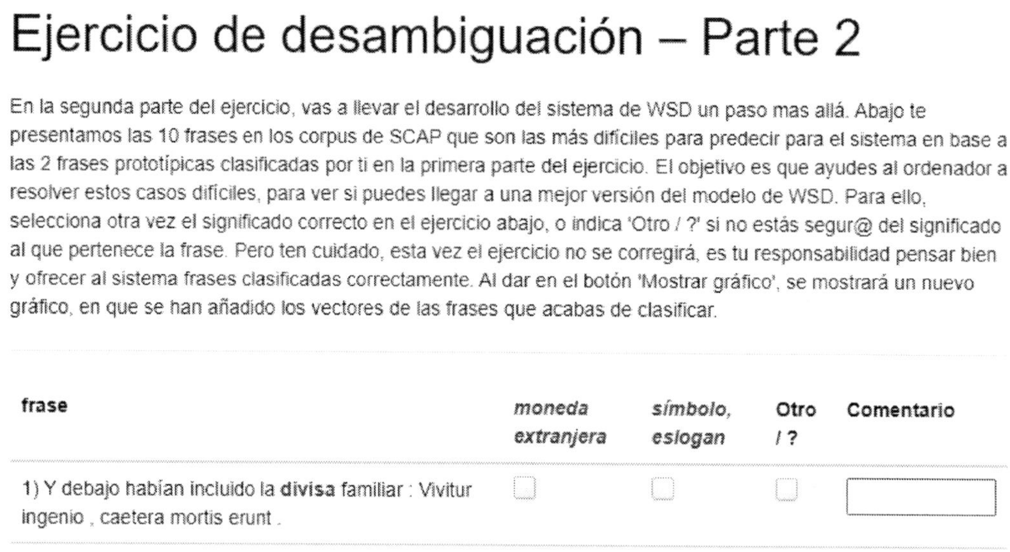

Figure 3: Screenshot of the all-embracing exercise in which students can train their own WSD model, for the item *divisa* ('foreign currency' / 'symbol, motto'). Before arriving at this part of the exercise, students first had to initialise their WSD model by assigning the prototypical example sentences from the sense inventory to the right sense. These labelled sentences were then converted into sense vectors and used to identify the ten most difficult sentences for the system (i.e. the ten sentences with the lowest cosine similarity difference between the two top maintained values) in a selection of unseen sentences taken from the SCAP corpora. In the exercise part shown in the screenshot, students are asked to assign these ten sentences to the correct sense, in order to provide the system with additional training data. Once finished, students are brought to the final part of the exercise, in which they can analyse the performance of their custom model on new sentences.

learn the different meanings of the ambiguous vocabulary item in question. Towards the end of the exercise series, students are also encouraged to consider lexical ambiguity from the perspective of the computer, and receive a brief introduction into the NLP technique of WSD. Finally, as an all-embracing exercise, they are offered the opportunity to train their own WSD models. Amongst other activities, this final exercise consists of assigning 10 unseen ambiguous sentences of a given target item to the correct sense (see Figure 3). These exercise responses are collected in order to be used as additional training data.

As all students are pre-assigned 8 vocabulary items for which they have to complete the entire exercise series (with the vocabulary items being evenly distributed across the students), for every vocabulary item at least 5 responses can be collected for each of the 10 unseen ambiguous sentences. Finally, a threshold-based filter is applied to the gathered data: all sentences for which at least 80% of the responses have been assigned to the same sense are considered suitable to be used as additional training data for that particular sense.

3.5 Evaluation

Since our WSD method is designed to be applied in a foreign language learning setting, it could not be evaluated using one of the (few) existing WSD datasets for Spanish (e.g. Màrquez et al., 2004). First of all, many of the 50 vocabulary items selected from the economic target corpus do not occur amongst the ambiguous words included in these datasets. Working with the words of the existing datasets instead of selecting the target items ourselves would have solved this problem, but none of the datasets includes a set of ambiguous items which could serve as input for the real-life vocabulary class as described in Section 3.1. Moreover, most datasets are labelled according to WordNet sense distinctions, which were not designed for the purpose of foreign language learning. In other words, all annotations would first have had to be manually converted to the sense distinctions made in our SFL-tailored inventory before they would become usable.

Therefore, we decide to create custom datasets, based on data from the SCAP corpora. For each of the 50 selected ambiguous items, all sentences in which the lemma of the item occurrs are extracted from the corpora. For this concordance search query, the minimal sentence length was put to 10 and the maximal length to 70, to ensure that noisy data are being kept out (e.g. short phrases with a lack of contextual information and paragraphs in which sentence splitting was not performed correctly). The resulting datasets per ambiguous item are then cleaned following an automatic, rule-based process, and randomly split into a 100-sentence test set and a "rest set" with all remaining sentences. Finally, the test sets are manually annotated by an SFL expert according to the sense distinctions made in the custom sense inventory.

To evaluate both the WSD method in general and the added value of using exercise responses as additional training data, two different input types (i.e. the training data which are used by the WSD system to make predictions) are determined. To make the system more robust, the first step of both input types consists of automatically identifying, for each sense of each ambiguous item, the 10 instances in the "rest set" with the highest cosine similarity compared to the contextualised sense vectors included in the sense inventory (see Section 3.3). The vectors corresponding to the ambiguous item in those sentences are then added as extra labelled training data on top of the original sense vectors. In the basic input type ("base"), no other training data are added after this step. In the second input type ("enriched"), however, the selected sentences from the interactive vocabulary exercise (see Section 3.4) are included as additional training instances.

Finally, the WSD method is applied twice to the test sets, once for every input type. To measure performance, weighted F1 scores are calculated: this score represents the harmonic mean of precision (i.e. the number of truly positive predictions divided by the number of truly positive and falsely positive predictions) and recall (i.e. the number of truly positive predictions divided by the number of truly positive and falsely negative predictions). By using the weighted variant of the metric, unequal label distributions are balanced out.

4 Results

First of all, the average results presented in Table 2 show that both input types outperform the most frequent sense (MFS) baseline by a large margin, highlighting the overall potential of the WSD method. Since, to the best of our knowledge, no benchmark exists for WSD for language learning purposes, to interpret the F1 scores we compare our results to Loureiro et al. (2021), a study with a similar setup as ours (see also Section 2.1). On a dataset of 20 English nouns, the fine-tuned large BERT model of Loureiro et al. (2021) obtains a top weighted F1 score of 0.975. However, it should be highlighted that they make use of labelled training sets with sizes up to 6421 instances. In this regard, the scores achieved by the best-performing model in our methodology, which only takes a few sentences as labelled input, can be considered highly satisfactory. Next, the results also reveal that the addition of the exercise responses as additional training data ("enriched") leads to a 0.01 increase in performance. Clearly, this increase is too small to make firm claims about the added value of resolving the most difficult cases (recall that the examples to be classified by the students correspond to the examples with the lowest cosine similarity difference between the two top maintained values) and adding them as training data.

As for the individual results, the scores reveal a mixed picture. First, for some items (*asociación*, *cuota*, *déficit*, *emisión*, *explotación* and *operación*) the addition of the exercise responses appears to cause a reverse effect. Although these non-neglegible decreases in performance are balanced out by the considerable improvements for *balance*, *comisión*, *compañía*, *descuento*, *división*, *entidad*, *gestión*, *ingreso*, *matriz*, *participación* and *valoración*, this finding suggests that new example sentences should be added with caution. When checking the added sentences, for *asociación*, *cuota* and *explotación* we found one or two sentences to be classified incorrectly by the students, which could explain part of the lower F1 score for those words. For the other items, resolving the most difficult cases seems to introduce "confusion" rather than clarity into the system. This finding could be an indication that we might need to reconsider the choice for taking this type of examples as our source for new training data. Switching to the exact opposite starting point, for instance, could be another approach worth studying: instead of integrating the sentences with the smallest cosine similarity differences into vocabulary exercises, the sentences with the largest differ-

Individual results							
Ambiguous item (Log Ratio)	#senses	F1_base	F1_enriched	Ambiguous item (Log Ratio)	#senses	F1_base	F1_enriched
acción (4.5)	4	.9909	.9547	entidad (8.5)	2	.8904	.9411
administración (7.1)	3	.909	.8623	explotación (6.1)	2	.9604	.8937
aplicación (5.4)	4	.8635	.8621	facturación (10.2)	3	.7997	.8372
área (5.1)	2	.8435	.8435	firma (5.7)	3	.8417	.8838
asociación (5.5)	2	.962	.9083	gestión (7)	2	.8877	.9809
balance (6.3)	2	.7755	.8493	implantación (6.4)	3	.8513	.8899
bono (9.3)	2	.9156	.9454	ingreso (6.8)	3	.9016	.9697
colocación (4.5)	3	.9417	.93	inversión (9)	3	.7226	.7664
comisión (6.8)	4	.9295	.9833	liquidación (6.7)	3	.7709	.775
compañía (5.5)	4	.7709	.9054	matriz (6.1)	3	.8547	.9622
competencia (6)	2	.9591	.949	mercado (7.2)	2	.9463	.964
concesión (5.1)	3	.9402	.9402	operación (6.2)	2	.9483	.8913
cotización (8.4)	3	.8129	.849	operador (8.7)	3	.7539	.7191
crecimiento (8.6)	2	.7786	.8211	organismo (5.1)	2	.9535	.9619
cuota (6.6)	2	.8719	.7231	participación (6.5)	2	.7863	.864
déficit (6.7)	2	.9804	.863	plataforma (4.5)	5	.9491	.9491
demanda (6.5)	2	.8698	.897	política (5.2)	2	.8368	.8368
descuento (6.8)	2	.9111	.9655	préstamo (5.7)	2	.9198	.9198
deuda (5)	2	.7048	.7379	rebaja (5.5)	2	.9482	.9482
distribución (6.4)	2	.9168	.8949	saneamiento (5.3)	2	.8024	.8024
divisa (5.6)	2	.9663	.9569	sector (6.8)	3	.8912	.8912
división (5.4)	6	.7146	.8376	segmento (8.8)	2	.9295	.9295
ejercicio (5.3)	4	.9259	.9172	subida (5)	2	.9879	.9879
emisión (7.3)	4	.8693	.7133	tasa (8.1)	3	.9218	.9218
empleo (5)	2	1	1	valoración (5.5)	2	.4713	.5806
Average results							
F1_base	.873						
F1_enriched	**.8836**						
MFS	.5901						

Table 2: Performance results on the custom 100-sentence test sets. The individual results report the weighted F1 scores for each item with "base" and "enriched" as the two different input types. Log Ratio values are added between brackets. For the average results, the mean of all 50 individual scores is taken. Here, also the most frequent sense (MFS) baseline is reported, a simple but often hard-to-beat dummy system which always predicts the most frequent sense of the ambiguous item (which was identified as the most frequent sense amongst the test set annotations).

ences could be taken as input for a new type of exercise. Finally, the individual results also highlight that a few items appear to be particularly challenging for the system (e.g. *valoración*: 'estimate' / 'appreciation, evaluation'), and will need to receive special attention. In this regard, a possible addition to the methodology could be to calculate the cosine similarity between the original sense vectors in order to determine an "inter-sense similarity" score. If, for a given ambiguous item, this score exceeds a certain threshold, the item could then be flagged so that more example sentences can be added before initialising the WSD method.

5 Conclusion and discussion

In this study, a novel WSD methodology for ICALL purposes is presented, applied to Spanish as the target language. The method makes use of a customised sense inventory in which all senses are accompanied by one or a few prototypical example sentences. By means of the RoBERTa-BNE model (Gutiérrez-Fandiño et al., 2021), these sentences are converted into unique "sense vectors", which can then be introduced into the cosine similarity classifier to predict the sense of an unseen ambiguous instance. Finally, we study the embedding of part of the training process into interactive vocabulary learning exercises for SFL students.

To assess performance, the method is applied to custom datasets for a selection of 50 ambiguous nouns related to the domain of economics. Overall, the WSD system achieves very promising results, with a top average weighted F1 score of 0.8836. Next, compiling additional training data through interactive vocabulary exercises leads to a 0.01 increase in performance compared to not using the exercise responses as additional training data. As the increase is only of a very small nature, additional research with a larger number of target items and/or larger test sets will be required to reach well-founded conclusions on this particular aspect. Finally, the analysis of the individual performance results indicates that adding the exercise responses does not per se lead to improved performance, especially (and perhaps logically) when incorrect classifications by the students passed the 80% threshold. Nevertheless, as more and more exercise responses will be collected over time, more sentences can be added (which could mitigate the "confusion" that is sometimes introduced) and more responses per sentence can be gathered (which could enable us to apply a more strict threshold for selecting suitable sentences). Additionally, switching to another type of input sentences in the exercises (e.g. the least difficult sentences instead of the most difficult ones) could also be a path worth exploring.

As the language model used to create the vectors is pretrained (and can thus be used off the shelf) and the exercise responses are filtered in an automated fashion, the prototypical example sentences are the only manually curated data needed to initialise the methodology. This architecture makes the WSD method scalable and applicable in real-life scenarios. Therefore, with this research we hope to contribute to implementing the distinction of word senses as an additional feature in corpus query tools, ICALL environments or computer-readable resources for didactic purposes (e.g. graded word lists), which would open a wide range of opportunities for the design of different language learning materials. These materials can range from lexical-semantic resources in which ambiguous items with similar polysemy patterns are grouped together, over disambiguated graded vocabulary lists, to exercises which start by presenting the so-called core meaning of polysemous items, a type of exercise which has proven to be beneficial for the long-term retention of those items (Verspoor and Lowie, 2003).

However, future research will still need to address the detection of low-performing items, and study how the performance of these items can be improved. For example, the cosine similarity between the original sense vectors could be calculated to determine an "inter-sense similarity" score. If, for a given ambiguous item, this score exceeds a certain threshold, the item could then be flagged. Similarly, the agreement rates between students on the interactive exercises can also be taken as a measure to detect possibly challenging items: if exercise responses show little consensus this should perhaps not be considered as a lack of inter-annotator agreement, but rather as a sign that (some of) the sense distinctions of the ambiguous word might be particularly challenging. Thirdly, we plan to carry out a follow-up study with a larger number of target items and multiple SFL students as test set annotators, and make the corresponding datasets publicly available so that they can be used to benchmark WSD methods for ICALL purposes. Finally, we also aim to expand our coverage to verbs and adjectives, which will likely entail other challenges given their different syntactic and morphological characteristics.

Acknowledgments

This research has been carried out as part of a PhD fellowship on the IVESS project (file number 11D3921N), funded by the Research Foundation - Flanders (FWO). For the elaboration of the custom sense inventory, we relied on the Clave dictionary, to whose contents we have access thanks to a research collaboration with the Fundación Santa María.

References

David Alfter and Johannes Graën. 2019. Interconnecting lexical resources and word alignment: How do learners get on with particle verbs? In *Proceedings of the 22nd Nordic Conference on Computational Linguistics*, pages 321–326.

Marsha Bensoussan and Batia Laufer. 1984. Lexical guessing in context in EFL reading comprehension. *Journal of Research in Reading*, 7:15–32.

Michele Bevilacqua, Tommaso Pasini, Alessandro Raganato, and Roberto Navigli. 2021. Recent Trends in Word Sense Disambiguation: A Survey. In *Proceedings of the Thirtieth International Joint Conference on Artificial Intelligence*, pages 4330–4338,

Montreal, Canada. International Joint Conferences on Artificial Intelligence Organization.

Terra Blevins, Mandar Joshi, and Luke Zettlemoyer. 2021. FEWS: Large-Scale, Low-Shot Word Sense Disambiguation with the Dictionary. In *Proceedings of the 16th Conference of the European Chapter of the Association for Computational Linguistics: Main Volume*, pages 455–465, Online. Association for Computational Linguistics.

Tamar Degani and Natasha Tokowicz. 2010. Ambiguous words are harder to learn. *Bilingualism: Language and Cognition*, 13(3):299–314.

Jasper Degraeuwe, Patrick Goethals, and Pauline Verhoeve. 2021. Ampliar la caja de herramientas del análisis del discurso asistido por el ordenador: el caso de los cinco sentidos en el discurso turístico. *Les Cahiers du GERES*, 12:91–109.

Christiane Fellbaum, editor. 1998. *WordNet: An Electronic Lexical Database*. The MIT Press.

Fundación SM. 2021. Diccionario Clave. Lengua española. `https://www.grupo-sm.com/es/book/diccionario-clave-lengua-espa%C3%B1ola`.

Goethals, Patrick. 2018. Customizing vocabulary learning for advanced learners of Spanish. In *Technological innovation for specialized linguistic domains : languages for digital lives and cultures, proceedings of TISLID'18*, pages 229–240. Éditions Universitaires Européennes. Event-place: Gent, Belgium.

Asier Gutiérrez-Fandiño, Jordi Armengol-Estapé, Marc Pàmies, Joan Llop-Palao, Joaquín Silveira-Ocampo, Casimiro Pio Carrino, Aitor Gonzalez-Agirre, Carme Armentano-Oller, Carlos Rodriguez-Penagos, and Marta Villegas. 2021. MarIA: Spanish Language Models. Publisher: arXiv Version Number: 5.

Andrew Hardie. 2014. Log Ratio: An informal introduction. *ESRC Centre for Corpus Approaches to Social Science (CASS)*, pages 1–2.

Eduard Hovy, Roberto Navigli, and Simone Paolo Ponzetto. 2013. Collaboratively built semi-structured content and Artificial Intelligence: The story so far. *Artificial Intelligence*, 194:2–27.

Adam Kilgarriff. 1997. I don't believe in word senses. *Language Resources and Evaluation*, 31(2):91–113.

Anagha Kulkarni, Michael Heilman, Maxine Eskenazi, and Jamie Callan. 2008. Word Sense Disambiguation for Vocabulary Learning. In Beverley P. Woolf, Esma Aïmeur, Roger Nkambou, and Susanne Lajoie, editors, *Intelligent Tutoring Systems*, volume 5091, pages 500–509. Springer Berlin Heidelberg, Berlin, Heidelberg. ISSN: 0302-9743, 1611-3349 Series Title: Lecture Notes in Computer Science.

Daniel Loureiro, Kiamehr Rezaee, Mohammad Taher Pilehvar, and Jose Camacho-Collados. 2021. Analysis and Evaluation of Language Models for Word Sense Disambiguation. *Computational Linguistics*, pages 1–57.

Lluis Màrquez, Mariona Taulé, Antonia Martí, Núria Artigas, Mar García, Francis Real, and Dani Ferrés. 2004. Senseval-3: The Spanish lexical sample task. In *Proceedings of SENSEVAL-3, the Third International Workshop on the Evaluation of Systems for the Semantic Analysis of Text*, pages 21–24, Barcelona, Spain. Association for Computational Linguistics.

Roberto Navigli. 2009. Word sense disambiguation: A survey. *ACM Computing Surveys*, 41(2):1–69.

Roberto Navigli. 2018. Natural Language Understanding: Instructions for (Present and Future) Use. In *Proceedings of the Twenty-Seventh International Joint Conference on Artificial Intelligence*, pages 5697–5702, Stockholm, Sweden. International Joint Conferences on Artificial Intelligence Organization.

Roberto Navigli and Simone Paolo Ponzetto. 2012. BabelNet: The automatic construction, evaluation and application of a wide-coverage multilingual semantic network. *Artificial Intelligence*, 193:217–250.

Ildikó Pilán, Elena Volodina, and Lars Borin. 2016. Candidate sentence selection for language learning exercises: From a comprehensive framework to an empirical evaluation. *Revue Traitement Automatique Des Langues*, 57(3):67–91.

Simón Ruiz, Patrick Rebuschat, and Detmar Meurers. 2021. The effects of working memory and declarative memory on instructed second language vocabulary learning: Insights from intelligent CALL. *Language Teaching Research*, 25(4):510–539.

Anaïs Tack, Thomas François, Piet Desmet, and Cédrick Fairon. 2018. NT2Lex: A CEFR-Graded Lexical Resource for Dutch as a Foreign Language Linked to Open Dutch WordNet. In *Proceedings of the Thirteenth Workshop on Innovative Use of NLP for Building Educational Applications*, pages 137–146, New Orleans, Louisiana. Association for Computational Linguistics.

Marjolijn Verspoor and Wander Lowie. 2003. Making Sense of Polysemous Words. *Language Learning*, 53(3):547–586.

Arianna Zanetti, Elena Volodina, and Johannes Graën. 2021. Automatic Generation of Exercises for Second Language Learning from Parallel Corpus Data. *International Journal of TESOL Studies*, 3:55–70.

Language learning analytics : designing and testing new functional complexity measures in L2 writings

Thomas Gaillat
LIDILE, Université de Rennes / Rennes, France
thomas.gaillat@univ-rennes2.fr

Abstract

This paper presents the initial stage in the design of an ICALL system. The objective is to develop a system that automatically generates linguistic analytics of L2 learner writings. Student texts will be processed with NLP tools producing different types of textual measures. We present the design of a new functional complexity metric aiming to capture the paradigmatic competition between forms mapped to the same communicative function, i.e. microsystems. More precisely, we analyze the variations of the FOR and TO prepositions in terms of frequency and probability of occurrence. Relative frequency shows significant correlations with CEFR levels suggesting its possible use in an analytics report system. More work is required to extend the approach to other microsystems.

1 Introduction

When using an L2, learners make assumptions about form-function mappings. They observe contexts in order to understand the meanings of specific forms. "The task facing the learner is to discover (1) which forms are used to realize which functions in the L2 and (2) what weights to attach to the use of individual forms in the performance of specific functions." (Ellis, 1994, p.375). In completing this task, learners modify their internal L2 system, gradually stabilise the mappings and improve proficiency.

Proficiency has been the focus of much research and it relies partly on the use of the *complexity* construct. Grammar complexity features form a major part of the elements used to operationalise this construct. Two ways of operationalising the construct have emerged. One based on holistic measures factoring in several grammar constituents such as the ratio between the number of dependent clauses and the total number of clauses in a text. The other one relies on frequency counts of different grammar patterns classified in terms of complexity. For all the benefits in both approaches, neither operationalises the variations between multiple forms mapped to one function. Previous work suggests that there are variations in mappings across proficiency levels (O'Keeffe and Mark, 2017). So capturing these mapping variations could help to identify factors of proficiency in L2 learners.

Form-function mappings could be operationalised as probability indicators in the use of one form over other forms mapped to the same function. These indicators could be generated by models stored in the expert module of an Intelligent Tutoring System (ITS). To achieve this, the models must be built with data trained on occurrences of the forms. In this paper, we present an illustration of the design of a new functional complexity measure operationalising the FOR, TO prepositions mapped to the communication function of "expressing purpose". We design a measure generated with a probabilistic model which is intended to be part of a proficiency predictor system.

2 Theoretical background

Structure complexity is a construct that includes functional complexity as one of its sub-types (Bulté and Housen, 2012, p.25). This construct relies on the mappings between forms and functions of linguistic forms. It has been operationalised in various ways such as specific parts of speech or dependency relations (Settles et al., 2018) or syntactic constituents as in CTAP's feature selector module (Chen and Meurers, 2016). The use of functional complexity features offers two advantages for studies in the field of Second Language Acquisition. First, based on learner corpora, these features can be used to design metrics exploited for modelling purposes in prediction tasks such as CEFR classification (Vajjala, 2018; Kyle, 2016;

Thomas Gaillat. Language learning analytics : designing and testing new functional complexity measures in L2 writings. *Proceedings of the 11th Workshop on Natural Language Processing for Computer Assisted Language Learning (NLP4CALL 2022).* Linköping Electronic Conference Proceedings 190: 55–60.

Pilán et al., 2016; Yannakoudakis et al., 2011). Secondly, they can be exploited for the design of specific linguistic feedback which is meaningful for learners and teachers (Riemenschneider et al., 2021).

Learners make confusions between forms of the same communicative function. They tend to hesitate between one form or the other when they want to express a specific function such as obligation, probability, purpose or reference. These hesitations illustrate one aspect of the competition model in which learners constantly resolve conflicts while choosing forms (MacWhinney et al., 1984), hence the notion of L2 microsystems. These microsystems are unstable as learners unexpectedly group forms that do not necessarily fall in the same functional paradigm (Py, 1980). Due to this instability in the mappings, the microsystems are transitional in nature (Gentilhomme, 1980). They include erroneous mappings which later are removed, leading the learner to better proficiency.

The microsystems can be analysed according to their paradigmatic relations. The following examples show the use of the FOR and TO prepositions in contexts expressing purpose, and more precisely followed by verbs and nominalised verbs with ING. In all three cases, the learners present difficulties to choose the right preposition within to-clause or prepositional phrase contexts. In (1), a more acceptable choice might have been FOR. There seems to be a confusion between the use of the complement to-clause controlled by *write* and the use of a prepositional phrase (PP) introduced by FOR. In (2) and (3), the learner clearly misused FOR instead of TO. In (2) the learner shows a confusion between the use of a complement extraposed to-clause and a PP. In (3), the confusion seems to be between a PP and an adverbial clause wrongly introduced by FOR (instead of *in order to* for instance).

1. Dear Mr or Madam : I am writing *to* enquiring about the possibility of requesting a loan (Sentence ID: 41038:1 Teaching level: 10 Learner nationality: Spain)

2. But, sincerly, I think that it's a strategy *for* promote his new movie. (Sentence ID: 3762:2 Teaching level: 7 Learner nationality: Spain)

3. Then, you go to the sport centre *for* doing sport. After, you walk the dog and you give it the food . (Sentence ID: 16950:7 Teaching level: 6 Learner nationality: Spain)

The underlying assumption in these examples is that there is an L2 specific microsystem in which FOR and TO compete paradigmatically to express purpose, be it in to-clauses or prepositional phrases including ING noun phrases. In the context of L2 automatic analysis, a challenge is to quantify the variations within this microsystem and others, which leads us to the following research questions: How can we capture variations between forms mapped to the same communicative function? Which form variations can be observed within a microsystem across CEFR levels? Answering these questions with computer models would provide the ground for the design of an NLP pipeline.

3 A learner language analytics system

The microsystem approach falls within a broader objective, i.e. the design of an ICALL system (see Figure 1) for teachers. The objective is to develop a computer system that automatically generates linguistic analytics of learner writings. The students will input their texts which will be processed with NLP tools producing different types of textual measures, some of which microsystem based. The system will provide visualisations of the measures for teachers to analyse their students' writing profiles.

Developing the system requires the validation of the textual measures in terms of correlations. A method to identify correlations between linguistic features and metadata including proficiency, task types, learning habits will be applied. This paper discusses the case of the statistical validation of the FOR, TO microsystem.

4 Method for the validation of the measures used in the system

4.1 Data

We used the Spanish subset of the EFCAMDAT corpus (Geertzen et al., 2013). It is made up of 8,187 texts written by EnglishTown students based in Spain. Table 1 provides the breakdown. The data was annotated in terms of 16 proficiency levels which can be converted in the six CEFR levels as described in the corpus manual[1].

[1]Available at https://corpus.mml.cam.ac.uk/faq/EFCamDat-Introrelease2.pdf (last access 24/11/2022)

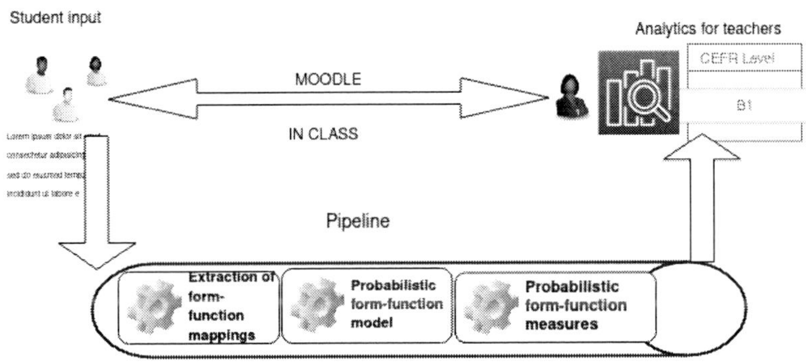

Figure 1: NLP pipeline - from data collection to visualisation

CEFR level	Writings	Mean of words
A1	2,571	106.75
A2	2,065	91.41
B1	2,004	120.3
B2	1,175	174.1
C1	340	193.8
C2	32	195

Table 1: Number of writings and mean number of words/text across CEFR levels in the Spanish subset of the EFCAMDAT learner corpus

4.2 Pre-processing and extraction

The texts were pre-processed with UDPipe (Straka et al., 2016) using the Stanford *english-ewt-ud-2.5-191206* English model in R. The tool provides grammatical annotation such as PoS, lemma, dependency relations and morphological features linked to the class of words (gender, number, case...). The CEFR levels were then appended to the resulting dataset.

The objective of the extraction was then to identify TO and FOR prepositions related to the function of "purpose". To extract the forms we proceeded twofold. Firstly, we only focused on actions (nominalised with ING or not) and retrieved verbs of any tense or aspect following the two forms. Secondly, following (Biber et al., 1999, p.693-751) on the identification of complement to-clauses, we applied queries that identified the forms according to a predetermined list of verbs and adjectives controlling to-clauses. We filtered by semantic class (Biber et al., 1999, p.700-705) keeping speech act verbs (e.g. ask, tell, warn), verbs of desire (e.g. hope, wish, like), verbs of intention or decision (e.g.decide, choose); verbs of effort (e.g. try, manage, fail). In the case of adjective controlling to-clauses, we filtered those referring to willingness (Biber et al., 1999, p.718). For the identification of prepositional phrases introduced by FOR and adverbial to-clauses (introduced by *in order to*, *so as to* or *to*, the heuristic identified forms immediately following a noun (plural or singular).

To measure extraction performance, we randomly sampled 100 occurrences of each form from dataset resulting from the first step. Each of these forms was then manually tagged as a purpose-related form or not. We then applied the heuristic to automatically identify the purpose-related forms. We then computed Recall, Precision and F1 metrics as shown in Table 2.

Forms	Precision	Recall	F1-Score
TO	0.56	0.42	0.48
FOR	0.73	0.66	0.69

Table 2: Precision, Recall and F1-Score for the extraction of FO and TO related to the purpose function

After the first step, we extracted 497 occurrences of FOR and 13,772 occurrences of TO. Applying the aforementioned heuristic resulted in a dataset of 9,820 occurrences of FOR (N=300) and TO (N=9,520). The distribution of the forms across levels is presented in Table 3.

4.3 Testing the significance of relative frequencies of microsystems as potential features of proficiency

To test the validity of the microsystem as a construct varying with proficiency, we analysed the relative frequencies of occurrence of the two forms (per 1,000 words) across the CEFR levels. We computed a one-way ANOVA to verify whether

CEFR	TO	FOR
A1	581	14
A2	1,328	43
B1	2,934	116
B2	2,441	91
C1	849	28
C2	69	0

Table 3: Distribution of FOR TO prepositions across CEFR levels

the differences between groups were significant.

4.4 Testing the significance of probabilities of microsystems as potential features of proficiency

We also wanted to measure the impact of microsystem internal probabilities on proficiency. To this end, we built a binomial logistic regression to model the microsystem forms. As we had an imbalanced number of forms, we first randomly extracted an even number of each preposition (N = 300 * 2). This was intended to prevent the classifier from assigning too much weight to the dominant class. We then split the dataset into a training (75%) and a test set (25%). The model was built with the *multinom()* function in the *nnet* R library (Venables and Ripley, 2002). We also computed a one-way ANOVA to verify whether the differences in the means of the probabilities between CEFR groups were significant.

5 Results

5.1 Relative frequencies as features

To test the significance of relative frequencies of the microsystem forms, we analysed their variations. We computed the means of frequencies in the texts across the six levels. Figure 2 shows the results. As frequencies of FOR were very low we plotted a barchart of the means. There seems to be a distinction in the use of TO at the A1 and C1 levels compared with the other levels. The use of TO seems to gradually decrease as proficiency increases. Regarding the FOR preposition, it appears to be favoured at the B1 level compared with the other five levels.

The one-way ANOVA for the TO prepositions reveals that the differences between the means of the CEFR groups are significant (F-value = 9.7, $p < 0.001$, Adjusted $R^2 = 0.01$) with an extremely low effect size. The ANOVA for the FOR prepositions shows that differences in means are not significant across the CEFR groups (F-value = 1.09, $p > 0.05$, Adjusted $R^2 = 0$).

5.2 Probabilities as potential features

To obtain relative probabilities of one component over the one one, we built a binomial model with the two microsystem prepositions as dependent variables, and parent and adjacent POS as independent variables. We first tested its classification power. The predicted probabilities of the TO vs FOR preposition (reference level) were extracted and matched to the true CEFR level of each observation of the test set. The model performance indicators show a 0.97 accuracy (95% CI (0.93-0.99) and p-value $< .001$). Precision and recall were 0.97 and 0.97 respectively.

We then analysed the distribution of the probabilities of TO vs FOR across the true CEFR levels in the fitted model over the training set. Figure 3 shows the variations of the data points including their variance and medians. If the variations overlap, medians appear to be quite distinct between levels. For instance, TO seems to be more likely to occur than FOR in the A1, A2 and C1 levels. The distribution of the FOR preposition is indirectly plotted as *1-P(TO)*, where *P(TO)* stands for probability of TO, i.e. a less-that-50% probability of TO implies a more-than-50% probability of FOR.

The one-way ANOVA showed that the differences between the means in the probabilities across the six CEFR groups are not significant (F-value = 1.49, $p > 0.05$, Adjusted $R^2 = 0$). A closer analysis shows that probabilities of the B1 level show $p = 0.05$.

6 Discussion and future work

In this paper, we have presented a new functional complexity metric which attempts to operationalises the paradigmatic competition between the TO and FOR prepositions used in the same communicative function which is "expressing purpose". The objective is to evaluate the metric as a proficiency criterial feature. This metric could be introduced in an ICALL system dedicated to generating analytics reporting measures of communicative functions for language teachers.

The experiment included the extraction of FOR and TO used with a meaning of purpose. The re-

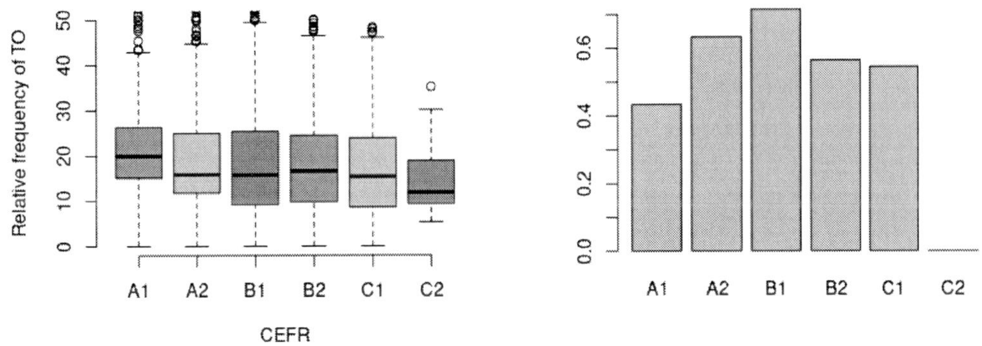

Figure 2: Distribution of relative frequencies of TO (left) and distributions in means of relative frequencies of FOR across CEFR levels in the EFCAMDAT Spanish subset

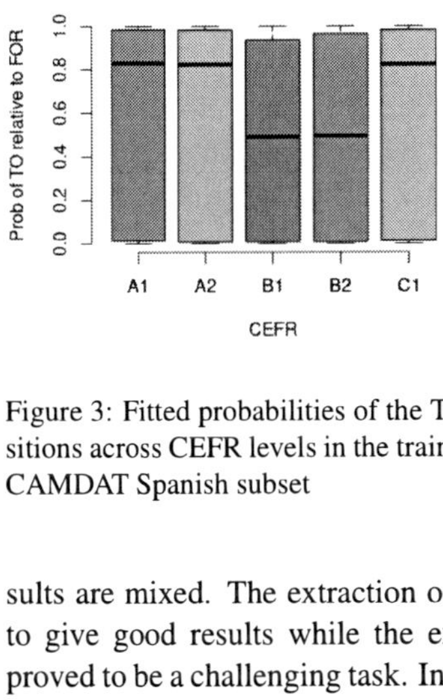

Figure 3: Fitted probabilities of the TO vs FOR prepositions across CEFR levels in the training set of the EFCAMDAT Spanish subset

sults are mixed. The extraction of FOR appeared to give good results while the extraction of TO proved to be a challenging task. In order to capture all possible learner uses (correct and incorrect), the heuristic is based on a list of words appearing in adverbial or complement to-clauses or in prepositional phrases introduced by FOR. The list needs further refinement regarding words introducing to-clauses. For instance, post-verification of the annotated sample showed a number of inconsistencies such as the presence of "have to" as a purpose expression.

The experiment's main objective was the statistical validation of the metric in terms of mean difference between the CEFR levels. The assumption was that if there were significant differences, the metric variations could be used as features of the system. We obtained mixed results. The model provides good classification power. The distributions of both the relative frequencies and the binomial logistic regression probabilities show variations across CEFR group. However, only the TO relative frequencies are significant, albeit with an extremely low effect.

These findings suggest that there are issues to solve before the metric could be used as a predictor in new texts. More testing needs to be done in order to validate the approach. Ultimately, the new measure should be tested as a feature in a proficiency predictor model. Finer-grained microsystem patterns could also be identified thanks to the work on the English Grammar Profile (O'Keeffe and Mark, 2017).

More microsystems are being designed. Following Gaillat et al. (2021), modals, articles, deictics are some of the forms that will be tested. The next stage is to create a program generating microsystem measures as part of a pipeline (see Figure 1). This pipeline will output its results in a MOODLE module (Dougiamas and Taylor, 2003) in the form of indicators linked to linguistic communicative purposes. Teachers will be able to interpret and diagnose their learners' linguistic profiles.

References

Douglas Biber, Stig Johanson, Geoffrey Leech, Susan Conrad, and Edward Finegan. 1999. *Longman Grammar of Spoken and Written English*. Longman, Harlow.

Bram Bulté and Alex Housen. 2012. *Defining and Operationalising L2 Complexity*. John Benjamins Publishing Company.

Xiaobin Chen and Detmar Meurers. 2016. CTAP: A Web-Based Tool Supporting Automatic Complexity Analysis. In *Proceedings of the Workshop on Computational Linguistics for Linguistic Complexity (CL4LC)*, pages 113–119. The COLING 2016 Organizing Committee. Event-place: Osaka, Japan.

Martin Dougiamas and Peter Taylor. 2003. Moodle: Using Learning Communities to Create an Open Source Course Management System. In *Proceedings of the EDMEDIA 2003 Conference, Honolulu, Hawaii*, pages 171–178, Hawaii. Association for the Advancement of Computing in Education (AACE).

Rod Ellis. 1994. *The Study of Second Language Acquisition*. Oxford University Press, Oxford, United Kingdom.

Thomas Gaillat, Andrew Simpkin, Nicolas Ballier, Bernardo Stearns, Annanda Sousa, Manon Bouyé, and Manel Zarrouk. 2021. Predicting CEFR levels in learners of English: The use of microsystem criterial features in a machine learning approach. *ReCALL*, 34(2). Publisher: Cambridge University Press.

Jeroen Geertzen, Theodora Alexopoulou, and Anna Korhonen. 2013. Automatic Linguistic Annotation of Large Scale L2 Databases: The EF-Cambridge Open Language Database (EFCamDat). In *Proceedings of the 31st Second Language Research Forum*, Carnegie Mellon. Cascadilla Press.

Yves Gentilhomme. 1980. Microsystèmes et acquisition des langues. *Encrages*, (Numéro spécial):79–84.

Kristopher Kyle. 2016. *Measuring syntactic development in L2 writing: Fine grained indices of syntactic complexity and usage-based indices of syntactic sophistication*. Dissertation, Georgia State University, Georgia.

Brian MacWhinney, Elizabeth Bates, and Reinhold Kliegl. 1984. Cue validity and sentence interpretation in English, German, and Italian. *Journal of Verbal Learning and Verbal Behavior*, 23(2):127–150.

Anne O'Keeffe and Geraldine Mark. 2017. The English Grammar Profile of learner competence: Methodology and key findings. *International Journal of Corpus Linguistics*, 22(4):457–489. Publisher: John Benjamins.

Ildikó Pilán, Elena Volodina, and Torsten Zesch. 2016. Predicting proficiency levels in learner writings by transferring a linguistic complexity model from expert-written coursebooks. In *Proceedings of COLING 2016, the 26th International Conference on Computational Linguistics: Technical Papers*, pages 2101–2111, Osaka, Japan. The COLING 2016 Organizing Committee.

Bernard Py. 1980. Quelques réflexions sur la notion d'interlangue. *Revue Tranel (Travaux neuchâtelois de linguistique)*, 1:31–54.

Anja Riemenschneider, Zarah Weiss, Pauline Schröter, and Detmar Meurers. 2021. Linguistic complexity in teachers' assessment of German essays in high stakes testing. *Assessing Writing*, 50:100561.

Milan Straka, Jan Hajič, and Jana Straková. 2016. UDPipe: Trainable Pipeline for Processing CoNLL-U Files Performing Tokenization, Morphological Analysis, POS Tagging and Parsing. In *Proceedings of the Tenth International Conference on Language Resources and Evaluation (LREC'16)*, pages 4290–4297, Portorož, Slovenia. European Language Resources Association (ELRA).

Sowmya Vajjala. 2018. Automated assessment of non-native learner essays: Investigating the role of linguistic features. *International Journal of Artificial Intelligence in Education*, (28):79–105. ArXiv: 1612.00729.

W. N. Venables and B. D. Ripley. 2002. *Modern Applied Statistics with S*, fourth edition. Springer, New York.

Helen Yannakoudakis, Ted Briscoe, and Ben Medlock. 2011. A New Dataset and Method for Automatically Grading ESOL Texts. In *Proceedings of the 49th Annual Meeting of the Association for Computational Linguistics: Human Language Technologies*, pages 180–189, Stroudsburg, PA, USA. Association for Computational Linguistics.

Generating and authoring high-variability exercises from authentic texts

Tanja Heck
Universität Tübingen / Germany
tanja.heck@uni-tuebingen.de

Detmar Meurers
Universität Tübingen / Germany
detmar.meurers@uni-tuebingen.de

Abstract

Integrating adaptivity into Task-Based Language Teaching requires exercises that transmit a specific content but whose complexity is adjusted to the learner's level. Thus, exercises of varying complexity based on the same text are needed. Revising generated exercise variants is time consuming and redundant where the same underlying linguistic annotations can be used for exercise generation. We present a fully implemented approach to generate generalized exercise specifications as an interim step before turning them into concrete exercises, as well as an interface for efficient reviewing of the specifications.

1 Introduction

For Computer-Assisted Language Learning (CALL), Task-Based Language Teaching (TBLT) can serve as a well-motivated, current pedagogical framework (Lai and Li, 2011). Putting a premium on the functional use of language with a focus on meaning, the TBLT perspective can offer a less monotonous learning experience than traditional grammar-focused instruction with decontextualized exercises (Doughty and Long, 2003). However, creating complex learning cycles with functional final tasks preceded by step-wise pre-task activities supporting practice of the task-essential language aspects requires considerable human effort. Form-based exercises, on the other hand, can be generated automatically in rule-based approaches or from authentic texts (Perez-Beltrachini et al., 2012).

Pursuing a kind of hybrid approach, Li et al. (2016) found that Task-Supported Language Teaching (TSLT), where working on a task follows explicit instruction, yielded better learning outcomes for grammar topics targeted in a cycle. Following a Presentation-Practice-Production (PPP) Model as backbone (Ur, 2018), TSLT explicitly teaches new concepts in the Presentation phase, uses traditional form-focused exercises in the Practice phase and more meaning-focused practice in the final task of the Production phase. In order to best support scaffolded learning preparing students for the Production task, the exercises in the Practice phase should preferably cover vocabulary and grammar topics relevant to that task.

The limited time available to teachers is not only an issue for the compilation of teaching materials, but also for taking into account the individual needs for additional support or practice (Aftab, 2015). Intelligent CALL systems can overcome this lack of differentiation through micro- and macro-adaptivity (Rus et al., 2015). Micro-adaptivity supports learners through scaffolded feedback when necessary. Macro-adaptivity adaptively selects and sequences exercises in the student's Zone of Proximal Development. The exercises thus provide practice opportunities for linguistic constructs where a learner struggles but can successfully complete the activity (when scaffolded). In TSLT, approaches to macro-adaptivity are especially valuable in the Practice phase in order to achieve effective and efficient proceduralization of language knowledge.

Macro-adaptivity usually relies on large pools of exercises in order to cover the vast space of possible ability levels a student can have across a range of linguistic constructs (Katinskaia et al., 2018). Since manual compilation of the required number of exercises is not feasible, automatic generation of exercises for the Practice phase become not only possible but necessary. While automatically generating exercises from authentic texts has been explored in various systems, they lack a systematic approach to generating large sets of exercises of varying complexity from source texts. In addition, proceduralization of linguistic knowledge requires exposure in a variety of contexts such as different syntactic structures, questions, or negation. Adaptive sequencing must therefore rely

Tanja Heck and Detmar Meurers. Generating and authoring high-variability exercises from authentic texts. *Proceedings of the 11th Workshop on Natural Language Processing for Computer Assisted Language Learning (NLP4CALL 2022)*. Linköping Electronic Conference Proceedings 190: 61–71.

on analyzing linguistic structures and differences in complexity of the source texts in order to provide the required variability and serve the needs of all students (Pandarova et al., 2019). This, however, does not allow instructors to also practice specific vocabulary or content at the same time.

Focusing on beginning to intermediate learners of English, the approach suggested by Heck and Meurers (2022a) fills this gap by systematically parameterizing exercises so that a single specification based on one sentence can be used to generate a range of exercises at varying levels of complexity. The approach, however, requires manually written specifications. While being more efficient than creating each exercise individually, the specifications still need to be composed manually, with the additional drawback of lacking intrinsically motivating authenticity (Peacock, 1997). We overcome this limitation by automatically generating the exercise specifications from authentic texts. Since this process might introduce errors, the generated specifications need to be reviewed and possibly revised. When conducting revisions at this stage of the exercise generation process, one only needs to check a single abstract specification instead of dozens of spelled out exercises. However, since each specification contains exercise elements relevant to a range of different exercise types, there is no readily-available authoring interface. We therefore introduce a prototype for a web-based interface serving this purpose.

In this paper, section 2 first reviews existing approaches to exercise generation in terms of their potential support for macro-adaptive systems. Section 3 describes the implementation of our approach with a focus on the user's interaction with the system throughout the exercise generation workflow. Section 4 evaluates the implementation before section 5 summarizes and concludes with an outlook.

2 Related Work

Addressing the shortcomings of prefabricated language material generally used in text-books, Authentic Intelligent CALL focuses on using authentic texts in language learning (Meurers, 2020). In particular, automatically generating grammar exercises from authentic texts has received considerable attention in the past as a means to meet the demand for practice material in Intelligent Language Tutoring Systems (ILTS) (Malafeev, 2015). Closed activity types such as Multiple Choice (MC) are especially popular due to their ability to automatically score the exercises based on the very restricted space of possible learner answers (Tafazoli et al., 2019), yet supported exercise formats vary from one system to the other. A number of tools integrate a variety of different formats: *MIRTO* automatically generates Fill-in-the-Blanks (FiB) as well as Mark-the-Words (MtW) exercises (Antoniadis et al., 2004); *Arik-Iturri* can generate MC, Error Detection, FiB and Word Formation exercises (Aldabe et al., 2006); an extension of the language aware search Engine *FLAIR*[1] (Heck and Meurers, 2022b) covers a wide range including FiB, MC, MtW, Memory, Jumbled Sentences and Drag and Drop exercises; *Sakumon* (Hoshino and Nakagawa, 2008) and *Cloze-Fox* (Jozef and Sevinc, 2010) support cloze exercises in FiB as well as MC format; *WERTi* (Meurers et al., 2010) and its multilingual extension *View* (Reynolds et al., 2014) in addition feature MtW exercises, the *Language Exercise App* Sentence Shuffling activities (Pérez and Cuadros, 2017), and Ferreira and Pereira Jr. (2018)'s *Verb Tenses System* True/False and Tense transposition exercises. While these systems can generate multiple exercises for a linguistic structure from the same source document, the actual number of exercises is usually quite limited. By varying exercise parameters such as the number of distractors, hints in parentheses, or the span of the target construction, variability can be increased. Notable examples making use of such parameterizations constitute MIRTO which provides parameters for the choice of target constructions, parentheses of FiB exercises and support elements such as reference pages (Antoniadis et al., 2004); the assistant system Sakumon which requires users to manually select target items and distractors from automatically generated suggestions (Hoshino and Nakagawa, 2008); the Language Exercise App where target constructions, distractors and parentheses of FiB exercises are parameterizable (Pérez and Cuadros, 2017); and FLAIR's exercise generation functionality which, in addition to providing parameters for target constructions, distractors and parentheses, allows users to influence the specificity of the exercise instructions (Heck and Meurers, 2022b). However, these systems require users

[1] http://sifnos.sfs.uni-tuebingen.de/FLAIR/

to specify each configuration individually so that generating large numbers of parameterized exercises involves considerable configuration effort as well as manual labour to review the generated exercises for correctness.

Many exercise generation tools provide support to post-edit the generated exercises, either within the tool (e.g., Toole and Heift, 2001; Hoshino and Nakagawa, 2008) or by providing an interface to general-purpose authoring interfaces such as Hot Potatoes[2] or the LMS Moodle[3] (e.g., Bick, 2000; Aldabe et al., 2006; Pérez and Cuadros, 2017). These interfaces are, however, designed to edit a single exercise at a time. Modifications of elements which affect all exercises generated from the same document thus have to be performed on each exercise individually.

There is a clear gap to generate large numbers of exercises from a document with different parameterizations as well as to allow for efficient editing of the generated exercises. We build on Heck and Meurers (2022a)'s approach to high-variability exercise generation by defining abstract exercise specifications as an intermediate step towards exercise generation. Our suggested approach generates specifications for conditionals and relative clauses automatically from authentic texts and provides an authoring interface for the specifications which allows to modify properties of all exercises generated from the same specification in a single step.

3 Implementation

As illustrated by the system architecture design in Figure 1, the implementation consists of three steps in-between which users are presented the interim results and can modify them if they wish to do so. This allows for maximally efficient user interactions as they can be performed on the most condensed representation layer containing the information to edit. The back-end code is implemented in a microservice architecture which supports flexible use of programming languages, thus facilitating the use of best-performing libraries across multiple programming languages.

The front-end implementation is still in its prototype state. It uses HTML, CSS and JavaScript, relying on Ajax for communication with the server.

[2]https://hotpot.uvic.ca

[3]https://moodle.org

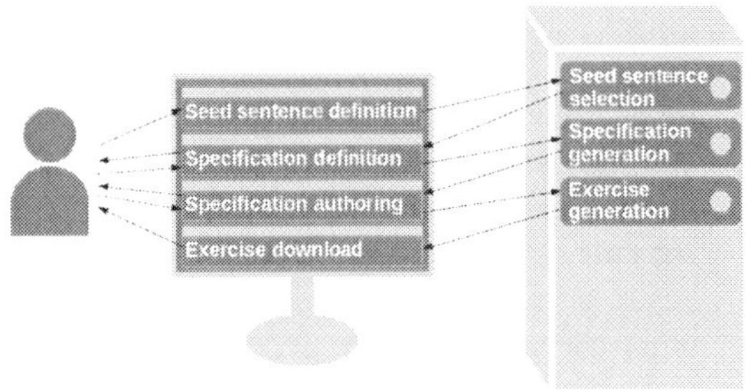

Figure 1: System architecture

The information flow between the user and the front-end, and between the front-end and the back-end is represented by arrows. Dashed arrows indicate optional information flow.

3.1 Seed sentence selection

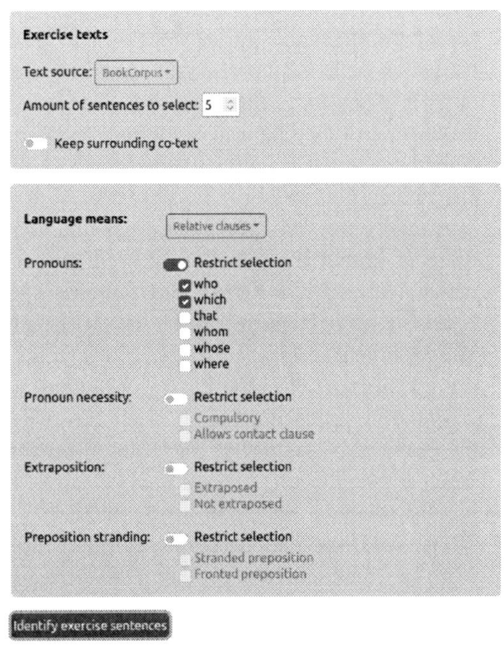

Figure 2: Seed sentence definition UI

Seed sentences, also referred to as *carrier sentences* or *candidate sentences* in the literature, are natural language sentences from which exercises are generated (Pilán et al., 2017). In our implementation, the selection of suitable sentences starts in the web interface shown in Figure 2. It supports three input sources: (1) the web, (2) the BookCorpus[4], and (3) custom texts. If users want

[4]The corpus based on an implementation by Kobayashi (2018) is available at https://the-eye.eu/public/AI/pile_preliminary_components/books1.tar.gz

to search the BookCorpus for candidate sentences, they need to specify the desired number of sentences. Since the space of possible parameter combinations grows exponentially with the number of parameters, the number of seed sentences to select can only be specified globally and not for specific parameter constellations. Crawling the Web in addition allows to search for sentences which appear in a defined semantic context so that users also need to specify a search term. Custom texts must be inserted into the provided input field. They can consist of manually compiled texts or any other texts copied from arbitrary sources.

An additional parameter determines whether some co-text is extracted along with the seed sentences or only the seed sentences themselves. If the co-text option is activated, the text in the same paragraph, delimited by line breaks, will be extracted as well. For contextualized exercises, the number of sentences cannot be specified. Instead, the exercise will contain all occurrences of the targeted linguistic structure in the paragraph as exercise items.

A final set of configuration parameters allows users to restrict the selection of seed sentences which will later be turned into exercise items. Available parameters depend on the targeted linguistic structures. For conditionals, they include the conditional type, the clause order, polarity, aspect, and sentence form. For relative clauses, the parameters consist of the relative pronoun, whether the pronoun is compulsory or can be left out, extraposition, and preposition stranding.

The seed sentence selection algorithm differs from one input source to another. For web texts, a google search is performed for the search term and the content of the search results is processed until the desired number of seed sentences has been extracted. For corpus texts, the documents of the corpus are searched instead, again until the required number of sentences has been identified. Custom texts are processed in their entirety.

For Natural Language Processing (NLP), the Java library Stanford CoreNLP[5], as well as the Python libraries NLTK[6], SpaCy[7] and Stanza[8] were considered. Table 1 summarizes the results of the evaluation of their reliability with respect to the annotations for seed sentence selection of conditionals and relative clauses. SpaCy and Stanza yielded similarly good results, with SpaCy performing considerably faster. Subsequent NLP analyses were therefore implemented based on SpaCy.

	Precision		**Recall**	
	RC	**C**	**RC**	**C**
NLTK	.89	.7	.7417	.9610
Stanza	.98	.81	.8976	.9927
SpaCy	.94	.86	.9039	.9902
Stanford CoreNLP	.96	.76	.7606	.9683
Sample size	100	100	635	410

Table 1: Evaluation of NLP libraries

Precision was computed for a random sample of 100 sentences from the BookCorpus. Recall values were determined for a collection of manually compiled example sentences. All metrics were determined for relative clauses (RC) and conditionals (Cond).

The algorithm processes the texts of all input sources in the same manner: A naive construction identification rule based on dependency parses determines whether a sentence could be a potential candidate. For conditionals, it searches for adverb clauses with some additional conditions such as the existence of a token with value *if* and the absence of a verb token contained in a manually compiled list of reported speech markers[9]. For relative clauses, the algorithm searches for relative clauses with a Wh-pronoun.

However, this rough filtering results in a considerable amount of noise in the sentence candidates. Pilán et al. (2017) identify a number of criteria for good seed sentences, including well-formedness, context independence, linguistic complexity and additional structural and lexical criteria. While we address most of the structural criteria, such as negated or interrogative contexts, with the parameters exposed to users, we deliberately do not restrict seed sentence selection based on lexical criteria, which are often user-dependent and better targeted by a macro-adaptive algorithm in the target ILTS (Gooding and Tragut, 2022). Compliance with context independence will be more likely when the co-text option is activated and can be addressed manually in the subsequent workflow step. In order to account for well-formedness and

[5] `https://stanfordnlp.github.io/CoreNLP`

[6] `https://www.nltk.org`

[7] `https://spacy.io`

[8] `https://stanfordnlp.github.io/stanza`

[9] Available lists (e.g. Tham and Nhi, 2021; Yilmaz and Özdem Erturk, 2017) contain predominantly affirmative markers. Since only question markers are relevant to confusions with conditional clauses, we compiled a list based on sampled evidence from the BookCorpus.

linguistic complexity, we apply further processing after the naive sentence selection: The algorithm extracts all the information relevant to exercise generation. This includes the exercise targets and their properties as well as properties of the sentences relevant to the configured parameters. The algorithm rejects the sentence as soon as one piece of information cannot be extracted or if it does not comply with the configured parameters. This not only ensures the highest possible success rate for exercise generation in the succeeding step, but also filters out most sentences which passed the naive filter but do not actually contain the targeted linguistic structure. In addition, we hypothesize that the NLP tools' inability to correctly process a sentence would reflect a beginning student's inability to do so, thus also eliminating sentences too complex for our target group.

The successfully parsed sentences are stored in a result list. If so specified by the user, the co-text of the paragraph is also stored in that list as individual elements. For seed sentences targeting conditionals, additional filtering is applied when the user has restricted the selection of the conditional type and selected both types. Since such a configuration is usually used for exercises targeting the distinction between conditional types, the seed sentence selection ensures that both conditional types occur in roughly equal numbers in the result list. If the result list already contains enough seed sentences for one conditional type, any subsequently found occurrences of that type will therefore be treated like sentences with no conditional construction. Similarly, a subtopic for relative clauses targets contact clauses for which students need to learn when the pronoun can be left out. It is therefore important to have seed sentences both with optional and with compulsory relative pronoun. If a user activates the selection restriction for pronoun necessity and selects both values, the algorithm therefore makes sure that sentences with compulsory and optional pronoun occur with similar frequency in the results.

Each element in the result list is tagged with its type of either co-text or exercise item. The list is used on the client to populate the user interface designed to configure exercise specification parameters.

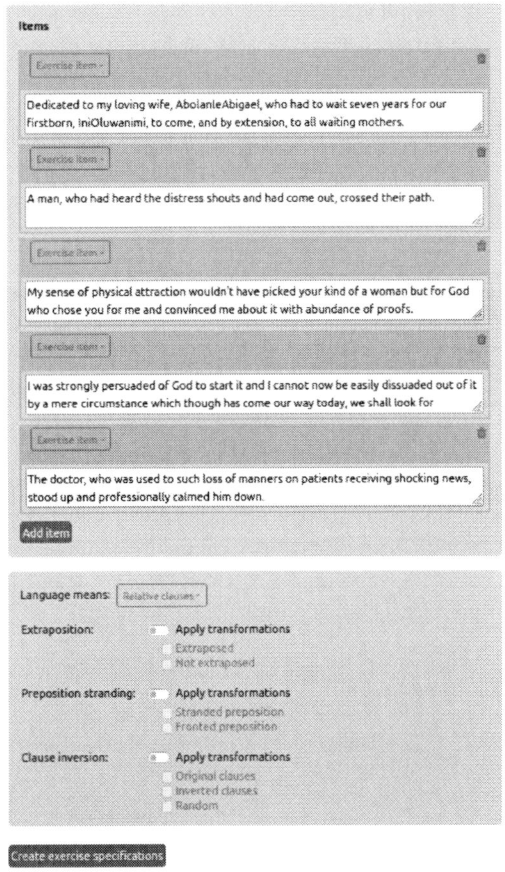

Figure 3: Specification definition UI

3.2 Exercise specification generation

The user interface to specify parameters of exercise specifications, shown in Figure 3, initially contains the exercise and co-text items extracted by the seed sentence selector. They can be edited, deleted, or their type changed from co-text to exercise item or vice versa. Additional items can be added manually. The order of all items can be changed through drag and drop mechanisms.

If no co-text items are specified, users can set additional parameters which will lead to the creation of linguistic transformations of the seed sentences. Transformations include for conditional sentences the aspect, conditional type, polarity, sentence form, and clause order. For relative clauses, preposition stranding, extraposition, and clause inversion are supported. The latter parameter transforms the original relative clause into a main clause and the original main clause into a relative clause, if possible. Whether a transformation results in a separate exercise specification or merely in an alternative sentence of the same specification depends on whether the target tokens, i.e., the pronoun of a relative clause or the verbs of conditional sentences, are affected by the transformation. For example, negating the main clause of the conditional sentence given in (1a) changes the verb from (*will go*) to *will not go* in (1b), thus requiring a new specification. Reversing the clause order in (1a) to that in (1c) does not affect the verb forms, therefore resulting in alternative sentences of the same specification. All transformations which result in a separate specification also offer the option to apply either of two realizations. In this case, the algorithm randomly applies one of the realizations of the transformation to each item while at the same time making sure that each realization is applied approximately the same number of times. This allows to generate exercises which practice a variety of linguistic phenomena.

(1) a. If he **gets** better, he **will go** to school.
b. If he **gets** better, he will not go to school.
c. He **will go** to school if he **gets** better.

Based on these configurations, the algorithm processes the texts declared as exercise items while keeping the co-text elements unchanged. Since it has been established in the previous step that the processed sentences must contain an occurrence of the targeted language means, the algorithm this time does not reject sentences which cannot be fully processed. Instead, it uses default values whenever a feature cannot be extracted. By shifting the focus from precision for seed sentence selection to recall for exercise specification generation, the same code can be used for both steps.

The extracted features are used to generate abstract exercise specifications which support a range of exercise types: Fill-in-the-Blanks, Single Choice, Memory, Jumbled Sentences, Short Answers, Mark-the-Words, and Categorization. These specifications are in addition enriched with exercise elements such as distractors for Single Choice exercises or parentheses for Fill-in-the-Blanks exercises. The distractor generation relies on Natural Language Generation (NLG). Since openly available Python libraries did not yield the desired output, the Java-based SimpleNlg[10] library is used to this purpose. The integration of this code is facilitated by the microservice architecture.

The generated exercise specifications are sent to the client where they are used to populate the exercise specification authoring interface.

3.3 Exercise generation

In order to finalize the specifications used for exercise generation, users can review them in the web interface shown in Figure 4. The grouping of multiple transformations into a single specification allows to reduce revision effort to a minimum. The transformations can be edited individually, deleted or added to. Each transformation can be marked as exercise seed from which to actually generate an exercise. If this option is not activated, the transformation merely serves as accepted correct answer alternative (provided the exercise context such as given prompts licenses the sentence). In order to make sure that all resulting exercises have an associated transformation for all items, the sentences are linked per parameter constellation across items. Deletion of one transformation therefore also deletes the corresponding sentence of all other items of the specification. Although some transformations of the same seed sentence require individual specifications, all specifications associated with the same seed sentences are linked by a common identifier. This enables adaptive systems using the generated exercises to avoid selecting similar activities in succession for the same learner. In addition to reviewing the generated exercise parameters such as target constructions, chunking, distractors, and hints in parentheses, the interface allows users to specify what exercises should be generated. As can be seen in Figure 5, this entails not only the exercise type, but also more specific parameters such as the number of distractors, whether to keep relative pronouns as individual chunks or combine them with adjoining ones, whether to insert exercise targets in both clauses or only one, or in which order to display the clauses from which to form relative sentences in the prompt. In addition, exercises can be generated for all linked items of a specification which are associated with the same transformation, as well as for a random choice of transformation of each item.

Based on these specifications, subsequent exercise generation is straightforward. All necessary information is already contained in the specifica-

[10] `http://github.com/simplenlg/simplenlg`

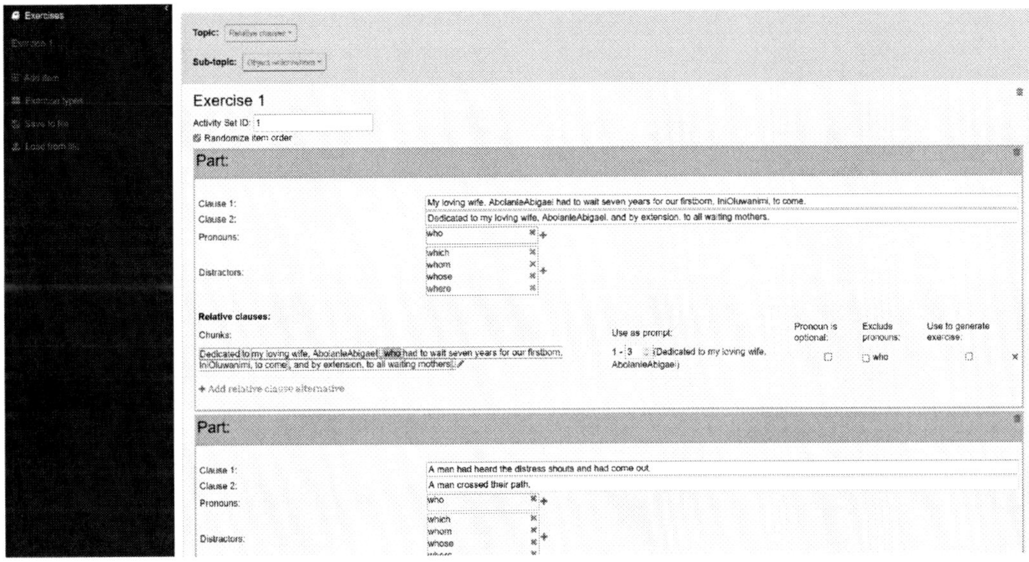

Figure 4: Specification authoring UI

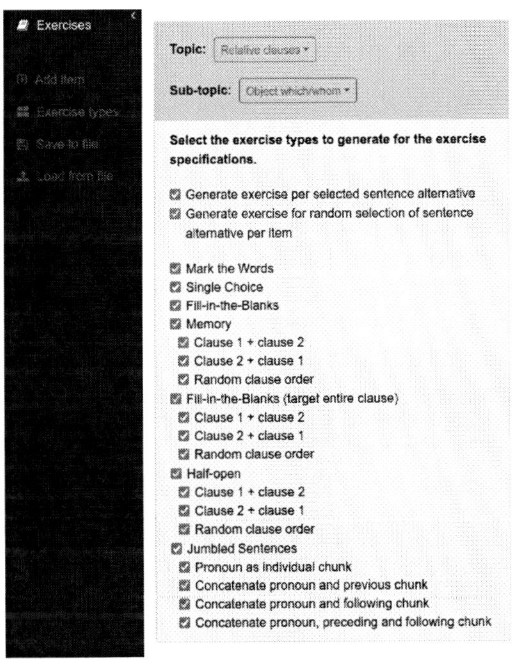

Figure 5: Exercise type definition UI

tions apart from instructions. These are stored in the code for each exercise type and linguistic structure. Apart from this, exercise generation consists in converting the specifications into the desired output format. Supported formats include the standardized H5P file format and a proprietary xml format for the in-house developed ILTS. The generated files are returned to the client where they can be downloaded by the user.

4 Evaluation

We evaluated precision and recall on candidate sentence selection for corpus texts and for manually compiled texts as well as the usability of the generated exercise specifications.

4.1 Methodology

We searched the BookCorpus for 100 occurrences of conditional sentences and relative sentences each with the naive sentence selection algorithm. The selection was not further restricted. We annotated them as *true positives* or *false positives* and computed precision values. We then determined which of these sentences were rejected by the sophisticated sentence selection algorithm and computed recall and precision values for this algorithm based on the data set obtained from the naive sentence selection. For a collection of 100 manually composed sentences for each of the two linguistic structures, we only applied the naive selection since for this input type, the sophisticated algorithm is bypassed. We computed recall values for the algorithm's acceptance of the input as seed sentences.

	RC	C	Corpus
Recall (N)	.91	1.0	M
Precision (N)	.93	.89	BC
Recall (S)	.3656	.7528	BC
Precision (S)	.8947	.9306	BC

Table 2: Evaluation of the seed sentence selection

Recall and precision were calculated for the naive (N) and for the sophisticated (S) algorithm. *Precision (S)* corresponds to overall precision. Recall of the naive algorithm was calculated on manually compiled texts (M), the remaining metrics on the BookCorpus (BC). For each metric, samples of 100 sentences were considered.

4.2 Results and Discussion

The results are summarized in Table 2: For seed sentence selection from the corpus, relative clauses obtain a precision of .93 on the naive selection. The precision of the sophisticated selection, which is also the precision of the overall seed sentence selection, is slightly lower at .8947. The decrease in precision is due to the high rejection rate, also resulting in a low recall of .3656, so that the percentage of accepted incorrect findings increases relative to the overall number of accepted sentences. While this might suggest that the additional filtering should be removed, the filtering also serves as a pre-selection with regard to the ensuing exercise generation from the specifications, thus rejecting sentences early on which cannot be processed successfully.

Results for conditionals are more in line with the expected behaviour. Precision on the corpus is already high (.89) for the naive sentence selection and increases further to .9306 with the sophisticated sentence selection. Recall of the sophisticated selection is also considerably higher than for relative clauses (.7528). Of the 89 sentences accepted as conditional sentences, 44 are actually not stereotypical conditional sentences taught in introductory language classes. They deviate in tense (e.g., Example 2a) or sentence structures such as using elliptical if-clauses (e.g., Example 2b). This highlights the relevance of parameters to restrict the selection of seed sentences which allows users to only select sentences with textbook properties.

(2) a. If I can't spoil my only daughter on her birthday, I'm not much of a father, now am I?

b. What if someone sees us?

Although the poor recall values indicate that a considerable amount of potential exercise sentences is lost in the process, this constitutes an accepted shortcoming when parsing large corpora. Considering the trade-off between fast performance and finding sentences lending themselves well to exercise generation, we put a focus on the latter criterion.

On the manually compiled sentences, the naive algorithm achieves recall values of 1.0 and .92 for conditionals and relative clauses respectively. Since each sentence of the data set contains a relevant construction, all conditional sentences are recognized by the algorithm while some relative clauses are rejected. These constitute either extraposed relative clauses such as example (3a) or sentences with the pronoun *whom* as in (3b). The issues can be traced back to incorrect parsing outputs obtained from the employed NLP tools.

(3) a. The kids screamed who are not from our school.

b. My parents called my teacher whom I saw today.

The number of exercises that can be generated from each seed sentence depends on three factors: (1) the user selections for sentence transformations in the specification definition UI and for exercise types in the specification authoring UI, (2) the algorithm's success in generating sentence transformations, and (3) the grammar subtopic.

$$\mathrm{e} = \mathrm{types} * \prod_{i=1}^{\substack{item-\\params}} \mathrm{options}_i * \prod_{i=1}^{\substack{alternatives-\\params}} \mathrm{options}_i \quad (4)$$

The maximum number of exercises breaks down according to the formula given in Equation 4: The number of generated exercise specification items constitutes the product of the options per activated transformation parameter of those parameters resulting in separate items. If all sentence alternatives are turned into exercises, the number of alternatives per exercise specification item is also considered. It constitutes the product of the options per activated transformation parameter of those parameters resulting in sentence alternatives. If instead only one randomly selected alternative is used per specification item, this number does not figure in the equation. The overall number of exercises constitutes the product of the number of exercise types with the number of exercise specification items and, if applicable, the number of sentence alternatives per item.

	C_{sent}	C_{diff}	RC_{pron}	RC_{cont}
types	34	21	16	3
items	81	81	3	3
$\mathbf{n_{rand}}$	**2754**	**1701**	**48**	**9**
alternatives	2	2	4	4
$\mathbf{n_{all}}$	**5508**	**3402**	**192**	**36**

Table 3: Maximum exercise counts

For random alternative selection (n_{rand}), the maximum number of generated exercises depends on the available exercise types and the number of specification items. If each alternative is turned into an exercise (n_{all}), the number of alternatives per exercise specification item is considered in addition. Available exercise types differ between the subtopic differentiating conditional types (C_{diff}), the remaining subtopics on conditionals (C_{sent}), contact clauses (RC_{cont}), and the remaining subtopics (RC_{pron}) on relative clauses.

Table 3 illustrates that applying this formula to the subtopics conditional sentences, differentiation of conditional types, relative clauses with relative pronouns, and contact clauses results in up to more than 5500 exercises for a single seed sentence.

5 Conclusion

We presented a fully implemented approach to step-by-step generation of form-based grammar exercises from authentic texts. We showed that our approach applying the annotation algorithm in the seed sentence selection step successfully eliminates false positives of more complex linguistic constructions such as conditionals, and it reduces issues for all language means in subsequent processing steps. We also found evidence in our evaluation that allowing users to specify selection restrictions can be crucial for the usability of the tool in classroom instruction to support the identification of pedagogically suitable sentences.

Future work will improve the user interface both in design and maintainability. The envisioned React[11] implementation will make use of state-of-the-art web technologies. We also plan to extend the implementation to additional language means. The generated exercises will be tested in the AI2Teach[12] project extending the FeedBook ILTS (Rudzewitz et al., 2017) successfully used in field studies in regular high schools in Germany (Meurers et al., 2019). This will yield further insights as to whether the authentic texts are suitably complex and of appropriate content for the target group.

[11] `https://reactjs.org`

[12] `https://fit.uni-tuebingen.de/Project/Details?id=7942`

References

Jaweria Aftab. 2015. Teachers' Beliefs about Differentiated Instructions in Mixed Ability Classrooms: A Case of Time Limitation. *Journal of Education and Educational Development*, 2(2):94–114.

Itziar Aldabe, Maddalen Lopez de Lacalle, Montse Maritxalar, Edurne Martínez, and Larraitz Uria. 2006. ArikIturri: An Automatic Question Generator Based on Corpora and NLP Techniques. In *Proceedings of the 8th International Conference on Intelligent Tutoring Systems (ITS'06), Jhongli (Taiwan)*, pages 584–594. Springer-Verlag.

Georges Antoniadis, Sandra Echinard, Olivier Kraif, Thomas Lebarbé, Mathieu Loiseau, and Claude Ponton. 2004. NLP-based scripting for CALL activities. In *Proceedings of the Workshop on eLearning for Computational Linguistics and Computational Linguistics for eLearning*, pages 18–25.

Eckhard Bick. 2000. Live use of Corpus data and Corpus annotation tools in CALL: Some new developments in VISL. *Nordic Language Technology, Årbog for Nordisk Sprogteknologisk Forskningsprogram*, 2004:171–185.

Catherine Doughty and Michael Long. 2003. Optimal psycholinguistic environments for distance foreign language learning. *Language Learning & Technology*, 7(3):50–80.

Kledilson Ferreira and Álvaro R. Pereira Jr. 2018. Verb tense classification and automatic exercise generation. In *WebMedia '18: Proceedings of the 24th Brazilian Symposium on Multimedia and the Web*, pages 105–108.

Sian Gooding and Manuel Tragut. 2022. One Size Does Not Fit All: The Case for Personalised Word Complexity Models. In *Findings of the Association for Computational Linguistics: NAACL 2022*, pages 353–365, Seattle, United States. Association for Computational Linguistics.

Tanja Heck and Detmar Meurers. 2022a. Automatic exercise generation to support macro-adaptivity in intelligent language tutoring systems. In *Intelligent CALL, granular systems and learner data: short papers from EUROCALL 2022*. Virtual.

Tanja Heck and Detmar Meurers. 2022b. Parametrizable exercise generation from authentic texts: Effectively targeting the language means on the curriculum. In *Proceedings of the 17th Workshop on Innovative Use of NLP for Building Educational Appli-*

cations (BEA 2022)*, pages 154–166, Seattle, Washington. Association for Computational Linguistics.

Ayako Hoshino and Hiroshi Nakagawa. 2008. A Cloze Test Authoring System and Its Automation. In *Advances in Web Based Learning – ICWL 2007*, pages 252–263, Berlin, Heidelberg. Springer Berlin Heidelberg.

Colpaert Jozef and Emre Sevinc. 2010. ClozeFox: Gap Exercise Generator with Scalable Intelligence for Mozilla Firefox. `https://github.com/emres/clozefox`. [Online; accessed 08-November-2022].

Anisia Katinskaia, Javad Nouri, and Roman Yangarber. 2018. Revita: a language-learning platform at the intersection of ITS and CALL. In *Proceedings of the eleventh international conference on language resources and evaluation (LREC 2018)*. European Language Resources Association (ELRA).

Sosuke Kobayashi. 2018. Homemade BookCorpus. `https://github.com/BIGBALLON/cifar-10-cnn`. [Online; accessed 08-November-2022].

Chun Lai and Guofang Li. 2011. Technology and Task-Based Language Teaching: A Critical Review. *CALICO Journal*, 28.

Shaofeng Li, Rod Ellis, and Yan Zhu. 2016. Task-Based Versus Task-Supported Language Instruction: An Experimental Study. *Annual Review of Applied Linguistics*, 36:205–229.

Alexey Malafeev. 2015. Exercise Maker: Automatic Language Exercise Generation. In *Computational Linguistics and Intellectual Technologies*, pages 441–452.

Detmar Meurers. 2020. Natural language processing and language learning. In Carol A. Chapelle, editor, *The Concise Encyclopedia of Applied Linguistics*, pages 817–831. Wiley, Oxford.

Detmar Meurers, Kordula De Kuthy, Florian Nuxoll, Björn Rudzewitz, and Ramon Ziai. 2019. Scaling up intervention studies to investigate real-life foreign language learning in school. *Annual Review of Applied Linguistics*, 39:161–188.

Detmar Meurers, Ramon Ziai, Luiz Amaral, Adriane Boyd, Aleksandar Dimitrov, Vanessa Metcalf, and Niels Ott. 2010. Enhancing authentic web pages for language learners. In *Proceedings of the 5th Workshop on Innovative Use of NLP for Building Educational Applications (BEA)*, pages 10–18, Los Angeles. ACL.

Irina Pandarova, Torben Schmidt, Johannes Hartig, Ahcene Boubekki, Roger Jones, and Ulf Brefeld. 2019. Predicting the Difficulty of Exercise Items for Dynamic Difficulty Adaptation in Adaptive Language Tutoring. *International Journal of Artificial Intelligence in Education*.

Matthew Peacock. 1997. The Effect of Authentic Materials on the Motivation of EFL Learners. *ELT Journal*, 51(2):144–156.

Naiara Pérez and Montse Cuadros. 2017. Multilingual CALL Framework for Automatic Language Exercise Generation from Free Text. In *Proceedings of the Software Demonstrations of the 15th Conference of the European Chapter of the Association for Computational Linguistics*, pages 49–52, Valencia, Spain. Association for Computational Linguistics.

Laura Perez-Beltrachini, Claire Gardent, and German Kruszewski. 2012. Generating Grammar Exercises. In *Proceedings of the Seventh Workshop on Building Educational Applications Using NLP*, pages 147–156. Association for Computational Linguistics.

Ildikó Pilán, Elena Volodina, and Lars Borin. 2017. Candidate sentence selection for language learning exercises: From a comprehensive framework to an empirical evaluation. *Traitement Automatique des Langues (TAL), special issue on NLP for learning and teaching*, 57.

Robert Reynolds, Eduard Schaf, and Detmar Meurers. 2014. A view of Russian: Visual input enhancement and adaptive feedback. In *Proceedings of the third workshop on NLP for computer-assisted language learning*, pages 98–112, Uppsala. ACL.

Björn Rudzewitz, Ramon Ziai, Kordula De Kuthy, and Detmar Meurers. 2017. Developing a web-based workbook for English supporting the interaction of students and teachers. In *Proceedings of the Joint 6th Workshop on NLP for Computer Assisted Language Learning and 2nd Workshop on NLP for Research on Language Acquisition*, pages 36–46.

Vasile Rus, Nobal B. Niraula, and Rajendra Banjade. 2015. DeepTutor: An Effective, Online Intelligent Tutoring System That Promotes Deep Learning. In *Association for the Advancement of Artificial Intelligence*.

Dara Tafazoli, Mª Elena Gómez Parra, and Cristina Huertas Abril. 2019. Intelligent language tutoring system: Integrating intelligent computer-assisted language learning into language education. *International Journal of Information and Communication Technology Education*, 15:60–74.

Duong My Tham and Tran Phuong Nhi. 2021. A Corpus-Based Study on Reporting Verbs Used in Tesol Research Articles by Native and Non-Native Writers. *VNU Journal of Foreign Studies*, 37(3).

Janine Toole and Trude Heift. 2001. Generating Learning Content for an Intelligent Language Tutoring System. In *Proceedings of NLP-CALL Workshop at the 10th Int. Conf. on Artificial Intelligence in Education (AI-ED). San Antonio, Texas*, pages 1–8.

Penny Ur. 2018. PPP: Presentation–Practice–Production. *The TESOL Encyclopedia of English Language Teaching*, pages 1–6.

Maide Yilmaz and Zeynep Özdem Erturk. 2017. A Contrastive Corpus-Based Analysis of the Use of Reporting Verbs by Native and Non-Native ELT Researchers. *Novitas-ROYAL (Research on Youth and Language)*, 11(2):112–127.

Bringing Automatic Scoring into the Classroom – Measuring the Impact of Automated Analytic Feedback on Student Writing Performance

Andrea Horbach[1], Ronja Laarmann-Quante[2], Lucas Liebenow[3], Thorben Jansen[3], Stefan Keller[4], Jennifer Meyer[3], Torsten Zesch[1] and Johanna Fleckenstein[3,5]
[1]CATALPA, FernUniversität in Hagen, Germany, [2]Ruhr-Universität Bochum, Germany,
[3]Leibniz-Institut für die Pädagogik der Naturwissenschaften und Mathematik, Kiel, Germany,
[4]Pädagogische Hochschule Zürich, Switzerland, [5]Universität Hildesheim, Germany

Abstract

While many methods for automatically scoring student writings have been proposed, few studies have inquired whether such scores constitute effective feedback improving learners' writing quality. In this paper, we use an EFL email dataset annotated according to five analytic assessment criteria to train a classifier for each criterion, reaching human-machine agreement values (kappa) between .35 and .87. We then perform an intervention study with 112 lower secondary students in which participants in the feedback condition received stepwise automatic feedback for each criterion while students in the control group received only a description of the respective scoring criterion. We manually and automatically score the resulting revisions to measure the effect of automated feedback and find that students in the feedback condition improved more than in the control group for 2 out of 5 criteria. Our results are encouraging as they show that even imperfect automated feedback can be successfully used in the classroom.

1 Introduction

Writing e-mails in English is an important skill in many academic and professional contexts and, thus, part of many secondary school curricula in English as a foreign language (EFL). However, scoring writing exercises manually and providing feedback is a time-consuming task for educators. Therefore, we present a study on how to automatically provide feedback based on automated scores. The study took place in the context of EFL education at secondary level in Switzerland and Germany. In contrast to other studies that focus only on the technical evaluation of a machine learning approach, we go one step further and directly measure the effects of using automatic scoring to provide feedback in the classroom. We conducted this experiment as a controlled randomized experimental study.

To this end, we first describe the dataset this study is based on. The eRubrix corpus (Keller et al., 2023) contains a total of 1,104 semi-formal e-mails written in response to three different prompts (see below for details).In these e-mail texts, five individual trait scores are annotated, assessing whether individual parts of an e-mail are addressed in an appropriate fashion. Table 1 shows an example from the dataset: the original draft as well as the five revisions produced by a participant in the feedback group.

We then describe an NLP pipeline used to automatically score this dataset analytically according to these five criteria. Besides the prompt-specific scoring used in our intervention study, we also provide additional experiments evaluating cross-prompt scoring performance in order to show the transferability of the approach to new writing prompts of a similar kind. In the subsequent experimental study, we show the usefulness of feedback generated from the automatic score, comparing the performance improvement of an intervention group (receiving informative tutorial feedback) with that of a control group (receiving scoring criteria only). In this study, we show that students in the feedback group improved more than students in the control group for two out of five criteria.

2 Related Work

In this section, we first contextualize our scoring task within the automatic scoring landscape and then introduce the psychological background of our intervention study.

Automatic Scoring The task tackled in this paper is an instance of essay scoring in which we assess texts both according to their linguistic quality and their content (Beigman Klebanov and Madnani, 2020). The setup in which different aspects of an essay are scored is similar to what is of-

Andrea Horbach, Ronja Laarmann-Quante, Lucas Liebenow, Thorben Jansen, Stefan Keller, Jennifer Meyer, Torsten Zesch and Johanna Fleckenstein. Bringing Automatic Scoring into the Classroom - Measuring the Impact of Automated Analytic Feedback on Student Writing Performance. *Proceedings of the 11th Workshop on Natural Language Processing for Computer Assisted Language Learning (NLP4CALL 2022)*. Linköping Electronic Conference Proceedings 190: 72–83.

E-mail Text	Criterion	Score
English questions Hello, Is a three- week course possible? I think two weeks courses for all levels, qualified from experienced teachers. And how much is the price? Who organized the activities and what of activities are organized? See you Kim Weber	Content Completeness	Pass
English **learning** Hello, Is a three- week course possible? I think two weeks courses for all levels, qualified from experienced teachers. **Could you tell me** how much is the price? **And** who organized the activities and what of activities are organized? See you Kim Weber	Greeting & Closing	Fail
English learning **Dear Mrs Black,** Is a three- week course possible? I think two weeks courses for all levels, qualified from experienced teachers. Could you tell me how much is the price? And who organized the activities and what of activities are organized? **Best wishes** Kim Weber	Subject Line	Pass
Questions at the Central School Dear Mrs Black, Is a three- week course possible? I think two weeks courses for all levels, qualified from experienced teachers. Could you tell me how much is the price? And who organized the activities and what of activities are organized? Best wishes Kim Weber	Interpersonal Dimension	Fail
Questions at the Central School Dear Mrs Black, **I'm writing to tell you my questions and I would like to ask you about the Central School.** Is a three- week course possible? I think two weeks courses for all levels, qualified from experienced teachers. Could you tell me how much is the price? And who organized the activities and what of activities are organized? **Thank you for answering my questions.** Best wishes Kim Weber	Register & Style	Fail
Questions at the Central School Dear Mrs Black, I'm writing to tell you my questions and I would like to ask you about the Central School. Is a three- week course possible? I think two weeks courses for all levels, qualified from experienced teachers. Could you tell me how much is the price? **Finally** ,who organized the activities and what of activities are organized? Thank you for answering my questions. Best wishes Kim Weber	Final Revision	-

Table 1: An example e-mail written in response to the 'Language School' prompt in the eRubrix dataset. We show the original e-mail together with its five revisions (edits are highlighted by the authors) and whether the e-mail passed or failed the respective criterion.

ten called trait-based essay scoring (Lee et al., 2010). However, an important difference is that in most work, essay traits are considered one dimension according to which to score a *whole text*, such as coherence (Yannakoudakis and Briscoe, 2012; Farag et al., 2018), topicality (Klebanov et al., 2016) or argumentation (Stab and Gurevych, 2014; Persing and Ng, 2015, 2016). In contrast, human judgments for each rubric in the eRubrix dataset only refer to *specific parts* of an essay and score them according to their appropriateness. This is similar to a holistic score for only a subpart of the text as in Horbach et al. (2017), where essays consist of a summary and a discussion part scored separately. (Note that in our automatic scoring, we nevertheless use the whole text as input in most cases, as we cannot reliably split the data into individual segments). This makes it similar to the task of facet-based short-answer scoring (Nielsen et al., 2009, 2008) where the presence of certain content units, so called facets, in the text is analyzed. However, one crucial difference is that in our case both content and form are scored together.

Further, the task of writing an e-mail or letter is well known in automated essay scoring. The ASAP-AES dataset, for example, also contains tasks where students have to write a letter.[1] However, such tasks are often framed in terms of a persuasive text that conveys the author's own position, whereas in our task, e-mails are written in order to gather information.

Feedback Intervention Study The aim of our intervention study is to investigate the effect of informative tutorial feedback based on automatically scored texts. In instructional contexts, feedback generally refers to any information given to a person during or after a learning process. It aims to reduce the gap between the current performance and the desired learning outcome (Mory, 2004; Narciss, 2008; Sadler, 1989). Feedback is deemed one of the most effective factors influencing student learning, however, meta-analyses show that the effects are heterogeneous (for feedback on learning in general: cf. Wisniewski et al., 2020; for feedback on writing: cf. Graham et al., 2015). Attempting to explain the inconsistent findings, certain moderators for feedback effectiveness have been identified (Bangert-Drowns et al., 1991; Black and Wiliam, 1998; Hattie and Timperley, 2007; Kluger and DeNisi, 1996; Mory, 2004; Shute, 2008). Feedback has a positive effect on learner performance only if it reduces uncertainty and cognitive load by presenting the information necessary to improve task performance. According to Narciss (2008), informative tutorial feedback should include both evaluative information (i.e., information on the current task performance) and tutorial information (i.e., elaborate information to improve task performance) in order to support learning effectively. Hattie and Timperley's 2007 feedback model summarizes the empirically identified effectiveness criteria using three questions: "Where am I going?" (transparency of learning goals), "How am I going?" (individual information on current task performance), and "Where to next?" (information on how to achieve learning goals).

In accordance with this model, feedback was conceptualized according to these criteria in our study. Learners were presented with evaluative information on their performance (aspect mastered/not mastered) as well as elaborative feedback (hints and examples for performance improvement).

The evidence on the effectiveness of automatic feedback on writing performance is also described as being heterogeneous (McNamara et al., 2015; Stevenson and Phakiti, 2014; Strobl et al., 2019). Fleckenstein et al. (in press) conducted a systematic review of individual writing support by intelligent tutoring systems (ITS). Whereas the effects of the interventions were promising in general, the authors found that there were only few studies with randomized controlled experimental designs (see, e.g., Kellogg et al., 2010; Palermo and Thomson, 2018; Wade-Stein and Kintsch, 2004; Wilson and Roscoe, 2020; Wilson and Czik, 2016; Xu and Zhang, 2022). Moreover, it was often unclear what type of tutorial support led to performance improvement as the interventions often included non-adaptive, confounding support measures (e.g., prewriting activities, strategy instruction, drill and practice) in addition to holistic and/or analytic automated feedback. Our intervention study is one of the few randomized controlled experiments that investigates the unconfounded effect of analytic feedback in the context of automated scoring.

[1] https://www.kaggle.com/c/asap-aes

Prompt	# e-mails	∅ # tokens (SD)
Language School	368	97.9 (± 33.0)
Burger Restaurant	369	104.1 (± 34.0)
Camping	367	105.0 (± 34.1)

Table 2: Basic dataset statistics.

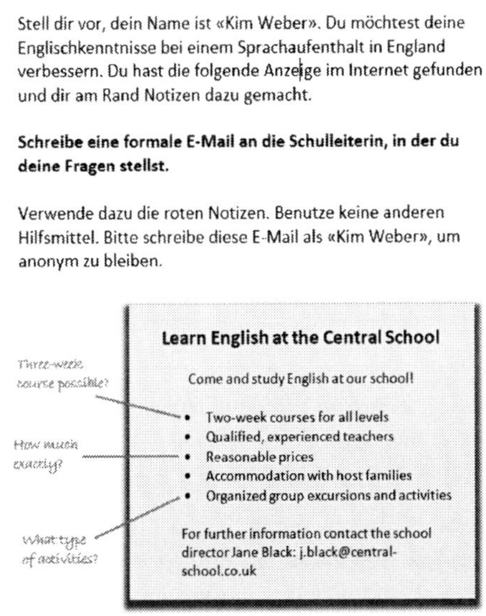

Figure 1: Instructions for the *language school* prompt. The German text translates as follows: *Imagine your name is Kim Weber. You want to improve your English language skills through a language stay in England. You have seen the following ad on the Internet. Write a formal e-mail to the school principal asking your questions. Use the notes printed in red. Do not use any other material. Write the e-mail as 'Kim Weber' to stay anonymous.*

3 Data

The eRubrix dataset contains three individual writing prompts, each asking the student to write an information-seeking e-mail. In the first task, students inquire about attending a course at a language school in the UK, in the second task, they respond to a job advertisement at a burger restaurant, and in the third, they gather information for a camping holiday.

One is an inquiry Table 2 shows basic statistics for the dataset. Figure 1 shows as an example of the language school prompt. Per prompt, about 370 individual e-mails were collected.

Each e-mail was scored with a binary label for each of the following criteria, corresponding to key elements of an e-mail. The description of each criterion closely follows the scoring rubrics described in Keller et al. (2023).

- **Content Completeness:** whether the e-mail asks for all three pieces of information required in the task.
- **Greeting & Closing:** whether the salutation at the beginning and the closing are adequate to the situation.
- **Subject Line:** whether the subject line adequately communicates the intention of the e-mail.
- **Interpersonal Dimension:** whether writers explain who they are, what the purpose of the mail is and describe at the end what kind of response they expect.
- **Register & Style:** whether the e-mail uses clear, detailed and adequate language and is free from mistakes which inhibit understanding.

Scoring was performed by two trained annotators, cases of disagreement were adjudicated by a third annotator. Table 3 shows inter-annotator-agreement (Cohen's kappa), as well as the label distribution by indicating the fraction of texts that mastered the respective criterion. We see that annotators were able to agree on the first four criteria well, while *Register & Style* seemed to be more problematic to annotate.

4 Automatic Scoring

In this section, we describe our automatic scoring procedure. After the experimental setup, we report experiments for prompt-specific scoring where one classifier is trained per prompt and per scoring rubric We also perform generic scoring with a model trained across prompts, i.e. on more training data. The prompt-specific model for the *language school* prompt is used in our intervention study. In order to show the transferability of our approach, we also report on additional experiments for cross-prompt training.

4.1 Experimental Setup

We use the Gradient Boosting classifier from scikit-learn[2] with a maximum tree depth of 6

[2] https://scikit-learn.org

Prompt	Content		Greeting		Subject		Interpersonal		Style	
	% corr.	IAA	% corr.	IAA	% corr.	IAA	% corr.	IAA	% corr.	IAA
All	87.6	-	31.2	-	72.6	-	62.0	-	19.7	-
Language School	87.5	.88	26.4	.90	67.9	.68	59.0	.91	22.0	.43
Burger Restaurant	87.5	.80	36.3	.93	89.5	.96	62.3	.94	19.5	.38
Camping	87.7	.85	30.8	.89	60.8	.75	64.9	.89	17.7	.47

Table 3: Label distribution (%corr. marks the percentage of essays where the criterion was fulfilled) and inter-annotator agreement for each scoring rubric, measured in Cohen's kappa.

Train	Test	Content		Greeting		Subject		Interpersonal		Style	
		acc	κ	acc	κ	acc	κ	acc	κ	acc	κ
All (CV)		.93	.59	.89	.75	.95	.88	.88	.75	.84	.38
Language School (CV)		.92	.60	.88	.67	.94	.87	.85	.69	.81	.35
Burger Restaurant (CV)		.94	.69	.92	.83	.99	.96	.82	.60	.82	.29
Camping (CV)		.91	.51	.89	.73	.93	.86	.77	.47	.82	.26
Burger & Camping	School	.83	.38	.76	.30	.81	.62	.89	.78	.68	.20
School & Camping	Burger	.93	.66	.85	.64	.67	.25	.85	.69	.82	.33
School & Burger	Camping	.50	.10	.75	.33	.71	.46	.84	.66	.85	.39

Table 4: Experimental results measured in accuracy and Cohen's kappa for cross-validation experiments on all data and per prompt (upper half) as well as prompt transfer between prompts (lower half).

and otherwise standard parameters and TF-IDF weighted unigram features. We evaluate using accuracy as well as Cohen's kappa (Cohen, 1960) as a way of measuring chance-corrected agreement.

4.2 Prompt-specific vs Generic Scoring

In a first set of experiments, we compare two different setups. We either train a generic model using data from all three prompts as training material or we train a prompt-specific model using only data from the same prompt for training and testing. In other words, we compare whether a model benefits from more training data coming from a different prompt. In both setups, we use ten-fold cross-validation.

The upper half of Table 4 shows the results. We see that we get a slight advantage for the two categories *Interpersonal* and *Style* when using more training data from other prompts, whereas this is only partially helpful for the other three criteria (*Content*, *Greeting* and *Subject*). We speculate that this is because the latter three are the most content dependent and therefore mainly rely on the specific lexical material for one prompt, while the other two contain also generic lexical material, like, e.g., "I am looking forward to your answer". Generally, we see that the highest prediction performance can be achieved for the *Subject* line, while *Style* is hardest to predict, which is probably due to the high class imbalance of this criterion, i.e., there are only few instances in the training data where the criterion is mastered. This criterion is also difficult to score for human raters as evidenced by the agreement scores, which are much lower than for the other criteria.

4.3 Cross-prompt Scoring

In order to asses the usability of the models in a real-life scenario where training data for a new prompt might not be readily available, we investigate model transfer to new prompts not used during training.

To do so, we train on all data from two prompts and test on the third prompt. The results are shown in the lower part of Table 4. We see that for most rubrics, the performance drops considerably compared to the within-prompt setting. However, for *Interpersonal* and *Style*, we partially find an improvement of the results in the cross-prompt setting. We assume that similar to our finding for the *All* setting above, these two rubrics rely a lot on generic wording. In addition, the Style rubric has a high class imbalance for the *Camping* setting, which might explain why this prompt is particularly susceptible to cross-prompt (and more balanced) training data.

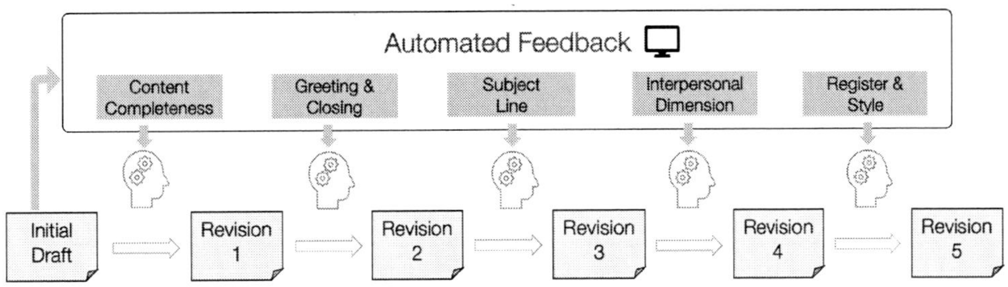

Figure 2: Students sequentially receive automated feedback on their original e-mail and are given the opportunity to revise based on the feedback.

5 Feedback Intervention Study

We investigated the following research questions: (1) Does the automated feedback lead to substantial improvement in students' writing performance? (2) What do we learn about the revision process by looking at stepwise text development? In the following, we first describe the procedure and results of our intervention study and then provide further insights into the resulting e-mail revision dataset.

5.1 Procedure

We conducted a randomized controlled field experiment with $N = 112$ lower secondary (ISCED level 2[3]) students to investigate the effect of a feedback intervention that was based on the automatic assessment. Seven students were excluded from the sample due to incomplete data, leaving a final sample of N = 105 students (*n* = 53 female; age *M* = 14.41, *SD* = 0.81) in grade 8 (*n* = 54) and grade 9 (*n* = 51) for the statistical analyses. Students were asked to respond to the 'language school' e-mail writing prompt (see Figure 1) that was then assessed using the scoring model for that specific prompt as described above.

As part of the intervention, students received automatic feedback on the five assessment criteria and were asked to revise their text accordingly. To communicate the feedback in the process of writing, a scoring rubric was used which contained the most important elements of the genre 'e-mail' (Keller et al., 2023). The elements were arranged in a stepwise manner based on the principle of communicative effectiveness (Widdowson, 1978), and presented to students in sequential order so that they could focus on one criterion at a time before moving on to the next one. In a process- and genre-based approach to writing (Hyland, 2007), feedback guided students towards writing good e-mails by focusing their attention on important generic elements by the principle of increasing communicative value.

Within the writing tasks set in this study, the most important element was to include all the questions mentioned in the task. Therefore, this element appeared as Step 1 in the rubric. If texts were found to be lacking one or several questions, the feedback suggested to go back to the task and make sure they had covered all required aspects. In subsequent steps, students were advised to contextualize their e-mails by finding appropriate formulas of salutation and closing (Step 2), to formulate clear and precise subject lines (Step 3), and to frame their e-mails with an introduction stating their name and the nature of their inquiry, and an indication of what type of answer they expected (Step 4). Finally, students were advised to check the grammar, lexis and spelling of their e-mail to make sure it did not contain any formal mistakes.

The decision to place formal correctness (*Reg ister & Style*) as the last step in the feedback process was based on the assumption that it is easier for learners to master the specific elements of a genre (which can be explicitly taught and learned) than to make progress in the general aspects of foreign language proficiency, such as syntax or lexical quality. Further, focusing their attention on formal mistakes too early would have risked students getting bogged down with questions of linguistic correctness, while the focus of the intervention lay on using language in a communicative way (Keller et al., 2023). Figure 2 visualizes the revision process.

Students were randomly assigned to the feed-

[3]`https://iqa.international/isced-levels/`

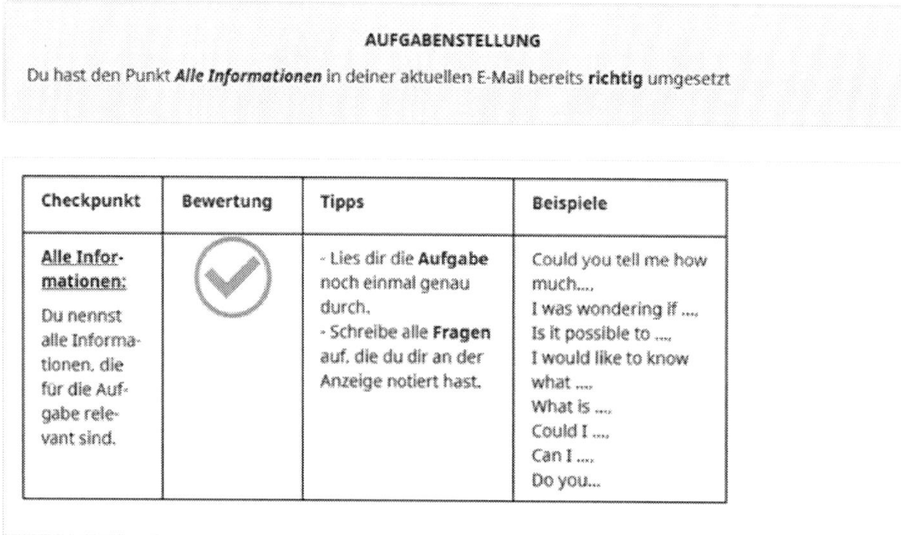
AUFGABENSTELLUNG

Du hast den Punkt ***Alle Informationen*** in deiner aktuellen E-Mail bereits **richtig** umgesetzt

Checkpunkt	Bewertung	Tipps	Beispiele
Alle Informationen: Du nennst alle Informationen, die für die Aufgabe relevant sind.	✓	- Lies dir die **Aufgabe** noch einmal genau durch. - Schreibe alle **Fragen** auf, die du dir an der Anzeige notiert hast.	Could you tell me how much...., I was wondering if ...., Is it possible to ...., I would like to know what ...., What is ...., Could I ...., Can I ...., Do you...

Figure 3: Example for a feedback message received in the category *Content*. Students from the control group were shown the requirements only (left column), while students in the feedback condition received their automatic score together with hints how to improve their writing.

back condition or the control condition. The feedback group was provided with informative tutorial feedback in German, including both evaluative and elaborative information on each scoring criterion including exemplary formulations in English. See Figure 3 for an example for the criterion *Interpersonal Dimension*. The first column specifies the requirements (e.g., 'Do you explain who you are and why you are writing?') for passing that criterion, the second one visualizes the predicted score. The third column contains hints how to improve the writing (e.g., 'Introduce yourself in the first sentence') while the fourth column contains concrete examples of appropriate formulations. The control group was provided with a description of the scoring criteria (i.e. only the first column in Figure 3), but did not receive individual feedback on their performance. All texts were scored on the five assessment criteria, using binary codes: 0 = *criterion not mastered* and 1 = *criterion mastered*.

We compared the performance on each criterion between the two groups before and after the feedback intervention, expecting the feedback group to show more substantial improvement. As the outcome was dichotomous (0/1), we analyzed the data using the R package nparLD (Noguchi et al., 2012), which allows for the nonparametric analysis of longitudinal data in factorial experiments. Wald-tests (Wald, 1943) were performed to test whether the interaction of group (control vs. feedback) and time (initial draft vs. final draft) was statistically significant for each of the five criteria.

5.2 Results

Performance Improvement Figure 4 shows the performance results based on the automatic scoring for the two groups on the first draft and on the final revised version. For each criterion, the graphs show what proportion of students had successfully mastered the criterion. For *content completeness*, the vast majority of students in both the control group (93 %) and the feedback group (82 %) had already met the requirement in their first draft. In the feedback group, 10 percent were able to improve in the revision whereas the control group remained at a consistently high level (95 %). The group differences in content completeness improvement, however, were not statistically significant, χ^2=3.22; *ns*. Only a small minority of the students mastered the criterion *Greeting and Closing* in their first draft (9 % in the control, 6 % in the feedback condition), showing little improvement in the control group (12 %) and substantial improvement in the feedback group (31 %). This difference in improvement between the groups was statistically significant, χ^2=9.88; p<.01. The criterion *subject line* was fulfilled by 44 percent (con-

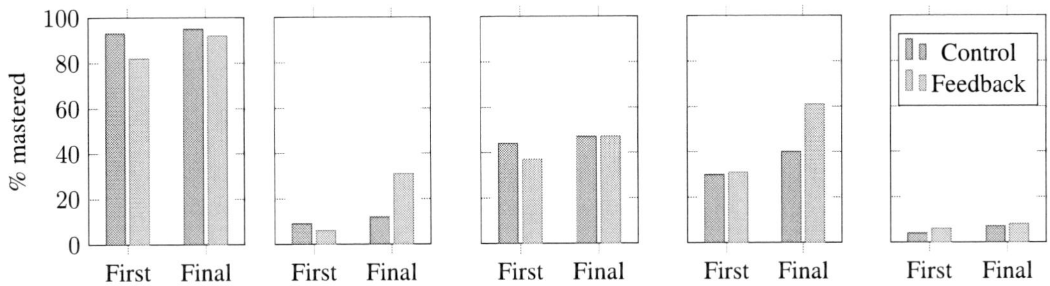

(a) Content (b) Greeting (c) Subject Line (d) Interpersonal (e) Register/Style

Figure 4: Improvements for control group and feedback group according to the automatic scoring model.

trol) and 37 percent (feedback), respectively, before the intervention, and by 47 percent in both groups after the intervention. While the descriptive results suggest that the feedback group was able to catch up, the effect was not significant, χ^2=1.19; *ns*. In both groups, almost a third of the students (30 % in the control, 31 % in the feedback condition) already mastered the criterion *interpersonal dimension* before the intervention. This percentage increased to 61 percent in the feedback condition and only 40 percent in the control condition. This effect was significant, χ^2=6.61; p <.01. The criterion *register and style* was only met by very few students before (4 % in the control, 6 % in the feedback condition) and after (7 % in the control, 8 % in the feedback condition) the intervention, yielding no significant differences, χ^2=0.29; *ns*.

5.3 Follow-up Analyses

The experiment resulted in an e-mail revision dataset where 5 revisions for each e-mail were recorded. This offers a unique opportunity to get insights into the properties of these revisions as well as the scoring behaviour of the trained model under realistic conditions.

E-mail Length As a first proxy for the extent of revisions we tracked e-mail length across revisions. Figure 5 shows the number of characters for each revision step in each condition.

We can see that there is a large variance of e-mail lengths at all revision steps, especially for the control group. In both groups, there is only a slight tendency that e-mails get longer across revisions, which indicates that the students do not primarily revise their texts by adding more content.

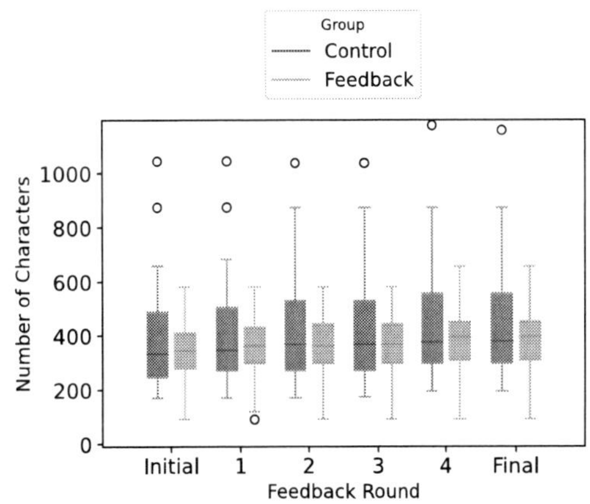

Figure 5: E-mail length (measured in characters) at each revision step.

Extent of Revisions To further investigate the nature of the revisions, we compute character-based edit distance between subsequent revisions, i.e. we count the minimal number of insertions, deletions or substitutions from one version to the next revision for both the feedback and the control condition.

Figure 6 shows that both groups display a similar pattern with most edits done after the initial step and the third revision. Manual inspection of essays from both groups showed that, in the first revision, students sometimes completed a not yet finished e-mail.

For the feedback group, we further looked separately at those students who were given the feedback that they had already mastered a criterion in contrast to those who were given the information that the criterion was not yet mastered. Figure 7 reveals that after the initial review, only those students which had not yet mastered a criterion made any revisions to their texts.

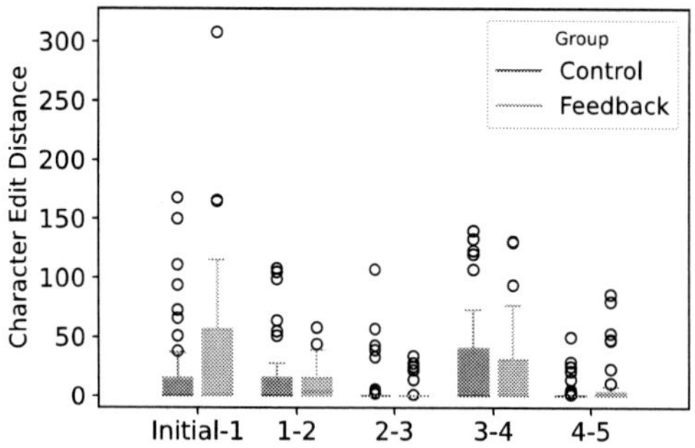

Figure 6: Edit distance between two consecutive revision steps (i.e. 2-3 is the edit distance between revision 2 and 3)

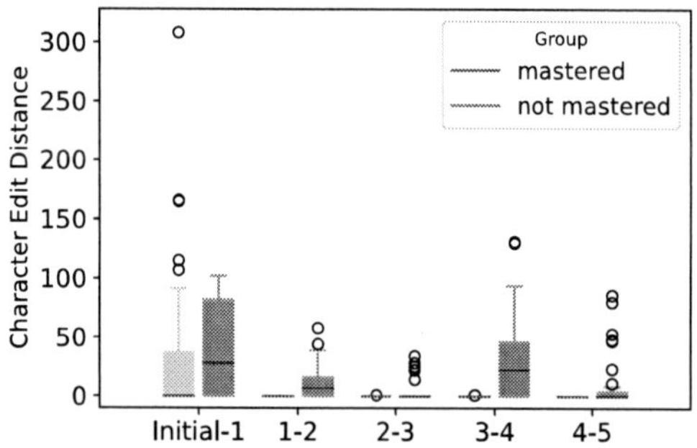

Figure 7: Edit distance between two consecutive revision steps (i.e. 2-3 is the edit distance between revision 2 and 3) for the Feedback group divided into those who passed or failed a certain criterion.

Automatic Scoring of E-mail Revisions While the study was initially conducted, only the first and final revision of an e-mail were scored automatically. We later scored each revision automatically according to each criterion in order to check whether improvements indeed mainly occurred after the respective feedback was received. Figure 8 indicates that for the feedback group, this expectation was confirmed, while the control group showed a less pronounced step-wise improvement.

Quality of Automatic Scores To check the automatic scoring performance on the newly collected e-mails, we manually scored the first as well as the final revision of each e-mail after the study was completed. Scoring was performed by a trained annotator who had already been involved in the scoring process of the eRubrix dataset. In doing so, we are able to validate the scoring performance of our automatic scoring model on this new data. For comparison, Table 5 contains cross

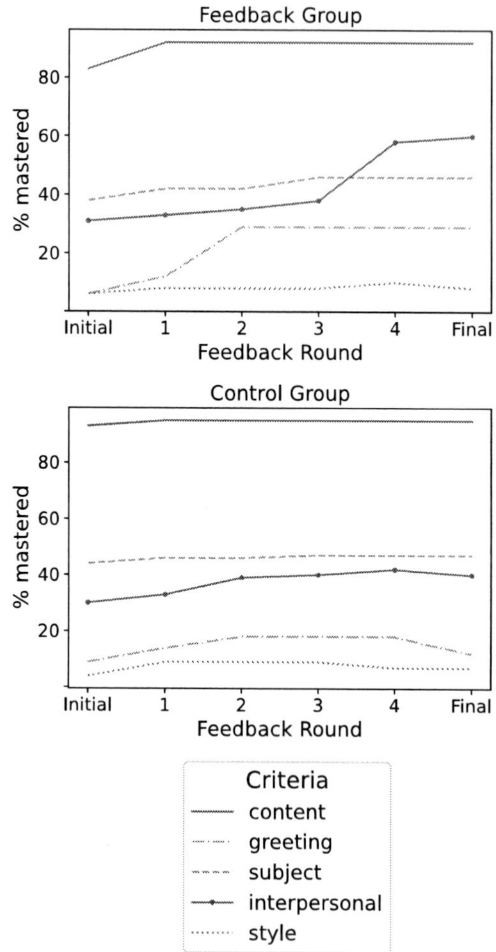

Figure 8: Percentage of students who mastered a criterion according to automatic scoring for each revision step.

validation results on the training data in the first line followed by scoring performance for the first and last draft of the e-mails from our intervention studies. For the two criteria *Greeting* and *Interpersonal*, performance is close to the performance in the training data, for *Content* and *Subject* performance deteriorates. For the latter criterion the cause might lie in issues of annotation where a single frequent subject line was scored differently between the texts in the eRubrix dataset and our study. In addition, we found population effects, where the new data contained formulations and lexical elements never encountered during training. The *Style* criterion could only be predicted unreliably in all conditions and was also the criterion with the lowest human-human agree-

Test data	Content		Greeting		Subject		Interpersonal		Style	
	acc	κ	acc	κ	acc	κ	acc	κ	acc	κ
eRubrix - CV	.92	.60	.88	.67	.94	.87	.85	.69	.81	.35
Intervention Study - First Draft	.78	.30	.95	.68	.70	.36	.85	.60	.78	.14
Intervention - Final Draft	.83	.29	.89	.63	.70	.41	.81	.62	.79	.27

Table 5: Scoring accuracy for the language school prompt used in our intervention study. We repeat the cross-validation experiments on the eRubrix data (first line) and then present results for the first and final draft in the intervention study.

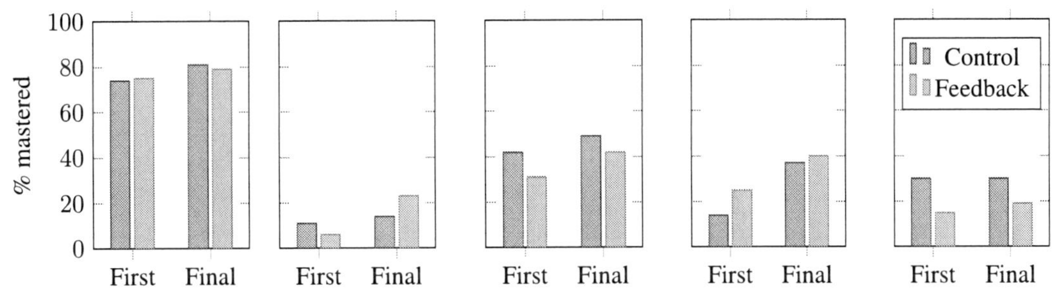

(a) Content (b) Greeting (c) Subject Line (d) Interpersonal (e) Register/Style

Figure 9: Improvements for control and feedback group according to the manual scoring.

ment. The two criteria with the best automatic scoring performance (*Greeting* and *Interpersonal*) also showed the highest improvement in the feedback group. We repeated the analyses described in 5.2 for the manual ratings. While the pattern of the results looks similar (see Figure 9), only one out of the five criteria showed statistically significant improvement. The only significant interaction was found for *Greeting and Closing* (χ^2=4.14; $p < .05$).

6 Discussion & Limitations

One limitation of our automated scoring approach is that for most scoring categories, we feed the whole text into the automatic classification model even though only certain parts are directly relevant (for example, to judge the appropriateness of the closing sentence it would be enough only to consider this particular sentence for scoring). To explore the options for further improvement, we therefore started to collect gold-standard annotations identifying the specific section where each element is located in the text so that we can use a two-stage approach in the future, where we first learn how to segment the text and then classify the appropriateness of the resulting segments.

In our intervention study, we were not able to separate effects of individual feedback components. Therefore we do not know the contribution of evaluative and elaborative feedback components. However, when looking at individual revisions, we saw a clear tendency that students relied on automatic feedback when deciding whether to revise their texts at all. Similarly, we used a very simple binary feedback that could be further improved, e.g. by highlighting relevant parts of an e-mail or by containing more specific hints for improvement.

We also scored only the first and last revision of the email automatically during the intervention study, while feedback (based on the first draft) was provided iteratively for each revision step. It is possible that students improved an aspect of the email that was only addressed later, so that feedback for that criterion was inaccurate at the point in time when the feedback was given. Our post-hoc automatic scores for each revision step (see Figure 8), however, indicate that this was rarely the case. Currently, we also do not know whether improvements will be long-term or whether students will be able to transfer them to new, unfamiliar e-mail writing prompts.

7 Conclusion

We presented a feedback intervention study based on automatic scores for an e-mail writing task scored according to different criteria. We found that students from the feedback groups improved more than students from the control groups for those two (out of five) criteria where the scoring algorithm worked best. Although much more work into similar directions is needed, especially with respect to the limitations discussed above, our study hints at the general usefulness of automatic scoring in the classroom.

8 Acknowledgements

This work was partially conducted in the framework of CATALPA - Center of Advanced Technology for Assisted Learning and Predictive Analytics" of the FernUniversität in Hagen, Germany, and partially within the KI-Starter project "Explaining AI Predictions of Semantic Relationships" funded by the Ministry of Culture and Science Nordrhein-Westfalen, Germany. We would like to thank our student assistant Sascha Meyer for his contributions to the automatic scoring model.

References

Robert L Bangert-Drowns, Chen-Lin C Kulik, James A Kulik, and MaryTeresa Morgan. 1991. The instructional effect of feedback in test-like events. *Review of educational research*, 61(2):213–238.

Beata Beigman Klebanov and Nitin Madnani. 2020. Automated evaluation of writing – 50 years and counting. In *Proceedings of the 58th Annual Meeting of the Association for Computational Linguistics*, pages 7796–7810, Online. Association for Computational Linguistics.

Paul Black and Dylan Wiliam. 1998. Assessment and classroom learning. *Assessment in Education: principles, policy & practice*, 5(1):7–74.

Jacob Cohen. 1960. A coefficient of agreement for nominal scales. *Educational and Psychological Measurement*, 20(1):37–46.

Youmna Farag, Helen Yannakoudakis, and Ted Briscoe. 2018. Neural automated essay scoring and coherence modeling for adversarially crafted input. *arXiv preprint arXiv:1804.06898*.

Johanna Fleckenstein, Raja Reble, Jennifer Meyer, Thorben Jansen, Lucas W. Liebenow, Jens Möller, and Olaf Köller. in press. Digitale Schreibförderung im Bildungskontext: Ein systematisches Review. In K. Scheiter and I. Gogolin, editors, *Bildung für eine digitale Zukunft (Edition ZfE, Band XX)*. Wiesbaden: VS Verlag für Sozialwissenschaften.

Steve Graham, Michael Hebert, and Karen R Harris. 2015. Formative assessment and writing: A meta-analysis. *The Elementary School Journal*, 115(4):523–547.

John Hattie and Helen Timperley. 2007. The power of feedback. *Review of educational research*, 77(1):81–112.

Andrea Horbach, Dirk Scholten-Akoun, Yuning Ding, and Torsten Zesch. 2017. Fine-grained essay scoring of a complex writing task for native speakers. In *Proceedings of the 12th Workshop on Innovative Use of NLP for Building Educational Applications*, pages 357–366, Copenhagen, Denmark. Association for Computational Linguistics.

Ken Hyland. 2007. Genre pedagogy: Language, literacy and l2 writing instruction. *Journal of second language writing*, 16(3):148–164.

Stefan D. Keller, Ruth Trüb, Emily Raubach, Jennifer Mayer, Thorben Jansen, and Johanna Fleckenstein. 2023. Designing and validating an assessment rubric for writing emails in English as a foreign language. *Research in Subject-matter Teaching and Learning (RISTAL)*.

Ronald T Kellogg, Alison P Whiteford, and Thomas Quinlan. 2010. Does automated feedback help students learn to write? *Journal of Educational Computing Research*, 42(2):173–196.

Beata Beigman Klebanov, Michael Flor, and Binod Gyawali. 2016. Topicality-based indices for essay scoring. In *Proceedings of the 11th Workshop on Innovative Use of NLP for Building Educational Applications*, pages 63–72.

Avraham N Kluger and Angelo DeNisi. 1996. The effects of feedback interventions on performance: a historical review, a meta-analysis, and a preliminary feedback intervention theory. *Psychological bulletin*, 119(2):254.

Yong-Won Lee, Claudia Gentile, and Robert Kantor. 2010. Toward automated multi-trait scoring of essays: Investigating links among holistic, analytic, and text feature scores. *Applied Linguistics*, 31(3):391–417.

Danielle S McNamara, Scott A Crossley, Rod D Roscoe, Laura K Allen, and Jianmin Dai. 2015. A hierarchical classification approach to automated essay scoring. *Assessing Writing*, 23:35–59.

Edna Holland Mory. 2004. Feedback research revisited. In *Handbook of research on educational communications and technology*, pages 738–776. Routledge.

Susanne Narciss. 2008. Feedback strategies for interactive learning tasks. In *Handbook of research on educational communications and technology*, pages 125–143. Routledge.

Rodney D. Nielsen, Wayne Ward, James Martin, and Martha Palmer. 2008. Annotating students' understanding of science concepts. In *Proceedings of the Sixth International Conference on Language Resources and Evaluation (LREC'08)*, Marrakech, Morocco. European Language Resources Association (ELRA).

Rodney D Nielsen, Wayne Ward, and James H Martin. 2009. Recognizing entailment in intelligent tutoring systems. *Natural Language Engineering*, 15(4):479–501.

Kimihiro Noguchi, Yulia R Gel, Edgar Brunner, and Frank Konietschke. 2012. nparld: an r software package for the nonparametric analysis of longitudinal data in factorial experiments. *Journal of Statistical software*, 50:1–23.

Corey Palermo and Margareta Maria Thomson. 2018. Teacher implementation of self-regulated strategy development with an automated writing evaluation system: Effects on the argumentative writing performance of middle school students. *Contemporary Educational Psychology*, 54:255–270.

Isaac Persing and Vincent Ng. 2015. Modeling Argument Strength in Student Essays. In *Proceedings of the 53rd Annual Meeting of the Association for Computational Linguistics and the 7th International Joint Conference on Natural Language Processing (Volume 1: Long Papers)*, pages 543–552.

Isaac Persing and Vincent Ng. 2016. End-to-End Argumentation Mining in Student Essays. In *Proceedings of the 2016 Conference of the North American Chapter of the Association for Computational Linguistics: Human Language Technologies*, pages 1384–1394.

D Royce Sadler. 1989. Formative assessment and the design of instructional systems. *Instructional science*, 18(2):119–144.

Valerie J Shute. 2008. Focus on formative feedback. *Review of educational research*, 78(1):153–189.

Christian Stab and Iryna Gurevych. 2014. Identifying Argumentative Discourse Structures in Persuasive Essays. In *Proceedings of the 2014 Conference on Empirical Methods in Natural Language Processing (EMNLP)*, pages 46–56.

Marie Stevenson and Aek Phakiti. 2014. The effects of computer-generated feedback on the quality of writing. *Assessing Writing*, 19:51–65.

Carola Strobl, Emilie Ailhaud, Kalliopi Benetos, Ann Devitt, Otto Kruse, Antje Proske, and Christian Rapp. 2019. Digital support for academic writing: A review of technologies and pedagogies. *Computers & education*, 131:33–48.

David Wade-Stein and Eileen Kintsch. 2004. Summary street: Interactive computer support for writing. *Cognition and instruction*, 22(3):333–362.

Abraham Wald. 1943. Tests of statistical hypotheses concerning several parameters when the number of observations is large. *Transactions of the American Mathematical society*, 54(3):426–482.

Henry George Widdowson. 1978. *Teaching language as communication*. Oxford university press.

Joshua Wilson and Amanda Czik. 2016. Automated essay evaluation software in english language arts classrooms: Effects on teacher feedback, student motivation, and writing quality. *Computers & Education*, 100:94–109.

Joshua Wilson and Rod D Roscoe. 2020. Automated writing evaluation and feedback: Multiple metrics of efficacy. *Journal of Educational Computing Research*, 58(1):87–125.

Benedikt Wisniewski, Klaus Zierer, and John Hattie. 2020. The power of feedback revisited: A meta-analysis of educational feedback research. *Frontiers in Psychology*, 10:3087.

Jinfen Xu and Shanshan Zhang. 2022. Understanding awe feedback and english writing of learners with different proficiency levels in an efl classroom: A sociocultural perspective. *The Asia-Pacific Education Researcher*, 31(4):357–367.

Helen Yannakoudakis and Ted Briscoe. 2012. Modeling coherence in esol learner texts. In *Proceedings of the Seventh Workshop on Building Educational Applications Using NLP*, pages 33–43.

Exploring Linguistic Acceptability in Swedish Learners' Language

Julia Klezl, Yousuf Ali Mohammed, Elena Volodina
University of Gothenburg, Sweden
name.surname1.surname2@svenska.gu.se

Abstract

We present our initial experiments on binary classification of sentences into linguistically correct versus incorrect ones in Swedish using the DaLAJ dataset (Volodina et al., 2021a). The nature of the task is bordering on linguistic acceptability judgments, on the one hand, and on grammatical error detection task, on the other. The experiments include models trained with different input features and on different variations of the training, validation, and test splits. We also analyze the results focusing on different error types and errors made on different proficiency levels. Apart from insights into which features and approaches work well for this task, we present first benchmark results on this dataset. The implementation is based on a bidirectional LSTM network and pretrained FastText embeddings, BERT embeddings, own word and character embeddings, as well as part-of-speech tags and dependency labels as input features. The best model used BERT embeddings and a training and validation set enriched with additional correct sentences. It reached an accuracy of 73% on one of three test sets used in the evaluation. These promising results illustrate that the data and format of DaLAJ make a valuable new resource for research in acceptability judgements in Swedish.

1 Introduction

Linguistic acceptability comes from the field of generative linguistics. It is based on native speakers' intuitive judgements of whether a sentence is acceptable or not (Schütze, 1996). While Lau et al. (2017) argue that acceptability is a gradient phenomenon, it generally is treated as a binary classification task (Warstadt et al., 2019). To create datasets for acceptability judgements, either existing incorrect sentences are collected, for example from linguistic literature (Lau et al., 2017; Lawrence et al., 2000), or correct sentences are manipulated (Marvin and Linzen, 2018). Using incorrect sentences by language learners has not been a common approach in this field so far.

There have been several studies on linguistic acceptability in English over the last years, using various forms of neural networks, targeting different error types, and focusing on different underlying aims. Neural networks trained to make acceptability judgements can yield for example theoretical insights into how language is perceived and acquired (Lawrence et al., 2000; Lau et al., 2017), or into what knowledge language models represent (Linzen et al., 2016; Jing et al., 2019). Practical applications of such models include evaluation of results from language-generating systems (such as question-answering or machine translation) or providing assistance in language learning.

Contrary to the field in English, we are aware of only one study on linguistic acceptability on the Swedish language (Taktasheva et al., 2021), where authors use synthetically manipulated data focusing on effects of word order errors on model predictions. Our study is inspired by the research on linguistic acceptability, however, we set it into the domain of second language acquisition. We formulate the task as a binary classification on a sentence level, similar to Daudaravicius et al. (2016), where the system output should classify a sentence as correct or incorrect (i.e. containing an error). We see this type of classification as a first step to future grammatical error detection (GED) and correction (GEC) systems for Swedish, and as a first step before generating feedback on errors.

In our work, we present an exploration of the binary sentence classification task on DaLAJ, a Dataset for Linguistic Acceptability in Swedish, where each sentence pair contains (1) a sentence with one error only and (2) a corrected sentence. Due to the fact that the dataset is new, and the task unprecedented in this form for Swedish, our study has a strong exploratory character. Our contributions include a first evaluation of the strengths,

Julia Klezl, Yousuf Ali Mohammed and Elena Volodina. Exploring Linguistic Acceptability in Swedish Learners' Language. *Proceedings of the 11th Workshop on Natural Language Processing for Computer Assisted Language Learning (NLP4CALL 2022).* Linköping Electronic Conference Proceedings 190: 84–94.

possibilities, and certain drawbacks of the dataset, a comparison of different input features to the neural network, and first benchmark results for this task.

In the next section, we briefly outline two comparable studies in English. In section 3, the data, features, and models are introduced, followed by the results in section 4, as well as a discussion and a conclusion with some ideas for future work in sections 5 and 6.

2 Related work

Comparing acceptability models is generally difficult, since there are big differences across languages, target errors, metrics and datasets. The following shared task and study are relatively similar in set-up and aim to our focus, so they provide some context to view our work in.

2.1 AESW 2016

The goal in the Automatic Evaluation of Scientific Writing shared task (AESW) 2016 was to identify sentences in need of correction in scientific articles written in English (Daudaravicius et al., 2016). This did not only include grammatical errors but also stylistic features inappropriate for the academic genre. Predictions were given both in a binary and a probabilistic version. The task organizers report that six teams participated, two of which used deep learning methods, two maximum entropy, and the remaining two logistic regression and support vector machines. The teams using deep learning ranked highest with F1-scores of 61.08 and 62.78 on the binary task (Daudaravicius et al., 2016). One of them used a convolutional neural network and pretrained word embeddings (Lee et al., 2016). The other team combined several character - and one word-based encoder-decoder models and a sentence-level convolutional layer by majority vote (Schmaltz et al., 2016).

2.2 CoLA

CoLA is the **Co**rpus of **L**inguistic **A**cceptability, a collection of "10,657 English sentences labeled as grammatical or ungrammatical from published linguistics literature" (Warstadt et al., 2019). It targets morphological, syntactic, and semantic errors. The authors also present first models trained on this dataset. The most successful one uses transfer learning with an encoder pretrained on artificial data and contextualized word embeddings. It reaches an in-domain accuracy of 77% and an out-of-domain accuracy of 73%. Regarding the different error types, they conclude that their models "do not show evidence of learning non-local dependencies related to agreement and questions, but do appear to acquire knowledge about basic subject-verb-object word order and verbal argument structure" (Warstadt et al., 2019).

3 Materials and methods

3.1 Data

Three data sources were used in this work. The main dataset is DaLAJ, a single-error derivation of the SweLL-gold corpus. In addition to this, sentences presenting correct samples from SweLL-gold and the COCTAILL corpus were used.

3.1.1 SweLL-gold

SweLL-gold is a subcorpus of the **Swe**dish **L**earner **L**anguage corpus, a collection of 502 pseudonymized, normalized, and correction annotated essays written by adult Swedish learners of beginner, intermediate, and advanced levels (Volodina et al., 2019). The tagset includes 35 error correction tags, including morphological, syntactical, orthographic, punctuation, and lexical ones as well as exceptions such as corrections made as a consequence to other corrections, corrections that do not fit into any of the categories, or markup of unintelligible strings. Rudebeck and Sundberg (2021) provide detailed information on correction annotation in the SweLL-gold data. The 502 SweLL-gold essays contain a total of

- 6,615 sentences containing one or more errors
- 1,706 correct sentences.

3.1.2 DaLAJ

DaLAJ is a single-error sentence-scrambled extension to the SweLL-gold corpus. The format is described in Volodina et al. (2021a), Volodina et al. (2021b), where the pilot version DaLAJ 1.0 was tested, based on four error types.[1] The full dataset used in our present study follows the same principles but contains 35 error types and therefore more sentence pairs. The basic principle of

[1] DaLAJ 1.0 is available as part of the SwedishGlue collection (https://spraakbanken.gu.se/en/resources/dalaj), while DaLAJ 2.0, the full version used for training and testing in this article, will be released at a later stage.

the DaLAJ format is that sentences that originally contained more than one error are included once for each error, with all other errors corrected. This has two advantages: Since larger parts of every sentence are correct, it is easier for the models to learn the patterns and structure of correct language than when sentences contain multiple errors. By splitting multi-error sentences into multiple single-error sentences, we obtain a DaLAJ version of the SweLL-gold corpus which is around five times bigger than the original SweLL-gold corpus. For every sentence, this dataset contains the wrong sentence, the corrected sentence, the pair of the wrong and correct tokens, and the error label as described above. In terms of metadata, it additionally has the education level of the course the student was taking when writing the text (split into beginner, intermediate, and advanced) (see Table 1). It also includes the student's first language, but this is not considered in the present work. The sentences are randomized, which excludes the possibility to reconstruct full essays. This way it is possible to avoid restrictions imposed by the GDPR (EU Commission, 2016).

Description	Example sentence
original sentence	§Den§ är en svår fråga .
corrected sentence	§Det§ är en svår fråga .
error-correction pair	§Den§–§Det§
error label	L-Ref
education level	Fortsättning

Table 1: Example sentence from DaLAJ

Here are a few statistics about the size and composition of DaLAJ 2.0 before preprocessing:

- Number of incorrect sentences: 26,652 with their corrected equivalents which represent 6,615 unique sentences
- Number of unique correct sentences: 6,615
- Number of tokens: 1,241,754
- Vocabulary size: 19,963

For effective model training, we need to have a balanced number of (unique) correct and incorrect sentences. However, as we can see from the statistics numbers, for the 26,652 sentences containing errors we have only 6,615 unique corrected sentences that are duplicated each time when a source original sentence has more than one error. To expose our models to sufficient number of correct sentences, we, therefore, ideally need to add further 20,000 correct sentences. 1,706 of those come from the SweLL-gold. To complement the rest, we use COCTAILL, a corpus of course books, as described below.

3.1.3 COCTAILL

COCTAILL was chosen as a source for the additional correct sentences because it comes from the realm of language learning and should therefore be similar in domain to DaLAJ. It also includes information about the level of the course at which the texts are used for teaching. We have, thus, a proficiency level label for each sentence in COCTAILL. We use this metadata to keep the original distribution of beginner (A-levels), intermediate (B-levels), and advanced (C-levels) sentences in the additional correct sentence.

COCTAILL stands for "**C**orpus **of** **C**EFR-based **T**extbooks **a**s **I**nput for **L**earner **L**evel's modelling" and contains texts from 12 Swedish course books from beginner to advanced learners (Volodina et al., 2014). Since it also contains a fair amount of incomplete sentences such as headings, lists, or word definitions, we applied some filtering steps. In total, 5,015 beginner, 2,468 intermediate, and 5,066 advanced sentences were replaced with sentences of equivalent level to keep the original distribution.

3.2 Preprocessing

3.2.1 DaLAJ 2.0

We divided the DaLAJ sentences into three splits of 80% for training and 10% each for validation and testing, making sure that, even with duplicates, no identical sentences occur in the training and test splits and that the distribution of beginner, intermediate, and advanced sentences is equal across splits.

In the next step, we removed

- sentences with a length over 50 tokens (incl. punctuation)
- duplicate incorrect sentences
- all sentences that contained error types that appear less than 100 times in total (M-Other, M-Adj/adv, S-Comp, L-FL, S-Other, P-Sent, S-Adv, S-WO, S-FinV, S-R, P-R, S-Type) and

- all sentences that contained error types that do not belong to the five main error groups (orthography, lexis, morphology, punctuation, syntax) - i.e. tags that correspond to comments of all types and indicate illegible/uninterpretable strings (C, Cit-FL, Com!, OBS!, X)

Lastly, all pseudonymized tokens (e.g. 'A-city') were replaced with names of existing city, country, or place names, as shown in the example:

- Original: §jag§ är född i *A-hemland* .
- Replaced: §jag§ är född i *Norge* .

3.2.2 Training and validation sets

We tried two approaches with regards to data balance: (1) In the first approach, we kept the duplicate corrected sentences. Even though duplicates do not add new information to a model, they do keep it balanced, so it does not adopt bias due to an unequal label distribution. (2) In the second approach, we removed duplicates from the training and validation sets and replaced them with correct sentences from COCTAILL, as described in section 3.1.3.

3.2.3 Test sets

The models were evaluated on three different test sets. This does not just give insights into the models' performance but also into the impact the different compositions of the test sets have on the scores.

Test set 1 is the regular test split as it occurs in the dataset. In order to get accurate results, the correct sentences in this split were manually checked and corrected, so some changes were made, but no additional sentences were added or removed. This means that this test set contains a high number of duplicate correct sentences (as does the original dataset and the training and validation data in Models 1 and 3).

Test set 2 is a test set that includes no duplicates. It has the same number of incorrect sentences as the first test set and also uses the manually checked correct sentences. However, all duplicates were excluded, leaving this set significantly smaller and unbalanced.

In **test set 3**, we balanced test set 2 (the set without duplicates) by adding correct sentences from the original SweLL-gold corpus. These are not part of the DaLAJ training and validation sets, so they are unseen by the models, but come from the same domain as the other test sentences. One drawback here is that there are not enough intermediate-level sentences in the replacements, so they were supplemented with advanced-level sentences to make up for the difference. Table 2 gives an overview of all training, validation, and test sets.

3.3 Features

Different features were used in our models, alone or in combination, and with varying degrees of success. In all of them, we used white-space tokenization and padded to the maximum length of 50 with zeros on the left side of the sentence, unless otherwise specified.

FastText: First, words were converted into 300-dimensional pretrained FastText embeddings[2] (Grave et al., 2018). Pseudo-random vectors were used for infrequent words (UNK) and words that are not part of the embedding vocabulary (ERR). Missing words in the incorrect sentences were represented by "§§"-tokens. In the training and validation sets, they got the "UNK"-label and vector, in testing they got skipped, since adding them would have given away information about the error to the model.

FastText + error word: FastText embeddings like above were used, but with the error word explicitly added to the end of the sentence. For training and validation, we got the embeddings for the sentence as well as the error word(s) as described above and then concatenated the two vectors. For testing, the "ERR"-embeddings were added when out-of-vocabulary words occurred. Otherwise, only padding was added to the sentence embedding.

BERT: Contextualized word embeddings from Swedish BERT[3] (Malmsten et al., 2020) were used. A pretrained BERT-tokenizer split the sentences into words or subwords, which were then put through the pretrained Swedish BERT model. For the embeddings, we summed the hidden states of the last four encoder layers for each word. This resulted in 768-dimensional word embeddings. The BERT embeddings were padded on the right side to be compatible with the BERT tokenizer.

Word indices: Each word was simply converted to an index in the vocabulary and later turned into

[2]https://fasttext.cc/docs/en/crawl-vectors.html

[3]https://huggingface.co/KB/bert-base-swedish-cased

Set	# sen total	# beginner sen	# intermediate sen	# advanced sen	vocab
Train (dupl.)	32,394	12,890	5,766	13,738	10,826
Train (COCTAILL)	32,394	12,890	5,766	13,738	21,936
Val (dupl.)	4,008	1,576	722	1,710	2,922
Val (COCTAILL)	4,008	1,576	722	1,710	6,203
Test (dupl.)	3,884	1,439	659	1,786	2,677
Test (no dupl.)	2,573	1,001	437	1,135	2,677
Test (SweLL)	3,884	1,564	518	1,802	4,005

Table 2: Dataset and vocabulary sizes

100-dimensional embeddings by an Embedding layer[4] in the neural network. Words that occurred less than three times were regarded as unknown.

Character embeddings/indices: The sentences were converted into sequences of character indexes. They were transformed to 50-dimensional embeddings by an Embedding layer in the neural network. The threshold for unknown characters was set to five occurrences.

One-hot encodings for error words: Finally, one-hot vectors were used to indicate the problematic parts of each sentence. For training and validation, the word(s) between the §-markers were represented by 1, all other words and padding with 0. For testing, only words that do not occur in the FastText vocabulary were marked as 1 based on the assumption that these are spelling mistakes; all other words - as 0.

In addition to the word representations, we tried adding explicitly linguistic features, POS-tags and dependency relations. These tags were extracted with the Sparv pipeline[5] (Borin et al., 2016), converted into numbers by indexing the respective tags, and also padded to a length of 50 with zeros on the left side.

For the gold standard and for analysing the results, each sentence has two labels. One is the binary gold target indicating whether a result should be predicted as correct (0) or incorrect (1). The second is the SweLL error tag, indicating what exactly is wrong in the sentence. Correct sentences do not have an error tag.

The PyTorch Dataset and Dataloader classes[6] were used to shuffle and batch the data (batch size 32) and load it to the models.

[4]https://pytorch.org/docs/stable/generated/torch.nn.Embedding.html

[5]https://spraakbanken.gu.se/verktyg/sparv

[6]https://pytorch.org/docs/stable/data.html#torch.utils.data.DataLoader

3.4 Models

All models are based on a bidirectional LSTM layer and a linear layer. The choice of bi-LSTM classifier is based on its previous successful uses for binary error detection reported in literature (Rei and Yannakoudakis, 2016; Kaneko et al., 2017; Kasewa et al., 2018; Bell et al., 2019; Deksne, 2019). BiLSTMs are useful for sequential data when long-distance dependencies also play a role and context on both sides of a token should be taken into account.

To get predictions from the output logits, softmax and argmax functions were used. The Adam optimizer was used with different learning rates. Loss was calculated with the Cross-Entropy Loss function. All models were trained for a maximum of 75 epochs with early stopping after 15 epochs without improvements in validation loss. The models differ in their specific hyperparameters, input, and structure. Many of the features and feature combinations did not give meaningful results or did not improve the results reached with simpler models. In the following, the successful models are described in more detail. For these, the respective results are discussed in section 4.

3.4.1 Model 1 & 2: FastText

The first two models took pretrained FastText embeddings as input with a hidden size of 100 and the learning rate 0.0001. Model 1 used the regular DaLAJ 2.0 data including duplicate correct sentences. Model 2 used the training and validation sets in which duplicate correct sentences were replaced by sentences from COCTAILL.

3.4.2 Model 3 & 4: BERT

Models 3 and 4 had the same basic structure but used contextualized BERT embeddings instead of FastText. The hidden size was 100, like in the models above, but the learning rate was reduced to 0.00005. As above, model 3 was trained using the regular single-error dataset without additional sentences, while model 4 used additional COCTAILL sentences in training and validation.

3.4.3 Other models

Further experiments included adding linguistic features (such as parts of speech and dependency relations, character embeddings, word indices, one-hot encodings for error words) to test if they can improve the performance. They have in general failed compared to Models 1-4, and we therefore do not report them here, but outline in an Appendix.

4 Results and analysis

The models were evaluated in multiple ways. First, an overall quantitative analysis compared the different models. In the second and third part, the best-performing model was analyzed in more detail, considering error types and education levels. Finally, a qualitative analysis of the best models' predictions was conducted.

For the quantitative analysis, the main focus is on the accuracy score. However, since related work is often evaluated with other metrics such as F1-score, F0.5-score, or precision and recall, these scores are also reported for the best-performing model.

4.1 Overall quantitative analysis

There are three things to consider in the overall results in Table 3: The comparison between different embeddings, different training and validation sets, and between different test sets. First, regarding the embeddings, the models trained on BERT embeddings (Model 3 and Model 4) clearly outperformed the ones trained on FastText across all combinations of training and test sets. Second, the highest score (for both embedding types) was reached on models trained and validated on the dataset where duplicates were replaced with sentences from COCTAILL. Third, the differences between test sets show that models performed better on test sets without duplicates. This pattern was not as clear in the models trained on data including duplicates.

Table 4 contains the full classification report for the best model on the best test set. A look into these more detailed results shows significantly higher precision, recall, and F-scores for the incorrect sentences than the correct ones. This indicates that the model learned more from the incorrect than the correct samples in the training, potentially because there is more variation in the incorrect sentences. A comparison between the individual scores shows very stable results. Within the two classes, precision and recall lie very close together. In binary classification, there is usually a certain trade-off between precision and recall, and which one is more important depends on the task and application. Our model here turned out to be very balanced in this regard, so the F1- and F0.5-scores are almost identical.

4.2 Performance by error type

For all further analysis, only Model 4, which has the best overall performance, is considered. The following results are taken from test set 2.

Due to our filtering and preprocessing steps, we used only 18 of the total 35 SweLL error types in our experiments. Table 5 shows the accuracy and number of samples in the test set for each of them, along with a short explanation of the types. For a table explaining all error types we refer the reader to the appendix of Volodina et al. (2021a). More detailed information can be found in the full correction annotation guidelines[7] (Rudebeck and Sundberg, 2021). This only takes the incorrect sentences into account, since the correct ones do not have an error type. Both the individual scores and the ranking of error types differed between different models. Therefore, the following observations only allow conclusions about this specific model.

First, the types with the highest accuracy are considered. Some of them are expected. *O, L-Der,* and *M-F*[8], for example, are types that often result in "words" that do not exist in correct Swedish and are thus not part of the word embeddings used to train the models. Other high-performing groups were more surprising. The high scores for *S-Clause, S-Ext*, and *S-Msubj* indicate that the model learns about more complex aspects of language, such as word order. The fact that *P-W* errors are among the most successful groups further supports the conclusion that this model has a decent understanding of Swedish sentence structure.

Second, *O-Comp* and *M-Num* are the types with the lowest accuracy in this model. *O-Comp* might be more difficult to predict than other errors since this aspect of a language often does not follow

[7]https://spraakbanken.github.io/swell-project/Correction-annotation_guidelines

[8]All correction codes are briefly explained in Table 5

Model	data	embeddings	test 1 (dupl.)	test 2 (no dupl.)	test 3 (SweLL)
1	DaLAJ	FastText	0.61	0.42	0.53
2	DaLAJ + COCTAILL	FastText	0.59	0.62	0.66
3	DaLAJ	BERT	0.66	0.67	0.65
4	DaLAJ + COCTAILL	BERT	0.61	0.73	0.69

Table 3: Accuracy of models 1-4 in three different test sets

Class	Precision	Recall	F1-score	F0.5-score	Sample number	Accuracy
0 (correct)	0.43	0.39	0.41	0.42	631	0.39
1 (incorrect)	0.81	0.83	0.82	0.81	1942	0.83
Total					**2573**	**0.73**

Table 4: Classification report for model 4 on test set 2

strict rules. For *M-Num* errors, there might be difficulties in learning longer-distance agreement when determiners, nouns, and adjectives are not directly adjacent. However, it is somewhat surprising that the related errors *M-Def* and *M-Gend* perform significantly better.

Model's performance by error group does not show a very clear pattern. Most groups include mixed success rates across their respective types. That being said, lexical and punctuation errors are generally closer to average, while morphological errors tend to perform lower and syntactical ones perform above average.

A last perspective for comparison is the number of samples of each type in the dataset. One might expect a strong positive correlation between number of samples and prediction accuracy of an error type. However, this was not quite the case here. It is true that the error types with low accuracy scores generally also have a low number of samples (e.g. *O-Comp*). This pattern does not hold for the entire set of results though, since some of the types with very high accuracy, such as *S-Ext* or *S-Msubj*, also have relatively low number of samples. Finally, *P-M* and *S-M* are two types with above-average sample sizes, but merely average accuracy scores, indicating that identifying missing tokens in a sentence might be inherently more difficult than identifying incorrect ones.

4.3 Performance by education level

Table 6 shows clear performance differences between sentences written by learners at different education levels. Beginner sentences are predicted with distinctly higher success than intermediate and advanced ones. This might partly be explained by the under-representation of intermediate-level sentences. Another reason is the unequal distribution of error types across levels. Some of the types that proved to be most successful in the section above, such as *O, O-Cap*, or *M-F* occur with higher frequency in the beginner set. At the same time, some of the overall less successful types, such as *M-Case, M-Num*, or *L-W*, occur more frequently in the sentences written by advanced learners.

4.4 Qualitative analysis

In this section we take a closer look at the predictions, especially the false negatives, of Model 4. Numbered example sentences can be found at the end of the section.

First, there are small issues in the dataset. Some sentences were apparently incorrect when annotated in the context of their text, but are correct when considered independently. Example [1] is one case which the model therefore "misclassifies" as correct. Another problem is that some sentences have essay titles or headings incorrectly attached to them, like in [2].

Apart from these issues, there are some specific errors the model frequently misses. One of them is agreement with longer distances between the respective words, for example in [3]. Another difficulty for the model seem to be preposition choices. Incorrect usage of for example *"i", "på", "för"*, or *"med"* is often not predicted as an error. Sentences in which the pronoun case is incorrect also appear frequently among the false negatives. One last group of errors that are not recognized well by the model are spelling mistakes in names.

One step in preprocessing, the naive replacement of pseudonymization tokens with city, country, or place names, resulted in some sentences of

Error tag	Explanation	# sen	# true	Acc
O-Comp	Orthography: Problem with compounding	18	13	0.72
O-Cap	Orthography: Wrong capitalization	29	25	0.86
O	Orthography: Regular spelling correction	261	235	0.90
L-Der	Lexical: Word formation problem (derivation or compounding)	58	49	0.84
L-Ref	Lexical: Choice of anaphoric expression	59	48	0.81
L-W	Lexical: Wrong word or phrase	319	257	0.81
M-Case	Morphology: Noun case correction (nom vs gen; nom vs acc)	31	24	0.77
M-Def	Morphology: Definiteness (articles; noun & adj forms)	280	222	0.79
M-F	Morphology: Grammatical category kept, form changed	24	21	0.88
M-Gend	Morphology: Gender correction	81	67	0.83
M-Num	Morphology: Number correction	81	59	0.73
M-Verb	Morphology: Verb corrections (inflections, auxiliaries)	202	173	0.86
P-M	Punctuation: Punctuation missing (added)	134	113	0.84
P-W	Punctuation: Wrong punctuation	38	33	0.87
S-Clause	Syntax: Change of clause structure, incl. synt. function	66	61	0.92
S-Ext	Syntax: Extensive and complex correction	26	24	0.92
S-M	Syntax: Word missing (added)	196	157	0.80
S-Msubj	Syntax: Subject missing (added)	39	36	0.92

Table 5: Accuracy and number of samples by error type (in the test set) in Model 4

Education level	# Samples	Accuracy
Beginner	1001	0.77
Intermediate	437	0.69
Advanced	1135	0.70

Table 6: Accuracy and number of samples (in the test set) by education level in Model 4

questionable logic, like [4]. Looking at the results, it does not seem to disturb the classifier, but more research into it would be needed to be sure. Finally, we found a pattern that longer sentences tend to get predicted as incorrect more often than shorter ones. This is not conclusive by itself but invites further research into the effect of sentence length on the models.

[1] *Jag §är§ väldigt bra .*

[Eng. I §am§ very good .]

[2] *Skrivuppgift 3 , 3 april 2018 Politiker som föredömen Får politiker vara §gott§ föredömen för medborgarna ?*

[Eng. Writing task 3 , 3 April 2018 Politicians as models Are politicians allowed to be §good§ models for citizens ?]

[3] *Han har svart hår , mörka ögon och en mun som alltid §ville§ skratta .*

[Eng. He has black hair , dark eyes and a mouth that always §wanted§ to smile .]

[4] *Ruinen ligger mellan Spanien och Danmark och §den§ hade inte tak §utan§ bara fyra väggar .*

[Eng. The ruins lie between Spain and Denmark and §it§ has no roof §but§ only four walls .]

5 Discussion

The first conclusion to be drawn from the results is that there are significant differences in the effectiveness of different types of word embeddings. The fact that the models trained on BERT embeddings perform higher than the ones trained on FastText across all combinations of training and test sets presents them as the better choice overall. Reasons for this could be the differences in training data, dimensionality, and that the method of getting embeddings from the context itself works better in this task.

Our second insight is that there are clear differences in how successfully each error type is predicted. These differences are only partially correlated with the types' representation in the training data. As a general tendency, spelling mistakes and simple word-order errors are predicted with exceptionally high success rates while morphological errors (especially agreement of non-adjacent words) perform worse. These trends have to be taken with caution, however. Some error types occur in very few samples in the test set, which might impact the score's reliability in these cases.

Furthermore, we found that there are differences in performance depending on the sentences' education level. Sentences written on the beginner level proved to be classified with significantly higher success than those on the intermediate and advanced level. One explanation could be the under-representation of intermediate-level sentences. Another one is that the distribution of error types is not equal across the proficiency levels.

A comparison with similar studies on English shows that our work lies well within the range of their results. For example, in the AESW 2016 task, teams reached F1-scores of up to 62% on sentence-level classification of scientific writing (Daudaravicius et al., 2016). Warstadt et al. (2019) reached 73% to 77% accuracy on their CoLA dataset. Their data consists of sentences that were purposefully written to illustrate certain errors and that are not originally embedded in the context of a text, which is a big difference to the DaLAJ data.

The fact that our results compare favorably to similar studies in English proves that the novel approach used to create DaLAJ dataset was successful. As explained in more detail in Volodina et al. (2021a), there are several advantages to using a dataset based on learner data for this task. Not only is the data realistic, it is also generally annotated by experts, and often includes detailed error labels. Advantages of the hybrid approach between authentic and synthetic data are that the number of available sentences is higher with this method, sentences are more informative than authentic ones, but still very similar to the originals. A minor drawback of this dataset is that the sentences were originally written and normalized (i.e. re-written in correct Swedish) in the context of a full essay and then classified in isolation, which caused some difficulties with predicting the correctness of for example anaphoric references.

The experiments with different training, validation, and test sets gave a clear indication that replacing duplicate sentences with unique ones from another source results in better models and better scores. By replacing the duplicates with correct sentences from a second corpus, they have far more relevant input and are able to generalize better.

6 Conclusions and future work

We presented promising benchmark results on the linguistic acceptability task in Swedish. The comparison of different input features showed that pre-trained word embeddings, especially contextualized BERT embeddings, are very successful while other ways of representing the sentences did not yield good results, and additional linguistic features did not improve the embedding-based model. Overall, the dataset proved to be big and informative enough to train such models, despite some minor drawbacks.

In future experiments, we plan to use this dataset for multi-class classification of errors, for token-level error detection, and for error correction. These experiments would be an important step towards a functioning automatic writing evaluation (AWE) system for Swedish, where feedback generation will need to rely on correctly detected and labeled error types. In connection to this, we will need to see whether models trained on distilled hybrid data like DaLAJ can be successfully applied to authentic data containing multiple errors per sentence. Finally, we will experiment with generation of synthetic data to study its influence over model performance and to improve our chances of getting accurate tools for language learners.

Acknowledgments

This work has been supported by a research grant from the Swedish Riksbankens Jubileumsfond *SweLL - research infrastructure for Swedish as a second language*, IN16-0464:1; by *Nationella språkbanken*, funded by the Swedish Research Council (2018-2024, contract 2017-00626) and their participating partner institutions; and by VINNOVA through its funding of *SwedishGlue: a benchmark suite for language models* (2020-02523).

References

Samuel Bell, Helen Yannakoudakis, and Marek Rei. 2019. Context is key: Grammatical error detection with contextual word representations. In *Proceedings of the Fourteenth Workshop on Innovative Use of NLP for Building Educational Applications*, pages 103–115, Florence, Italy. Association for Computational Linguistics.

Lars Borin, Markus Forsberg, Martin Hammarstedt, Dan Rosén, Roland Schäfer, and Anne Schumacher. 2016. Sparv: Språkbanken's corpus annotation pipeline infrastructure. In *SLTC 2016. The Sixth Swedish Language Technology Conference*, pages 17–18, Umeå University, Sweden.

Vidas Daudaravicius, Rafael E. Banchs, Elena Volodina, and Courtney Napoles. 2016. A report on the automatic evaluation of scientific writing shared task. In *Proceedings of the 11th Workshop on Innovative Use of NLP for Building Educational Applications*, pages 53–62, San Diego, CA. Association for Computational Linguistics.

Daiga Deksne. 2019. Bidirectional LSTM tagger for Latvian Grammatical Error Detection. In *International Conference on Text, Speech, and Dialogue*, pages 58–68. Springer.

EU Commission. 2016. General data protection regulation. *Official Journal of the European Union*, 59:1–88.

Edouard Grave, Piotr Bojanowski, Prakhar Gupta, Armand Joulin, and Tomas Mikolov. 2018. Learning word vectors for 157 languages. In *Proceedings of the International Conference on Language Resources and Evaluation (LREC 2018)*.

Wang Jing, Matthew A. Kelly, and David Reitter. 2019. Do we need neural models to explain human judgments of acceptability? *CoRR*, abs/1909.08663v1.

Masahiro Kaneko, Yuya Sakaizawa, and Mamoru Komachi. 2017. Grammatical error detection using error-and grammaticality-specific word embeddings. In *Proceedings of the Eighth International Joint Conference on Natural Language Processing (Volume 1: Long Papers)*, pages 40–48.

Sudhanshu Kasewa, Pontus Stenetorp, and Sebastian Riedel. 2018. Wronging a right: Generating better errors to improve grammatical error detection. *CoRR, abs/1810.00668*.

Jey Han Lau, Alexander Clark, and Shalom Lappin. 2017. Grammaticality, acceptability, and probability: A probabilistic view of linguistic knowledge. *Cognitive Science*, 41(5):1202–1241.

Steve Lawrence, C. Lee Giles, and Sandiway Fong. 2000. Natural language grammatical inference with recurrent neural networks. *IEEE Transactions on Knowledge and Data Engineering*, 12(1):126–140.

Lung-Hao Lee, Bo-Lin Lin, Liang-Chih Yu, and Yuen-Hsien Tseng. 2016. The NTNU-YZU system in the AESW shared task: Automated evaluation of scientific writing using a convolutional neural network. In *Proceedings of the 11th Workshop on Innovative Use of NLP for Building Educational Applications*, pages 122–129, San Diego, CA. Association for Computational Linguistics.

Tal Linzen, Emmanuel Dupoux, and Yoav Goldberg. 2016. Assessing the ability of LSTMs to learn syntax-sensitive dependencies. *Transactions of the Association for Computational Linguistics*, 4:521–535.

Martin Malmsten, Love Börjeson, and Chris Haffenden. 2020. Playing with words at the national library of sweden - making a swedish BERT. *CoRR*, abs/2007.01658v1.

Rebecca Marvin and Tal Linzen. 2018. Targeted syntactic evaluation of language models. In *Proceedings of the 2018 Conference on Empirical Methods in Natural Language Processing*, pages 1192–1202, Brussels, Belgium. Association for Computational Linguistics.

Marek Rei and Helen Yannakoudakis. 2016. Compositional sequence labeling models for error detection in learner writing. *Proceedings of the 54th Annual Meeting of the Association for Computational Linguistics (Volume 1: Long Papers)*.

Lisa Rudebeck and Gunlög Sundberg. 2021. SweLL correction annotation guidelines. Technical report, GU-ISS Research report series, Department of Swedish, University of Gothenburg. http://hdl.handle.net/2077/69434.

Allen Schmaltz, Yoon Kim, Alexander M. Rush, and Stuart Shieber. 2016. Sentence-level grammatical error identification as sequence-to-sequence correction. In *Proceedings of the 11th Workshop on Innovative Use of NLP for Building Educational Applications*, pages 242–251, San Diego, CA. Association for Computational Linguistics.

Carson T. Schütze. 1996. *The Empirical Base of Linguistics : Grammaticality Judgments and Linguistic Methodology*. University of Chicago Press, Chicago, Il.

Ekaterina Taktasheva, Vladislav Mikhailov, and Ekaterina Artemova. 2021. Shaking syntactic trees on the sesame street: Multilingual probing with controllable perturbations. *arXiv preprint arXiv:2109.14017*.

Elena Volodina, Lena Granstedt, Arild Matsson, Beáta Megyesi, Ildikó Pilán, Julia Prentice [Grosse], Dan Rosén, Lisa Rudebeck, Carl-Johan Schenström, Gunlög Sundberg, and Mats Wirén. 2019. The SweLL language learner corpus: From design to annotation. *The Northern European Journal of Language Technology*, 6:67–104.

Elena Volodina, Yousuf Ali Mohammed, and Julia Klezl. 2021a. DaLAJ - a dataset for linguistic acceptability judgments for Swedish. In *Proceedings of the 10th Workshop on Natural Language Processing for Computer Assisted Language Learning (NLP4CALL 2021)*, pages 28–37.

Elena Volodina, Yousuf Ali Mohammed, and Julia Klezl. 2021b. DaLAJ - a dataset for linguistic acceptability judgments for Swedish: Format, baseline, sharing. *CoRR*, abs/2105.06681.

Elena Volodina, Ildikó Pilán, Stian Rødven Eide, and Hannes Heidarsson. 2014. You get what you annotate: A pedagogically annotated corpus of coursebooks for Swedish as a second language. In

Proceedings of the third workshop on NLP for computer-assisted language learning, pages 128–144, Uppsala, Sweden. LiU Electronic Press.

Alex Warstadt, Amanpreet Singh, and Samuel R. Bowman. 2019. Neural network acceptability judgments. *Transactions of the Association for Computational Linguistics*, 7:625–641.

Appendix A. Failed experiments

Character embeddings/indices: Since words with orthographic and morphological errors often do not occur in the word embeddings used, we hypothesized that character-level representations might be better-suited. Therefore, we trained a model on character instead of word embeddings. Apart from that, it had the same structure as the models with pretrained word embeddings. This model performed better than chance, but clearly worse than the FastText and BERT models, reaching accuracies of 55% to 64%. A possible reason for the low performance is the relatively low amount of data for training embeddings. Future approaches might be to separately train a character-level language model on a bigger correct dataset and use that for the embeddings or to try other methods of capturing subword information, such as byte-pair encodings.

Word indices: The next experiment used the same index-based approach, but on the word level again. Since the word embeddings used in this experiment are trained on very different data (Wikipedia, newspaper articles, etc.) than learners' essays, we tried using in-domain embeddings. Similar to the model above, it reached accuracy scores of 52% to 60%, possibly also due to the comparatively small dataset.

FastText + error word: We had two reasons for adding the error word to the FastText embeddings. First, it introduced more variety among the correct sentences in the models with duplicates. Second, repeating the wrong word could have helped the model learn what exactly is wrong in a sentence. This model did reach higher validation accuracy (up to around 70%), but accuracy on the test set remained at or around 50%. This indicates that the additional information is useful to the model to some extent, but it cannot transfer that knowledge to sentences where the error word is not explicitly repeated.

One-hot encodings for error words: This feature was again combined with the pretrained word embeddings. Both input vectors went through separate biLSTM layers, and the outputs were concatenated before the linear layer. Validation accuracy improved, but not test accuracy, so the problem seems to lie in the transfer of information to the test sentences, which mainly consist of only zeros (except for spelling errors). An idea for improving this is to randomly replace the one-hot vectors for some sentences in the training and validation data with zeros-only vectors, forcing the model to generalize to data with only zeros. Another approach might be to use a more advanced model with an attention mechanism instead.

Evaluating Automatic Spelling Correction Tools on German Primary School Children's Misspellings

Ronja Laarmann-Quante
Department of Linguistics
Faculty of Philology
Ruhr University Bochum, Germany

Lisa Prepens and **Torsten Zesch**
CATALPA - Center of Advanced Technology for Assisted Learning and Predictive Analytics
FernUniversität in Hagen, Germany

Abstract

Most existing spellcheckers have been developed for adults and it is yet understudied how well children's texts can be automatically spellchecked, e.g. to build tools that assist them in spelling acquisition. This paper presents a detailed evaluation of six tools for automatic spelling correction on texts produced by German primary school children between grades 2 and 4. We find that popular off-the-shelf tools only achieve a correction accuracy of up to 46 % even when local word context is taken into account. For many misspellings, the desired correction is not even among the suggested candidates. A noisy-channel model that we trained on similar errors, in contrast, achieves a correction accuracy of up to 69 %. Further analyses show that this approach is very successful at candidate generation and that a better re-ranking of correction candidates could lead to a correction accuracy of ~90 %. Most of the remaining misspellings are so distorted that they are hard to correct without broader context. Furthermore, we analyze how the tools perform at different grade levels and for misspellings with different edit distances.

1 Introduction

Assisting children in learning to spell correctly is a time-consuming task and it requires solid diagnostic skills in order to tell different kinds of spelling errors apart. For example, misspelling the German word *Hund* ('dog') as **Hunt* includes an error of final devoicing, which does not change the word's pronunciation (we mark incorrect spellings with an asterisk). In contrast, misspelling the word as **Hunb* comprises a mirrored letter in the first place and the pronunciation is affected. Thus, the different kinds of errors require different feedback or different kinds of practice exercises for the child.

Therefore, automated tools for spelling error classification have been proposed (Berkling and Lavalley, 2015; Laarmann-Quante, 2017). However, when children are free to write whatever they want, in contrast to dictations, it is a non-trivial task to find out which words they wanted to write before the spelling errors can be analyzed. In the above example, the popular spellchecking tool Hunspell[1] would correct **Hunt* to *Hund* but **Hunb* to *Hub* '((vertical) lift)', leading to a wrong analysis of the child's errors. Hence, before the types of errors can be analyzed, misspellings first have to be detected and corrected. In the following, we will concentrate on the automatic correction step.

The aim and contribution of this paper is an evaluation of six existing spelling correction tools on misspellings of German primary school children taken from the Litkey Corpus (Laarmann-Quante et al., 2019). We examine how well the existing approaches perform in order to be used e.g. in an automatic spelling error diagnosis tool. Thereby, we set a baseline for future approaches tailored towards German children's spellings. Furthermore, we analyze the spelling correction performance of the tools for errors with different edit distances and for different grade levels. We assume that over time, children's errors get more adult-like, leading to a better performance of the tools.

The remainder of this paper is structured as follows: Section 2 introduces related work about the evaluation of spellcheckers and approaches for the correction of children's errors. In Section 3, we introduce the Litkey Corpus, which is used as the data basis for our spelling correction experiments. The experimental setup for the evaluation study is explained in Section 4, and Section 5 presents the results including some further analyses.[2]

2 Related Work

Spelling correction tools have mostly been compared on English data and often artificial errors

[1] http://hunspell.github.io

[2] Data and experimental code from this study are available under https://github.com/catalpa-cl/spellchecker-evaluation-german-children.

Ronja Laarmann-Quante, Lisa Prepens and Torsten Zesch. Evaluating Automatic Spelling Correction Tools on German Primary School Children's Misspellings. *Proceedings of the 11th Workshop on Natural Language Processing for Computer Assisted Language Learning (NLP4CALL 2022).* Linköping Electronic Conference Proceedings 190: 95–107.

(see e.g. Näther, 2020). However, it is well-known that conventional spellcheckers are tailored towards errors produced by proficient adults (e.g. typos) and struggle with errors containing multiple edits, as e.g. produced by language learners (Rimrott and Heift, 2008; Flor et al., 2019). Bexte et al. (2022) introduced a multilingual benchmark data set of spelling errors produced by language learners in order to compare spellcheckers on. They found that for the Litkey data, correction performance was poorer compared to data of Italian children and data of second-language learners of German, indicating that spelling errors of German children are rather hard to correct. However, they only compared three spellchecking tools (Hunspell, LanguageTool and DKPro-Spelling, which was introduced in their paper) and used an uncleaned version of the Litkey Corpus. In the corpus, some proper names occur so frequently that they could potentially bias the correction performance as they do not appear in the spellcheckers' dictionaries. In the study we present in this paper, we will do some data cleaning in order to reduce corpus-specific artifacts and compare six spellcheckers on the data, some of them trained on similar errors. Furthermore, we will provide a more in-depth analysis of the tools' performances across different grade levels and for errors with different edit distances.

While several spellchecking approaches that target errors of foreign language learners have been proposed (e.g. Boyd, 2009; Hovermale, 2011; Flor and Futagi, 2012; Nagata et al., 2017), children's errors have rarely been addressed. Downs et al. (2020, 2022) present a spelling correction approach for English children based on phonetic similarity, which outperforms existing spellcheckers. For German, a similar approach was taken by Stüker et al. (2011). However, they found that the phonetic model alone could not outperform Hunspell. Therefore, in our study, we focus on the performance of existing spellchecking tools to set a baseline for future approaches that target German children's errors.

3 Data Set

We base our study on the Litkey Corpus (Laarmann-Quante et al., 2019), which is a freely-available longitudinal corpus consisting of 1,922 German texts written by 251 primary school children between the second half of grade 2 and the end of grade 4 (= end of primary school). Every few months, at ten testing points in total, the same children were asked to write down a story that was shown in a sequence of six pictures. At the end of each school year, i.e. at the second, sixth and tenth testing point, the same picture story was used, all other picture stories were different.

The corpus includes the manual transcription of the handwritten texts (which we refer to as *orig* in the following), as well as a target hypothesis for each word with a manual correction of orthographic errors (referred to as *target*). Note that the target hypothesis does not correct grammatical or other kinds of errors.

3.1 Data Cleaning

The original data set consists of 212,505 orig-target pairs (6,364 target types). For our experiments, we removed the following kinds of tokens:

- (target) tokens with less than 2 alphabetic characters in order to only capture words and not punctuation marks or artifacts like *(grade) 4b*
- words that are marked in the corpus as non-identifiable, non-existing/non-standard or as containing illegible characters
- the proper names *Lea*, *Lars* and *Dodo* because they are specific to the corpus and appear multiple times in every text so they would distort the statistics
- words that contain a dot (capturing abbreviations)

Furthermore, we removed all special annotation marks from the remaining tokens, e.g. linebreak markers. This leaves us with 162,426 orig-target pairs in total.

3.2 Misspelling Statistics

In the present study, we are not looking at pure capitalization errors because they are a special type of error which require knowledge of sentence structure and morphosyntax (in German, the head of a noun phrase is capitalized). Therefore, in this paper, we do not count tokens as misspellings if orig and target only differ with regard to letter case. We also ignore wrong word separations, e.g. when the child wrote **aufeinmal* for *auf einmal* ('suddenly') or **zu frieden* for *zufrieden* ('pleased'). This leaves us with a total of 24,601 misspellings.

On average, the (cleaned) texts consist of 84 ($\pm$ 40) words with an average misspelling rate of

	total	**misspelled**
# orig-target pairs	162,426	24,601
# unique orig-target pairs	15,188	9,484
# unique target words	5,675	3,154

Table 1: Basic statistics of the cleaned data set.

17 % (± 11). Only 9 texts contain no misspelling at all. Some further statistics about the cleaned data set and the number of misspellings are shown in Table 1.

For some target words, we find many different spelling variants. The top 3 are *Fundbüro* 'lost-and-found office' (68 variants), *glücklich* 'happy' (56 variants) and *Karton* 'cardboard box' (51 variants).

A particular challenge for automatic spellchecking are origs that have to be corrected to different targets, depending on the context. For example, *bas* is corrected to *dass* 'that', *Bus* 'bus' and *pass* 'pay (attention)', respectively, in the gold standard correction. In our data set, we find 935 such origs (1,855 if also different letter case is taken into account). This number also includes real-word errors such as *als* 'as', which is found as a correct word but also as a misspelling of *alles* 'all' in the corpus.

3.3 Development over Testing Points

Due to the longitudinal design of the Litkey Corpus, it is possible to analyze the development of misspellings over a time period of 2.5 years. Table 2 shows some statistics for each of the ten testing points in the cleaned Litkey data set. Since the number of available texts per testing point differs, some testing points contribute more errors to the whole data set (in absolute numbers) than others. Furthermore, we see that over time, the children produce longer texts but that the error rates per text decrease.

testing point	**grade**	**∅ err. rate/text**	**∅ # errors/text**	**∅ text length**	**# errors abs.**	**# texts abs.**
01	2	.29	16	54	1,716	141
02	2	.26	17	68	2,154	165
03	3	.26	17	67	2,028	162
04	3	.25	21	86	2,520	173
05	3	.22	20	92	2,527	173
06	3	.18	19	104	2,924	231
07	4	.18	18	105	2,900	223
08	4	.18	22	124	3,046	215
09	4	.13	17	126	2,549	217
10	4	.12	15	120	2,237	222

Table 2: Basic statistics for each testing point.

We hypothesize that the children's increasing spelling competence is not only reflected by a decrease in error rate but also that the errors become more adult-like so that they are easier to correct by conventional spellchecking systems. As discussed in Section 2, spellcheckers typically struggle with misspellings that have a high edit distance to the target word. Figure 1 shows the proportion of errors with a particular edit distance per testing point. We use an edit distance where deletions, insertions and substitutions each have a cost of 1. We see a clear trend that over time, misspellings with an edit distance > 1 become rarer. There is some oscillation, which may be due to the fact that different picture stories elicited very different words but if we compare testing points 02, 06 and 10, where the same picture story was used, we find a steady decrease of higher edit distances. Nevertheless, it is noteworthy that already in grade 2, more than two thirds of the errors only have an edit distance of 1. Recall that pure capitalization errors are not part of our misspelling data set so that the prevalence of an edit distance of 1 that we see here is not attributable to words that only differ in letter case.

4 Experimental Setup

Spelling correction is typically seen as a two-step process, consisting of misspelling detection and misspelling correction (see e.g. Hládek et al., 2020). The misspelling detection step usually relies on a dictionary lookup and its performance is largely dependent on the coverage of the dictionary. Bexte et al. (2022) achieved an F-Score of up to .79 for error *detection* in German primary school children's texts from the Litkey Corpus, which is higher than the results for most second-language learner corpora that were investigated in that study. Hence, in this paper, we only concentrate on the correction step, which has been shown to be much more problematic for children's texts. That is, we use the gold standard set of misspellings as the basis for our experiments.

4.1 Spellcheckers

While the number of existing spellchecking approaches is abundant (see e.g. Hládek et al., 2020), we restrict our comparison to six correction systems available for German. Four of them are usable off-the-shelf and the other two have to be trained based on a list of misspellings and their correc-

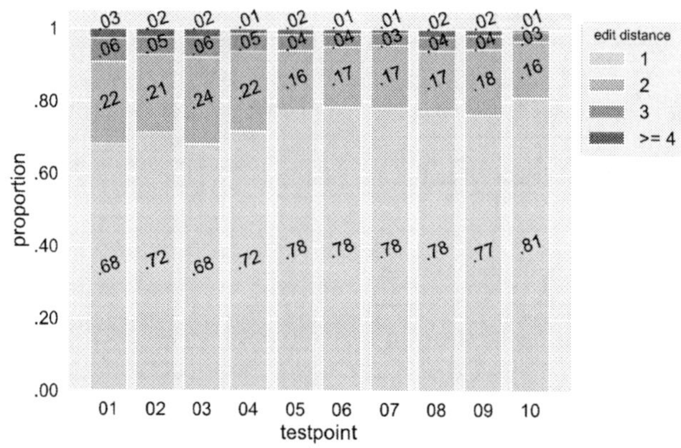

Figure 1: Distribution of edit distances between orig and target for each testing point.

tions. We exclude neural approaches, which are not readily available for German and would require more training data. For those spellcheckers which allow to specify a full-form dictionary (which are the two trainable ones and DKPro-Spelling), we try two different ones, namely **Hun-dict**, which is the Hunspell dictionary converted into a full-form word list that was also used for the correction experiments reported in Bexte et al. (2022) and **childLex** (Schroeder et al., 2015), which is compiled from 500 German children's books.

4.1.1 Off-the-Shelf Spellcheckers

We use all off-the-shelf spellcheckers with default configurations unless noted otherwise.

Hunspell is one of the most popular spellchecking libraries and used e.g. in OpenOffice and macOS. It finds correction candidates by different means, e.g. by applying edit operations to the misspelled string or by computing the similarity with words in the dictionary.[3] For our experiments, we use Hunspell with the German dictionary it comes with and simply feed all misspelling types into the system, as there is no context awareness.

Nuspell[4] is similar to Hunspell and can be used with the same dictionaries. Like Hunspell, it supports rich morphology and complex word compounding, which is important for German.

LanguageTool[5] is an open-source proofreading tool with add-ons for several popular programs like MS Word or Google Docs. It has a built-in dictionary (based on Hunspell with extensions) and mainly relies on handcrafted rules, which are partly context-sensitive. Therefore, we use LanguageTool in two configurations: firstly, we only feed individual misspellings into the tool, i.e. we ignore the context, and secondly we spellcheck the words in the context of the whole text to benefit from context-sensitive rules. Note that in this case we do not clean the texts as rigorously as described in Section 3.1. We only remove special annotation marks (e.g. linebreak markers) as well as words that are marked as non-identifiable or as non-existing word forms in order to maintain the necessary context information. For spellchecking whole texts with LanguageTool, we first disabled two internal rules, i.e. capitalization at the beginning of a sentence (UPPERCASE_SENTENCE_START) and spaces before/behind commas and brackets (COMMA_PARENTHESIS_WHITESPACE). The reason is that these rules would always fire first and prevent the search for a proper correction candidate. For example, a misspelled word at the beginning of a sentence would only be corrected to uppercase although it is still misspelled (e.g. **dan* → **Dan* rather than *Dann* 'then').

DKPro-Spelling[6] (Bexte et al., 2022) is a spellchecking toolkit that can be integrated into an NLP processing pipeline in the DKPro framework (Eckart de Castilho and Gurevych, 2014). It is highly customizable but also comes with a preconfigured setting, which we use for our experiments. In this setting, three correction candidates are chosen from a dictionary based on the smallest edit distance on the character level. Note that in the case of ties, DKPro-Spelling returns more than

[3] See https://zverok.space/spellchecker.html for details.

[4] https://nuspell.github.io

[5] https://github.com/languagetool-org/languagetool

[6] https://github.com/catalpa-cl/ltl-spelling

three candidates. In a second step, the candidates are re-ranked based on a Web1T trigram language model (Brants, 2006).

4.1.2 Trainable Spellcheckers

We train the two trainable spellcheckers in our experiment on a total of 7,488 unique misspellings (case-sensitive) and their manual corrections from two other German spelling corpora that consist of children's texts. These are the H1 corpus (Berkling, 2016), which includes texts from second and third grade and the Osnabrücker Bildergeschichtenkorpus ('Osnabrück picture story corpus'; Thelen, 2000, 2010), which mainly contains texts of children in second grade. While we ignore pure capitalization errors in our data set, for the remaining errors we will include a case-sensitive evaluation (see Section 4.3), which is why we keep letter case information in the training data.

Brill & Moore We use a Java implementation of the noisy channel approach presented in Brill and Moore (2000)[7]. The model learns the probability of certain edits from the training data, which can also comprise several characters at once. For example, from orig-target pairs like **faren - fahren* ('to drive'), **Fart - Fahrt* ('drive'), the model may learn that instead of the sequence *ahr*, children often write *ar*. That is, it uses contextual information in that it does not only learn that *h* is often omitted but also in which context. Thus, the model is able to learn specific error patterns of children that are present in the training data. Note that the model is only context-sensitive in the sense that it can take into account the context of an edit on the character level but not the broader context of the surrounding words. The tool outputs a fixed number of 10 correction candidates per default and we leave it like that.

Norma[8] (Bollmann, 2012) was originally developed for spelling normalization of historical language data but can be used on all kinds of nonstandard language. It is a toolchain that combines different normalization techniques. We use the default setting in which first, whole word forms are mapped to one another. If no mapping is applicable, context-sensitive character rewrite rules are applied, and third, if no rules are applicable, the correction is chosen based on weighted Levenshtein distance by choosing the word from the dictionary with the lowest distance. All steps are learnt from training data. Note that Norma always only outputs the one most probable correction candidate.

[7] https://github.com/adrianeboyd/BrillMooreSpellChecker

[8] https://github.com/comphist/norma

4.2 Upper Bound

For most texts, spellcheckers are not able to achieve 100 % correction accuracy simply because some of the target words are not part of the underlying dictionary and hence cannot be suggested as correction candidates (e.g. certain proper names or rare compounds). We therefore compute the upper bound for the performance of each spellchecker in our experiments.

For Hunspell and LanguageTool, we determine the upper bound by feeding the target words into the respective tool. If no suggestion is made, the word is recognized as correct, i. e. the target word is contained in the dictionary. In order to find the upper bound when letter case is ignored, we capitalize all target words, since e.g. verbs and adjectives are recognized as correct even if they are capitalized, but nouns are recognized as false if they are lowercased.

For the other spellcheckers, the upper bound can be determined directly by checking how many of the target words are contained in Hun-dict and childLex, respectively. Note that DKPro-Spelling uses an adapted version of childLex where only words that occur in at least ten children's books are considered (45k types) whereas Brill & Moore and Norma use the full childLex word list (158k types), which results in slightly different upper bounds.

4.3 Evaluation Setup

We measure the correction performance of a spellchecker in two ways: We evaluate a) how often the target word is ranked at the first rank of the suggestion list of the respective spellchecker (FIRST) and b) how often the target word is contained somewhere in the suggestion list (ALL). We suppose that all spellcheckers provide an internal ranking, so that the most probable candidate is ranked first, although it is often not made explicit (except for DKPro-Spelling and Brill & Moore). Hence, the FIRST metric, which we also call correction accuracy, is relevant for fully automatic spelling correction and therefore the one we are most interested in here. The ALL metric is not directly comparable across spellcheckers because they produce different numbers of suggestions (see Table 3). However, it tells us how often a spellchecker does in principle generate the right correction candidate.

	avg. # suggs		
Hunspell	4.8	±	4.3
Nuspell	5.3	±	4.9
LangTool (words)	15.2	±	8.4
LangTool (texts)	15.2	±	7.9
DKPro (childlex)	9.0	±	8.7
DKPro (hun-dict)	10.1	±	10.0
Brill & Moore	10.0	±	0.0
Norma	1.0	±	0.0

Table 3: Average number of suggestions per spellchecker, including cases with 0 suggestions.

Pushing the candidate to the first rank could then be achieved via a second step where the candidates are re-ranked e.g. based on the context.

We furthermore distinguish between an evaluation based on types versus tokens as well as a case-sensitive and a case-insensitive evaluation, resulting in four different conditions, see Table 4. By the distinction of tokens vs. types, we mean that when we evaluate the spellcheckers based on tokens, we count every single occurrence of a misspelling and whether it was corrected successfully or not. When we look at types, we count the correction of every unique misspelling (= unique orig-target pair) only once.[9] Hence, when spellcheckers do not take the context into account and correct the same misspelling always in the same way, the evaluation on a token base can be strongly influenced by misspellings that occur very frequently. The evaluation on a type base, in contrast, shows more clearly the correction performance on different errors. If a spellchecker performs better on tokens than on types, it means that (some) misspellings with a high frequency are corrected more successfully than low-frequency misspellings and vice versa.

Capitalization is highly context-dependent (see Section 3.2). Therefore, the performance of a spellchecker may be underestimated when letter case is taken into account. We are mostly interested in how often a spellchecker is able to suggest the correct word, irrespective of lettercase. Nevertheless, we also report the case-sensitive results in order to see what large a role capitalization plays for a successful automatic correction.

[9]Note that, for example, **Hunt* - *Hund* and **Hunb* - *Hund* are two different types although they share the same target word. Likewise, *alls* - *als* ('when') and *alls* - *alles* ('all') share the same orig word but we treat them as two different types.

5 Results

Table 4 shows the performance of each spellchecker based on the FIRST and ALL metric and the upper bound (UB) for each of the four evaluation conditions (types vs. tokens, case-sensitive vs. case-insensitive). The upper part of the table contains the off-the-shelf spellchecking tools and the lower part the trained spellcheckers. DKPro-Spelling is special in that it is the only off-the-shelf spellchecker in which the default configuration comes with a re-ranking of candidates based on local context. Therefore, the same misspelling may be corrected differently based on context, hence there is no type-based evaluation for this spellchecker. The respective dictionary is indicated in brackets. Recall that for LanguageTool, we tried two configurations, a) based on a list of errors (*LangTool words*) and b) based on the errors within context (*LangTool texts*). Hence, there is again no type-based evaluation for the latter configuration. Since Norma only outputs one correction candidate, the results for the FIRST and ALL metric are identical. Therefore, we only list them under FIRST.

Among the **off-the-shelf spellcheckers**, DKPro-Spelling has the best performance. Regarding the FIRST metric, this may be due to the context-based re-ranking of candidates. Therefore, we will reconsider the other spellcheckers with language model re-ranking in Section 5.1. Among Hunspell, Nuspell and LanguageTool, differences are not large. None of them is able to rank the correct candidate on first rank in more than 40 % of cases. We see that this rather poor result is not primarily due to a bad ranking of suggestion candidates. Even when all correction candidates are considered, the correct one is only available for 62-71 % of all tokens. This means that even with a better re-ranking, the spellcheckers would not be able to correct every third to fourth word appropriately because the right correction is not even considered. Note that LanguageTool achieves slightly better results when only an error list is provided rather than the errors in context, which can be explained by more rules firing in the latter case that lead to an inappropriate correction.

The **trained spellcheckers** largely outperform the off-the-shelf tools in all conditions. Norma has a correction accuracy of up to 62 %. This shows that even without knowledge of the context, quite a good correction accuracy can be achieved when children's error patterns are taken into account. We

	Token (case ins.)			Token (case sens.)			Type (case ins.)			Type (case sens.)		
	FIRST	ALL	UB	FIRST	ALL	UB	FIRST	ALL	UB	FIRST	ALL	UB
Hunspell	.34	.62	(.94)	.33	.59	(.94)	.35	.56	(.93)	.32	.51	(.92)
Nuspell	.35	.64	(.94)	.34	.61	(.94)	.36	.59	(.93)	.34	.54	(.92)
LangTool words	.39	.71	(.98)	.37	.68	(.97)	.38	.72	(.99)	.35	.66	(.96)
LangTool texts	.37	.68	-	.36	.65	-	-	-	-	-	-	-
DKPro (chL)	.46	.80	(.92)	.44	.77	(.91)	-	-	-	-	-	-
DKPro (Hun)	.45	.76	(.93)	.44	.73	(.89)	-	-	-	-	-	-
Brill&Moore (chL)	.57	.92	(.97)	.53	.91	(.97)	.58	.84	(.95)	.52	.83	(.94)
Brill&Moore (Hun)	.53	.86	(.93)	.51	.83	(.89)	.48	.77	(.90)	.45	.73	(.86)
Norma (chL)	.62	-	(.97)	.56	-	(.97)	.54	-	(.95)	.50	-	(.94)
Norma (Hun)	.57	-	(.93)	.52	-	(.89)	.49	-	(.90)	.45	-	(.86)

Table 4: Overall evaluation results based on the FIRST and ALL metric for each of the four evaluation conditions (types vs. tokens, case-sensitive vs. case-insensitive). The dictionary used (childLex or Hun-dict) and the upper bound (UB) for each spellchecker are given in brackets.

see that the error patterns in two other German corpora of children's texts that were used for training generalize well enough to achieve good correction results also on the Litkey corpus. Most remarkably, for the Brill & Moore spellchecker, the desired correction is among the 10 correction candidates in > 90 % of cases on the token level. Hence, a successful automatic correction is mainly a matter of candidate ranking here.

Some general observations can be made across all spellcheckers: The difference between **case-sensitive** and **case-insensitive** evaluation is rather small, indicating that proper capitalization is only a minor issue with regard to spelling correction in the children's texts.

With regard to **type-based** versus **token-based** evaluation, we see only small differences for most spellcheckers with a slight tendency towards better results on a token base. This indicates that the more frequently occurring misspellings are easier to correct than the rare ones. The difference is most pronounced for Norma, which may be explainable due to the fact that this tool stores particular correction patterns.

Finally, we can observe that the **upper bound** is mostly $> .90$ up to .99, which shows a very good coverage of the underlying dictionaries. For spellcheckers that we used with different dictionaries, we find that generally, childLex outperforms Hun-dict, i.e. a more child-directed dictionary is useful. For the following analyses, we therefore only use the results based on childLex for these spellcheckers.

5.1 Language Model Re-Ranking

A re-ranking of correction candidates based on local word context has been shown to be beneficial (Bexte et al., 2022). Therefore, we add a re-ranking to all spellchecker outputs based on the trigram model built from voxforge.org speech data that comes with the CMU Sphinx toolkit[10]. Unlike the Web1T model used by DKPro, this model is freely available and we suppose that speech data are close to the language that primary school children use in their writing. We try different conditions: re-ranking a) all candidates, b) only the top 5 and c) only the top 3 candidates. Table 5 shows for each condition, how often the desired correction ended up on the first rank.

For comparison, the first column shows the result without re-ranking or with default re-ranking in the case of DKPro-Spelling. Recall that for Norma, no re-ranking can be done since only one candidate is given. For DKPro-Spelling, although it comes with re-ranking off-the-shelf, we re-rank the candidates again with the CMU Sphinx language model for comparability. Note that DKPro-Spelling only outputs three correction candidates by default but it can be more if there are ties prior to re-ranking. We consider all these candidates for re-ranking, which is why we only report our new re-ranking results under "all candidates".

We see that for all spellcheckers, our re-ranking is beneficial, except for LanguageTool and DKPro-Spelling, where the default ranking works better. The best re-ranking results are achieved when

[10] https://cmusphinx.github.io/wiki/download/

	def.	3 cand.	5 cand.	all cand.
Hunspell	.34	.40	.40	.39
Nuspell	.35	.42	.41	.41
LTool words	.39	.36	.33	.24
DKPro	.46	-	-	.42
Brill & Moore	.57	.69	.64	.51
Norma	.62	-	-	-

Table 5: Correction accuracy (=first suggestion) after language model re-ranking (case insensitive). For comparison, the column *def.* ('default') repeats the first column of Table 4, i.e. the performance without re-ranking or default re-ranking in the case of DKPro.

only the top 3 candidates are re-ranked, indicating that the spellcheckers' original ranking (without knowledge of the context) is already quite useful in that lower-ranked candidates introduce more noise. Among the off-the-shelf spellcheckers, the improvements are only moderate, though, and none of them outperforms DKPro-Spelling. This means, the top result of a spellchecker that can be used off-the-shelf is a correction accuracy of 46 %, which means that fully automatic spelling correction would get more than every second word wrong.

For Brill & Moore, re-ranking the top 3 candidates improves the result by 12 percentage points, thereby outperforming Norma. Hence, the best result that could be achieved overall in this study is a correction accuracy of 69 % (we checked that only re-ranking the top 2 candidates did not improve the results any further). Given that in over 90 % of cases the desired correction is among the top 10 candidates for this spellchecker, there is still room for improving the re-ranking in future work to achieve a very high correction accuracy with this approach.

5.2 Comparison by Edit Distance

As stated in Section 2, common spellcheckers typically struggle with higher edit distances. For the trained spellcheckers in this study, we hypothesize that this is not so much the case because they can learn correction patterns that comprise several edits. To analyze the performance of the spellcheckers for different edit distances, we look separately at all misspellings with a particular edit distance and note how often the desired correction is at the first rank or another rank within the top 3 candidates (after re-ranking). The results for Brill & Moore and DKPro-Spelling (representing the best trained spellchecker and the best off-the-shelf spellchecker) are shown in Figure 2, the results for the other spellcheckers can be found in Appendix A. For DKPro-Spelling we use the default re-ranking here because it performed better than our re-ranking.

We see that for an edit distance of 1, all spellcheckers are able to find the desired correction for the majority of misspellings. However, even for the lowest edit distance, the trained spellcheckers Brill & Moore and Norma outperform the off-the-shelf spellcheckers, which shows that learning error patterns is even beneficial for seemingly easy errors. All spellcheckers have in common that the higher the edit distance, the less likely they are to provide the right correction. However, this is most pronounced for the off-the-shelf spellcheckers. For misspellings with an edit distance ≥ 4, off-the-shelf spellcheckers only correct a tiny fraction of words correctly, whereas Brill & Moore still includes the correct candidate in half of the cases.

5.3 Spellchecking Performance over Time

We saw earlier (Figure 1) that over the time course of primary school, the edit distances of the misspellings get smaller, which is why we expect the spellcheckers to work better on later testing points than on earlier testing points.

To analyze this, we look at the top 3 candidates (after re-ranking) at each of the ten testing points individually and note how often the desired correction is at the first rank or at one of the other ranks. Figure 3 shows the results for Brill & Moore and DKPro-Spelling (the latter again with default re-ranking). The results for all other spellcheckers are given in Appendix B.

We see that for Brill & Moore, the testing point does not have a big influence, which could be explained by the fact that the edit distance does not have such a big impact on this spellchecker (as was shown in Figure 2). In contrast, for the off-the-shelf spellcheckers such as DKPro-Spelling, where we saw a larger impact of edit distance, we can observe the expected trend that later testing points are easier to correct than early ones. However, we also find a lot of oscillation between testing points and in total, the differences are not very large. So even by the end of primary school, correction performance remains rather poor compared to the trained spellcheckers.

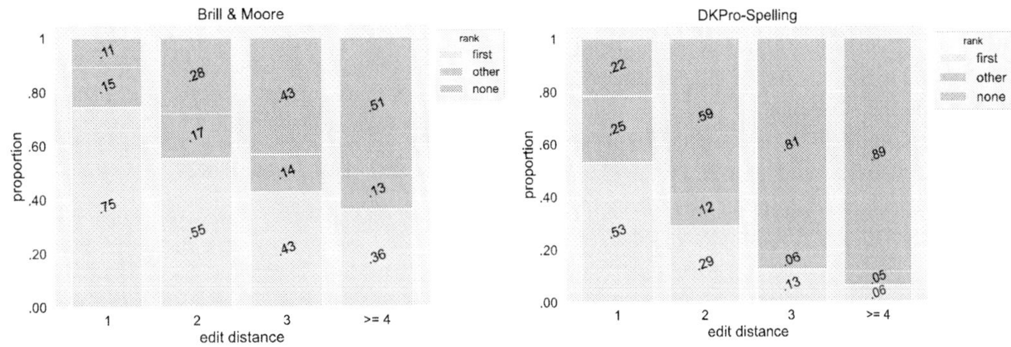

Figure 2: Correction performance per **edit distance** for Brill & Moore (left) and DKPro-Spelling (right). The coloring of the bars indicates from bottom to top how often the desired correction is ranked at the first rank, another rank or not among the suggestions when the top 3 candidates after re-ranking are considered (case-insensitive).

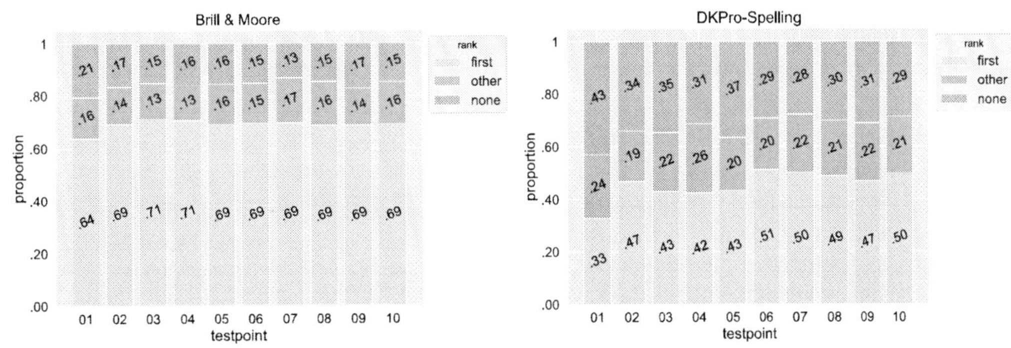

Figure 3: Correction performance per **testing point** for Brill & Moore (left) and DKPro-Spelling (right). The coloring of the bars indicates from bottom to top how often the desired correction is ranked at the first rank, another rank or not among the suggestions when the top 3 candidates after re-ranking are considered (case-insensitive).

5.4 Failure Analysis

In the following, we explore for what kinds of misspellings even the best spellchecking approach in this study (the **Brill & Moore** implementation) failed to find the right target word. We saw that on the (case-insensitive) type level, the Brill & Moore spellchecker had the right correction among the top 10 candidates in 84 % of cases given the childLex dictionary, with an upper bound of 95 % achievable corrections. In total numbers, this means that for 981 misspelling types (10.3 %), the target word was not among the top 10 candidates, although it would have been findable in the dictionary.

A deeper analysis shows that 23 % of these cases are real-word errors, i.e. the misspelling itself is contained in childLex. The remaining misspellings that could not be corrected have very high edit distances between orig and target, namely 2.4 on average. If we take the length of the target word into account (since an edit distance of 2 is more severe for short words than for long words), we find that on average, 46 % of the characters in the non-correctable words are wrong. Hence, the words are so distorted that without having broader context information in the first place, finding the right target word is almost impossible, even for humans. Some examples are given in Table 6.

orig	target	dist.	transl.
gawen	kaufen	3	'buy'
niegs	nichts	3	'nothing'
feid	fällt	4	'falls'
glugeis	glücklich	6	'happy'
sagras	zerkratzt	7	'scratched'

Table 6: Examples of highly distorted words that the Brill & Moore spellchecker was not able to correct.

6 Conclusion

We compared six different spelling correction tools on German primary school children's texts. We found very different performance behaviors between off-the-shelf tools on the one hand and tools that are trained on texts from other primary school children on the other hand.

We could see that off-the-shelf spellcheckers perform rather poorly across all grade levels. They only reach an overall correction accuracy of up to 46 % (including a trigram-model based re-ranking of candidates), which is certainly insufficient in order to be used e.g. in an automatic spelling error diagnosis tool. Furthermore, we saw that these spellcheckers are often not able to include the right correction in their suggestion lists at all, so that a better re-ranking would not help much.

Spellcheckers that learn error patterns from other German children's corpora are more successful in correcting, leading to an overall correction accuracy of up to 69 %. Most notably, the noisy-channel approach turned out to be very successful in candidate generation: in up to 92 % of cases, the target word was among the top 10 candidates. This means that there is the potential for future work to improve the fully automatic correction by finding more effective means of re-ranking the candidates. With regard to the remaining misspellings, we saw that they often include real-word errors and very distorted words, which could potentially be tackled by neural approaches where more context is taken into account but which also need more training data.

Acknowledgments

This work was partially conducted in the framework of CATALPA – Center of Advanced Technology for Assisted Learning and Predictive Analytics of the FernUniversität in Hagen, Germany. We would like to thank Marie Bexte for her support with DKPro-Spelling, Katrin Ortmann for her contributions in compiling the training data and the anonymous reviewers for their helpful comments.

References

Kay Berkling. 2016. Corpus for children's writing with enhanced output for specific spelling patterns (2nd and 3rd grade). In *Proceedings of the Tenth International Conference on Language Resources and Evaluation (LREC 2016)*, pages 3200–3206.

Kay Berkling and Rémi Lavalley. 2015. WISE: A Web-Interface for Spelling Error Recognition Description and Evaluation of the Algorithm for German. In *International Conference of the German Society for Computational Linguistics and Language Technology*, GSCL, pages 87–96.

Marie Bexte, Ronja Laarmann-Quante, Andrea Horbach, and Torsten Zesch. 2022. Lespell - a multilingual benchmark corpus of spelling errors to develop spellchecking methods for learner language. In *Proceedings of the Language Resources and Evaluation Conference*, pages 697–706, Marseille, France. European Language Resources Association.

Marcel Bollmann. 2012. (Semi-)automatic normalization of historical texts using distance measures and the Norma tool. In *Proceedings of the Second Workshop on Annotation of Corpora for Research in the Humanities (ACRH-2)*, Lisbon, Portugal.

Adriane Boyd. 2009. Pronunciation modeling in spelling correction for writers of English as a Foreign Language. In *Proceedings of Human Language Technologies: The 2009 Annual Conference of the North American Chapter of the Association for Computational Linguistics, Companion Volume: Student Research Workshop and Doctoral Consortium*, pages 31–36, Boulder, Colorado. Association for Computational Linguistics.

Thorsten Brants. 2006. *Web 1T 5-gram Version 1*. Linguistic Data Consortium.

Eric Brill and Robert C Moore. 2000. An improved error model for noisy channel spelling correction. In *Proceedings of the 38th Annual Meeting of the Association for Computational Linguistics*, pages 286–293.

Richard Eckart de Castilho and Iryna Gurevych. 2014. A broad-coverage collection of portable NLP components for building shareable analysis pipelines. In *Proceedings of the Workshop on Open Infrastructures and Analysis Frameworks for HLT*, pages 1–11, Dublin, Ireland. Association for Computational Linguistics and Dublin City University.

Brody Downs, Oghenemaro Anuyah, Aprajita Shukla, Jerry Alan Fails, Sole Pera, Katherine Wright, and Casey Kennington. 2020. KidSpell: A child-oriented, rule-based, phonetic spellchecker. In *Proceedings of the 12th Language Resources and Evaluation Conference*, pages 6937–6946, Marseille, France. European Language Resources Association.

Brody Downs, Maria Soledad Pera, Katherine Landau Wright, Casey Kennington, and Jerry Alan Fails. 2022. KidSpell: Making a difference in spellchecking for children. *International Journal of Child-Computer Interaction*, 32:100373.

Michael Flor, Michael Fried, and Alla Rozovskaya. 2019. A benchmark corpus of English misspellings and a minimally-supervised model for spelling correction. In *Proceedings of the Fourteenth Workshop on Innovative Use of NLP for Building Educational Applications*, pages 76–86, Florence, Italy. Association for Computational Linguistics.

Michael Flor and Yoko Futagi. 2012. On using context for automatic correction of non-word misspellings in student essays. In *Proceedings of the seventh workshop on building educational applications Using NLP*, pages 105–115.

Daniel Hládek, Ján Staš, and Matúš Pleva. 2020. Survey of automatic spelling correction. *Electronics*, 9(10):1670.

D. J. Hovermale. 2011. *Erron: A Phrase-Based Machine Translation Approach to Customized Spelling Correction*. Ph.D. thesis, Ohio State University.

Ronja Laarmann-Quante. 2017. Towards a tool for automatic spelling error analysis and feedback generation for freely written German texts produced by primary school children. In *Proceedings of the Seventh ISCA Workshop on Speech and Language Technology in Education (SLaTE)*, pages 36–41.

Ronja Laarmann-Quante, Katrin Ortmann, Anna Ehlert, Simon Masloch, Doreen Scholz, Eva Belke, and Stefanie Dipper. 2019. The Litkey Corpus: A richly annotated longitudinal corpus of German texts written by primary school children. *Behavior Research Methods*, 51(4):1889–1918.

Ryo Nagata, Hiroya Takamura, and Graham Neubig. 2017. Adaptive spelling error correction models for learner English. *Procedia Computer Science*, 112:474–483.

Markus Näther. 2020. An in-depth comparison of 14 spelling correction tools on a common benchmark. In *Proceedings of the 12th Language Resources and Evaluation Conference*, pages 1849–1857, Marseille, France. European Language Resources Association.

Anne Rimrott and Trude Heift. 2008. Evaluating automatic detection of misspellings in german. *Language Learning & Technology*, 12(3):73–92.

Sascha Schroeder, Kay-Michael Würzner, Julian Heister, Alexander Geyken, and Reinhold Kliegl. 2015. childLex: A lexical database of German read by children. *Behavior Research Methods*, 47(4):1085–1094.

Sebastian Stüker, Johanna Fay, and Kay Berkling. 2011. Towards context-dependent phonetic spelling error correction in children's freely composed text for diagnostic and pedagogical purposes. In *Twelfth Annual Conference of the International Speech Communication Association*.

Tobias Thelen. 2000. Osnabrücker Bildergeschichtenkorpus: Version 1.0.0.

Tobias Thelen. 2010. *Automatische Analyse orthographischer Leistungen von Schreibanfängern*. Ph.D. thesis, Universität Osnabrück.

A Correction Performance per Edit Distance

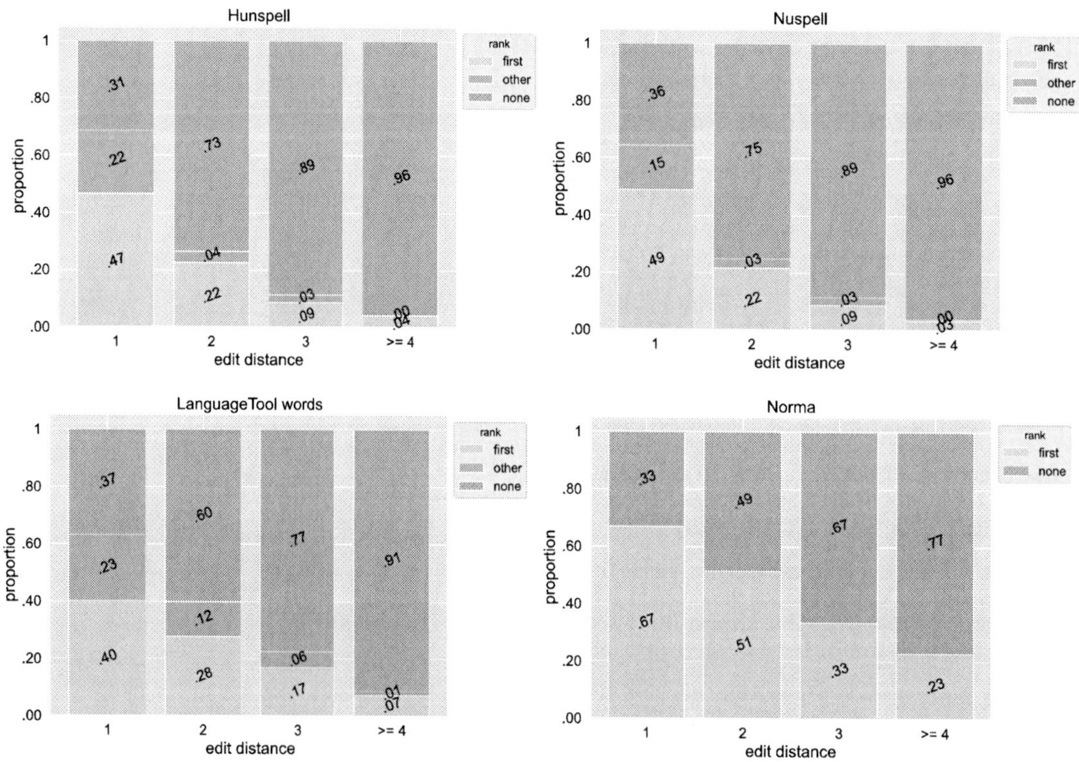

B Correction Performance per Testing Point

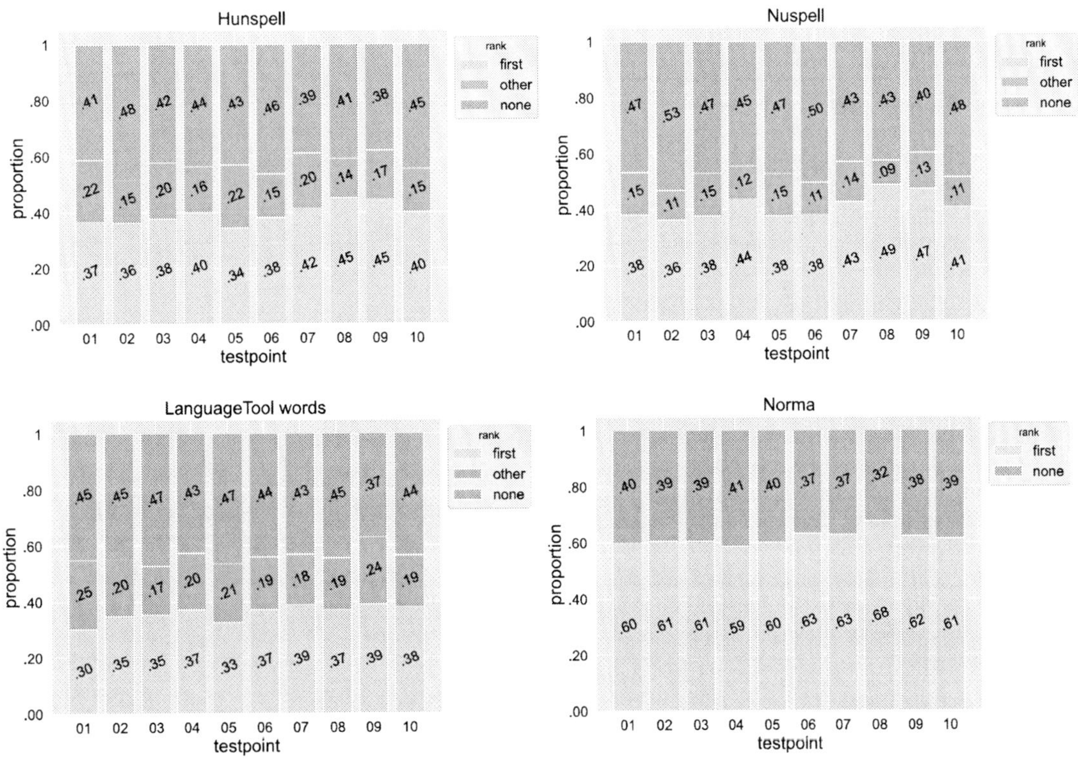

Metadata Formats for Learner Corpora: Case Study and Discussion

Herbert Lange
IDS Mannheim
lange@ids-mannheim.de

Abstract

Metadata provides important information relevant both to finding and understanding corpus data. Meaningful linguistic data requires both reasonable annotations and documentation of these annotations. This documentation is part of the metadata of a dataset. While corpus documentation has often been provided in the form of accompanying publications, machine-readable metadata, both containing the bibliographic information and documenting the corpus data, has many advantages. Metadata standards allow for the development of common tools and interfaces. In this paper I want to add a new perspective from an archive's point of view and look at the metadata provided for four learner corpora and discuss the suitability of established standards for machine-readable metadata. I am are aware that there is ongoing work towards metadata standards for learner corpora. However, I would like to keep the discussion going and add another point of view: increasing findability and reusability of learner corpora in an archiving context.

1 Introduction

Research data, including linguistic corpus data, usually is not just published as-is, but instead is enriched with so-called metadata. Metadata subsumes a wide range of additional information. Two main functions of metadata are to allow the data to be found and also to be understood by giving additional context.

For researchers the first point might seem more obvious and relevant. If someone publishes data, they typically want other people to be able to find this data. This is accomplished by providing bibliographic or catalog metadata. This kind of metadata can be used in repositories and registries to be able to provide relevant data to a user. Within the CLARIN infrastructure, the Virtual Language Observatory (VLO) (Goosen and Eckart, 2014) provides such a registry harvesting metadata from a wide range of repositories and providing a uniform interface to look for corpus data based on the provided metadata.

But findability is only one of the important aspects. There is also a growing interest in making data reusable. A very vocal initiative promoting this among other values is the FAIR initiative (Wilkinson et al., 2016). FAIR stands for Findable, Accessible, Interoperable, and Reusable and is connected to the Linked Open Data (LOD) movement. Linking various forms of data together enriches its value for future research. Suitable metadata can provide suitable linking.

2 Background: Established Metadata Standards for Corpora

There exist many formats used to provide metadata. They vary in expressively and their use can also depend on the file format used for the corpus data itself. Instead of covering many different formats I will focus on three formats that seem most relevant for learner corpora available in public archives.

2.1 CMDI

The Component Metadata Initiative (CMDI, Broeder et al., 2011) is the metadata standard established within the CLARIN infrastructure. It is used in the CLARIN VLO to find corpus data. Using standardized interfaces such as OAI-PMH[1], it can be automatically harvested from the repository providing the data. As a modular format, researchers

[1] http://www.openarchives.org/OAI/openarchivesprotocol.html

Herbert Lange. Metadata Formats for Learner Corpora: Case Study and Discussion. *Proceedings of the 11th Workshop on Natural Language Processing for Computer Assisted Language Learning (NLP4CALL 2022)*. Linköping Electronic Conference Proceedings 190: 108–113.

can define profiles matching their data and annotations. It is a very powerful standard which already with a basic profile provides catalog metadata as well as information about the file structure of the corpus.

2.2 Coma

The EXMARaLDA Corpus Manager (Coma) metadata format is often used in combination with EXMARaLDA Partitur-Editor (Schmidt and Wörner, 2014) annotations for audiovisual data. It can contain catalog metadata compatible with Dublin Core. Furthermore, it is designed to provide information about the corpus structure as well as information about the speakers and events. The documentation states: "Coma is [...] used for managing the relation of metadata, transcriptions, recordings, external annotations, and further related files, tying all related data together into a single corpus document." (Schmidt and Wörner, 2014, p. 413) This format can be especially relevant for spoken learner data.

2.3 TEI Header

Another common metadata format is TEI headers. Not a stand-alone format as the other formats, it is a standard for header information to be included in corpus data encoded following the guidelines of the Text Encoding Initiative (TEI, TEI Consortium, 2022). It can contain five main parts:

- a file description containing the bibliographic or catalog information
- an encoding description describing the relationship between an electronic text and its source or sources
- a text profile containing classification and contextual information about the text, such as its subject matter, the situation in which it was produced, the individuals described by or participating in producing it, and so forth
- a container element for other metadata formats allowing easy inclusion of metadata from non-TEI schemes
- a revision history providing a history of changes made during the development of the electronic text

Depending on the application, a TEI header can be quite a simple or a very complex and structured object. Because TEI is more dominant for written data, TEI headers are more relevant for corpora containing written learner data, but it should be noted that the TEI guidelines also cover transcription of spoken language which would make TEI headers also relevant for spoken learner data.

3 Case Study Learner Corpora

To evaluate the current situation of metadata provided for learner data, I selected four corpora out of the large collection of available datasets. Three of these corpora, DISKO, MIKO, and HMAT, are hosted at the IDS, either in the IDS repository[2] or as part of the database of spoken German (DGD, Schmidt, 2017)[3] and thus relevant for all archiving efforts at the IDS. The fourth corpus, SweLL, was selected to include a dataset that is not hosted in-house at the IDS. The selected corpora cover both written and spoken data.

The most relevant aspect of this case study is the metadata formats used. As shown in the overview of metadata formats, the choice of a metadata format is also influenced both by the annotation tools used and the repository hosting the data. Thus, this information is also summarized for each of the datasets.

3.1 SweLL

The Swedish Learner Language corpus (SweLL, Volodina et al., 2019) consists of two sub-corpora, SweLL-pilot and SweLL-gold. Both are collections of written learner essays. The learners are adults learning Swedish. The pilot corpus has been anonynimized and graded according to CEFR levels, the gold corpus has been pseudonymized, normalized and correction annotated. The annotations, sucha as normaliza-tion/correction annotation and pseudonymization, have been created using the SVALA annotation tool (Wirén et al., 2019) and are available in a plain text format and as JSON. Export to XML is possible.

The metadata description is available in human-readable form as Markdown and PDF

[2]https://repos.ids-mannheim.de/

[3]https://dgd.ids-mannheim.de/

following the guidelines by Granger and Paquot (2017b). In addition, learner metadata as well as statistics about pseudonymization and correction labels for the gold corpus are provided as MS Excel spreadsheets. SweLL is hosted at the Swedish Language Bank (Språkbanken Text)[4].

3.2 HaMaTaC

The Hamburg Mapping Task Corpus (HaMaTac, HZSK, 2010) is a spoken learner corpus with elicited speech data using a map task and involves multilingual speakers learning German. The recordings have been transcribed using the EXMARaLDA Partitur-Editor. Manual annotations include disfluency and phonetic phenomena. Part-of-speech tags using a modified STTS tag set (Schiller et al., 1999) as well as lemmatized forms have been added automatically using TreeTagger.

Metadata is provided using the Coma format and additional speaker metadata is present as headers in the transcription files. The Coma file covers catalog metadata following Dublin Core as well as transcription and annotation metadata including annotation structure. The corpus is available both via the Hamburg Center for Language Corpora (HZSK)[5] and as part of the Database of Spoken German (DGD). The HZSK is part of the CLARIN infrastructure, consequently some metadata are also available as CMDI. In addition to machine-readable metadata, corpus documentation is present as PDFs.

3.3 MIKO

The "Mitschreiben in Vorlesungen: Ein multimodales Lehr-Lernkorpus" corpus (MIKO, Spiegel et al., 2022) is a multimodal corpus containing recordings of lectures as well as lecture notes created by students, both L1 and L2 speakers of German. Most of the lectures are transcribed and annotated using EXMARaLDA and stored as machine-readable data. The lecture notes are based on photos of the notes which have been anonymized and stored as PDFs.

Coma metadata is included in the corpus to document speaker information. Additional metadata about both lectures and lecture notes are included as CSV tables. Finally, human-readable corpus documentation as well as description of the metadata variables is included as PDFs. MIKO is also available as part of the DGD. Furthermore, MIKO is present in the IDS repository which is part of the CLARIN infrastructure and thus requires some CMDI metadata.

3.4 DISKO

Finally, the "Deutsch im Studium: Lernerkorpus" corpus (DISKO, Wisniewski et al., 2022) is a written learner corpus consisting of several subcorpora. It was created in the context of the same project as MIKO and shares some similarities. The two main corpora consist of texts created for a writing exercise repeated up to three times with one year intervals by both L1 and L2 speakers of German. Additional corpora are based on language tests for students. Unusual for a written corpus, annotations have been created using an extension of the EXMARaLDA Partitur-Editor. Besides the EXMARaLDA files the data is also available as plain text and ANNIS data as well as the original handwritten documents as PDFs.

For the main parts DISKO L1 and L2 the metadata contain extensive information about the participants including language and socio-economic background. For the other subcorpora a limited set of metadata is available. Despite the use of EXMARaLDA, no Coma data is present, but the transcription files contain extensive information in the file headers. Also, similar to MIKO, metadata is present as CSV files and documentation of both the corpus itself and the metadata is available as PDFs. DISKO is available in the IDS repository and consequently requires some metadata available as CMDI.

4 Discussion

As one can see from these datasets listed in Section 3, both the metadata formats used and the information included are quite diverse. That shows that we are quite a bit away from an ideal of a single machine-readable metadata standard for learner corpora.

Several good reasons can be listed both in favor of expressive machine-readable metadata

[4] https://spraakbanken.gu.se/en/projects/swell

[5] https://corpora.uni-hamburg.de/hzsk/en/

for (learner) corpora and against it. One reason against the enforcement of metadata standards, e.g., before archiving the created data is the additional overhead. Already the creation of a dataset is time-consuming and sometimes even tedious. Adding the strict requirement for complete, extensive, machine-readable metadata and documentation can be seen as gate-keeping and too high a threshold. Some people might even consider withholding their data instead of releasing it if they have to meet such requirements for publication.

One major point in favor of standardized metadata and corpus documentation is the ability to automatically check for issues in the data set. Especially when archiving corpus data it is necessary to assess the quality of the data to guarantee later reuse. For example within the QUEST project (QUality ESTablished – Testing and Application of Curation Criteria and Quality Standards for Audiovisual Annotated Language Data)[6] it was demonstrated how a semi-automatic quality assurance process can profit from machine-readable corpus information (Arestau, 2022; Wamprechtshammer et al., 2022). For example, as long as the annotation schema is known, either because it follows some standard or if it is documented in a suitable way, it can be checked to be consistent and coherent across the whole data set.

It is also not the case that we have to start completely from scratch. There has been previous work on metadata standards for learner corpora such as (Granger and Paquot, 2017b,a). However, they lack visibility and are currently not generally applied. Another issue is that the draft by Granger and Paquot only specifies the data model, i.e., which fields have to be included and which values are acceptable, but not the representation. Consequently, the standard can be met both by human-readable metadata expressed for example using XML or JSON but also by only human-readable documentation such as MS Word documents or PDFs. Both issues, however, will hopefully be solved soon. Following the 6th International Conference for Learner Corpus Research (LCR 2022), a public call for feedback on a new draft of the core metadata standard has been sent to several relevant mailing lists[7]. Furthermore, at the same conference König et al. (2022) presented their approach to testing the core metadata standard on several corpora and expressing it using CMDI.

The question of representation of metadata is the final issue to be discussed here. As I summarized in the introduction, there is a number of viable and established metadata formats for learner corpora. Most of them are sufficiently expressive or extensible to be used for machine-readable corpus documentation. And there can be good reasons to prefer one over the other, e.g., good integration in the annotation software or in the infrastructure in which the data should be deposited. Sometimes several formats can be "competing" by providing similar functionality: both CMDI and OLAC (Bird and Simons, 2001) formats can be used in metadata harvesting, CMDI within CLARIN infrastructure and OLAC with the Open Language Archives Community. However, each metadata format requires understanding its philosophy to be able to use it in the most suitable way. This can be partially mitigated by using dedicated software for metadata creation and management such as the EXMARaLDA Corpus Manager, LAMETA (Hatton et al., 2021) or various CMDI tools in the CLARIN infrastructure but requires learning how to use the software instead. A minimum viable solution could be based on spreadsheets which are both easy to create and edit and can be automatically read by software. However, spreadsheets lack additional semantics such as a hierarchical structure or controlled vocabulary.

5 Conclusion

There are many good reasons for metadata standards, especially from the perspective of archiving and research data infrastructure. It is easier to deposit data in a repository if a supported set of metadata is provided in a standardized format. Furthermore, having access to suitable metadata, it is possible to auto-

[6]https://www.slm.uni-hamburg.de/ifuu/forschung/forschungsprojekte/quest.html

[7]LINGUIST list archive: https://web.archive.org/web/20221124163838/https://list.elra.info/mailman3/hyperkitty/list/corpora@list.elra.info/message/5ITI7JXPYWAADXQ2MWTEXIQITWSVV332/

matically check relevant aspects of the corpus data. These two points would improve both findability and reusability of the deposited data. Especially the increased findability of the created datasets should ideally motivate corpus creators to include a sufficient set of metadata information in addition to their corpus data.

Furthermore, there are established machine-readable metadata formats with infrastructure and ecosystem surrounding them. For example CMDI is already omnipresent for all data published within CLARIN and can be modified to fit the data using profiles. As show by König et al. (2022), it could form a starting point for a unified representation for learner corpora metadata. And because it is a standard format within a large infrastructure, existing tools can be used to create and modify the metadata for learner corpora. Finally, having one metadata format as a pivot for conversion into other formats could be suitable for any additional metadata requirements such as specific formats for a certain archive outside CLARIN as well as for Linked Open Data.

A major challenge is to balance the interests of all parties involved. From an infrastructure point of view it is essential to have machine-readable metadata usable for ingesting the corpus data and providing means for finding relevant data. But when establishing a machine-readable metadata standard we also need to reduce the additional work loaded onto the researcher to document their data. The whole discussion is only relevant when corpus creators are willing to prepare and submit their data. Consequently, we have to collaborate on establishing standards acceptable for all parties.

Acknowledgements

Parts of this work have been funded by the QUEST project by the German Federal Ministry of Education and Research (BMBF) grant 16QK09B (06/2019–05/2022) as well as Text+ funded by the German Research Foundation (DFG) project number 460033370.

I would also like to thank Elena Arestau for the collaboration on quality standards for learner corpora as part of QUEST.

References

Elena Arestau. 2022. Curation of learner corpora. Technical report, University of Hamburg. https://www.slm.uni-hamburg.de/ifuu/forschung/forschungsprojekte/quest/ueber-das-projekt/projektergebnisse/arestaulearnercorpora.pdf.

Steven Bird and Gary Simons. 2001. The OLAC Metadata Set and Controlled Vocabularies. In Proceedings of the ACL 2001 Workshop on Sharing Tools and Resources.

Daan Broeder, Oliver Schonefeld, Thorsten Trippel, Dieter Van Uytvanck, and Andreas Witt. 2011. A pragmatic approach to XML interoperability – the Component Metadata Infrastructure (CMDI). In Proceedings of Balisage: The Markup Conference 2011, Montréal, Canada, August 2 - 5, 2011, volume 7 of Balisage Series on Markup Technologies, Montréal, Canada.

Twan Goosen and Thomas Eckart. 2014. Virtual language observatory 3.0: What's new. In CLARIN Annual Conference, Soesterberg, The Netherlands.

Sylviane Granger and Magali Paquot. 2017a. Core metadata for learner corpora. Draft 1.0.

Sylviane Granger and Magali Paquot. 2017b. Towards standardization of metadata for L2 corpora. In Invited talk at the CLARIN workshop on Interoperability of Second Language Resources and Tools, 6-8 December 2017, University of Gothenburg, Sweden.

John Hatton, Gary Holton, Mandana Seyfeddinipur, and Nick Thieberger. 2021. Lameta. https://github.com/onset/laMETA/releases.

HZSK. 2010. HAMATAC - the Hamburg MapTask Corpus. Archived in Hamburger Zentrum für Sprachkorpora. Version 0.3. Publication date 2010-09-16.

Alexander König, Jennifer-Carmen Frey, Egon W. Stemle, Glaznieks Aivars, and Magali Paquot. 2022. Towards standardizing lcr metadata. In 6th International Conference for Learner Corpus Research (LCR 2022), 22.9.2022–24.9.2022, Padova.

Anne Schiller, Simone Teufel, Christine Stöckert, and Christine Thielen. 1999. Guidelines für das Tagging deutscher Textkorpora mit STTS (Kleines und großes Tagset). Technical report, Institut für maschinelle Sprachverarbeitung, Universität Stuttgart and Seminar für Sprachwissenschaften, Universität Tübingen. https://www.ims.uni-stuttgart.de/documents/ressourcen/lexika/tagsets/stts-1999.pdf, accessed 2022-01-03.

Thomas Schmidt. 2017. DGD – die Datenbank für Gesprochenes Deutsch. Mündliche Korpora am Institut für Deutsche Sprache (IDS) in Mannheim. 45(3):451 – 463.

Thomas Schmidt and Kai Wörner. 2014. EXMARaLDA. The Oxford handbook of corpus phonology, pages 402 – 419. Oxford Univ. Press, Oxford.

Leonore Spiegel, Maria Parker, Tim Feldmüller, Lisa Lenort, and Katrin Wisniewski. 2022. Mitschreiben in Vorlesungen in der Studieneingangsphase: Das multimodale Lehr-Lernkorpus MIKO. In Katrin Wisniewski, Wolfgang Lenhard, Leonore Spiegel, and Jupp Möhring, editors, Sprache und Studienerfolg bei Bildungsausländerinnen und Bildungsausländern. Waxmann Verlag, Münster.

TEI Consortium. 2022. TEI P5: Guidelines for Electronic Text Encoding and Interchange. Text Encoding Initiative Consortium. Version 4.4.0. Last updated on 19th April 2022, revision ff9cc28b0.

Elena Volodina, Lena Granstedt, Arild Matsson, Beáta Megyesi, Ildikó Pilán, Julia Prentice, Dan Rosén, Lisa Rudebeck, Carl-Johan Schenström, Gunlög Sundberg, and Mats Wirén. 2019. The SweLL Language Learner Corpus : From Design to Annotation. Northern European Journal of Language Technology (NEJLT), 6:67–104. Special Issue of Selected Contributions from the Seventh Swedish Language Technology Conference (SLTC 2018).

Anna Wamprechtshammer, Elena Arestau, Jocelyn Aznar, Hanna Hedeland, Amy Isard, Ilya Khait, Herbert Lange, Nicole Majka, Felix Rau, and Gabriele Schwiertz. 2022. QUEST: Guidelines and specifications for the assessment of audiovisual, annotated language data. Technical report, QUEST project. Forthcoming.

Mark D. Wilkinson et al. 2016. The FAIR Guiding Principles for scientific data management and stewardship. Scientific Data, 3(1):160018.

Mats Wirén, Arild Matsson, Dan Rosén, and Elena Volodina. 2019. Svala: Annotation of second-language learner text based on mostly automatic alignment of parallel corpora. In Selected papers from the CLARIN Annual Conference 2018, Pisa, 8-10 October 2018 :, number 159 in Linköping Electronic Conference Proceedings, pages 222–234.

Katrin Wisniewski, Elisabeth Muntschick, and Annette Portmann. 2022. Schreiben in der Studiersprache Deutsch. Das Lernerkorpus DISKO. In Katrin Wisniewski, Wolfgang Lenhard, Leonore Spiegel, and Jupp Möhring, editors, Sprache und Studienerfolg bei Bildungsausländerinnen und Bildungsausländern. Waxmann Verlag, Münster.

A Transformer for SAG: What Does it Grade?

Nico Willms
Hochschule für Technik
Stuttgart, Germany

Ulrike Padó
Hochschule für Technik
Stuttgart, Germany
ulrike.pado@hft-stuttgart.de

Abstract

Automatic short-answer grading aims to predict human grades for short free-text answers to test questions, in order to support or replace human grading. Despite active research, there is to date no wide-spread use of ASAG in real-world teaching. One reason is a lack of transparency of popular methods like Transformer-based deep neural networks, which means that students and teachers cannot know how much to trust automated grading. We probe one such model using the adversarial attack paradigm to better understand their reliance on syntactic and semantic information in the student answers, and their vulnerability to the (easily manipulated) answer length. We find that the model is, reassuringly, likely to reject answers with missing syntactic and semantic information, but that it picks up on the correlation between answer length and correctness in standard training. Thus, real-world applications have to safeguard against exploitation of answer length.

1 Introduction

Automated short-answer grading (ASAG) promises to support or replace human grading decisions for student-constructed answers to test questions and in this way avoid human error and save teachers' time and effort. In the context of formative testing for frequent feedback, online teaching and self-study, ASAG is especially attractive, since human grading effort is significant due to repeated testing or large groups, and the need for feedback can arise at any time of day or night in the case of self-study (Burrows et al., 2015).

ASAG models are not currently in wide-spread use in real-world teaching contexts (e.g., Lee and Shin (2020); Wilson et al. (2021) for the related task of essay scoring). Three requirements for their adoption are reliable performance on small-scale, real-word data, ease of development for non-experts and transparency of model decision making, both for teachers and students.

Transformer-based models like BERT (Devlin et al., 2019) and RoBERTa (Liu et al., 2019) have been recently successfully explored for ASAG (Camus and Filighera, 2020; Bexte et al., 2022). Given the relatively small size of available training data for ASAG (in the low ten thousands of data points), the great advantage of these models is that they are freely available pre-trained on large data sets and require only relatively small data sets for fine-tuning to a specific task. Another advantage is that they require no manual feature engineering, as relevant patterns are derived by the complex neural networks from word distributions in the very large pre-training data sets. Transformer-based models therefore seem like good candidates to address the reliability on small data sets and ease of development criteria.

However, the grading decisions made by neural models are intransparent. This makes it hard for teachers to understand how to best use ASAG on specific data sets - are the predictions reliable enough to replace human grades, should they be manually revised, or are the available models unreliable altogether for their data? A related question is what the model predictions are based on - do they consider the content of the short answers, as intended, or do they also rely on extraneous signals, and can they be swayed by trivial manipulations of the input that would not convince a human grader? Since real-world grading applications have to gain the trust of teachers and students alike, these questions are highly relevant for practical application. This paper aims to further understand the functioning and limitations of a standard Transformer-based ASAG model.

Since ASAG is a semantic task (similar to the Natural Language Inference and Paraphrase Detection sub-tasks in the GLUE benchmark, which BERT does well on, see Devlin et al. (2019)), we

Nico Willms and Ulrike Pado. A Transformer for SAG: What Does it Grade?. *Proceedings of the 11th Workshop on Natural Language Processing for Computer Assisted Language Learning (NLP4CALL 2022)*. Linköping Electronic Conference Proceedings 190: 114–122.

hope to see sensitivity to the content of the input beyond keyword spotting. At the same time, trivial manipulations of the input should not affect the predicted grade.

One strategy for probing model behaviour and representations are adversarial attacks (Goodfellow et al., 2015), modifications of the input data that allow us to evaluate model behaviour in a controlled experiment. The strategy has been used before to establish relevant insights about neural ASAG: Ding et al. (2020) established that a recursive neural network was sensitive to combinations of content words (rather than just keywords, for example) for ASAG. Looking at the possibility of fooling the model, Filighera et al. (2020) were able to identify two-word trigger phrases that in some cases suffice to switch the predictions of a BERT-based model when added to student answers – while not altering the content of the student answer in a meaningful way.

We present several experiments to investigate a Transformer-based model's sensitivity to syntactic and semantic information in ASAG student answers, as well as a confounding (and potentially exploitable) length effect. Experiment 1 (Section 4) investigates the system's reaction to removal of syntactic information (namely, word order and function words). Experiment 2 (Section 5) explores the extent of the system's reliance on content words from different word classes and its robustness in case they are removed. Finally, Experiment 3 (Section 6) investigates the impact of input length.

We find that the model uses syntactic information (such as word order and function words for English), but its loss is not catastrophic for model performance. Removing nouns from the input data has the most tangible effect in Experiment 2, reducing the model's ability to identify a correct answer to 50% (when a human grader would likely be similarly affected). These results underscore that the model does rely on the meaning of the short answers to arrive at its grade prediction, as we had hoped.

However, we also find that the model is easily swayed by input length: Longer answers are much more likely to be graded *correct*. This pattern is visible in the training data and clearly picked up by the model. This result is alarming, since the length signal is easy to manipulate.

2 Related Work

Traditionally, extensive feature engineering on the lexical, syntactic and semantic level has been employed for ASAG (see Burrows et al. (2015) for an overview). More recently, neural network-based approaches have been tested, for example in work by Riordan et al. (2017) using an LSTM (Long Short-Term Memory, Hochreiter and Schmidhuber (1997)) or by Sung et al. (2019) or Camus and Filighera (2020) using the Transformer-based BERT (Devlin et al., 2019) or RoBERTa (Liu et al., 2019) models.

While Riordan et al. (2017) report that their LSTM-based model approaches the state of the art, the BERT-based approach of Sung et al. (2019) is the first to improve on the state of the art for a standard ASAG data set. The use of domain-specific data in pre-training and fine-tuning proves helpful, but makes performance brittle in unknown domains. Camus and Filighera (2020) demonstrate that fine-tuning on tasks related to ASAG (like Natural Language Inference, where systems decide whether a hypothesis follows from a premise) yields more robust improvements, even though the fine-tuning data has little connection to the topic domain of the test data.

To date, the state of the art on standard benchmark data sets is set by combinations of neural and traditional machine learning approaches: Saha et al. (2018) and Sahu and Bhowmick (2020) combine word and sentence embeddings with string-based similarity methods. Since these approaches inherit both the need for feature engineering and for extensive pre-training of the embeddings, they are harder to re-create for the application of ASAG methods in teaching practice. We therefore focus on the Transformer-based models in this paper due to their comparable ease of use.

BERT and related models have been investigated extensively with different strategies over the last years, finding that BERT learns syntactic (Hewitt and Manning, 2019; Tenney et al., 2019) and semantic representations (Ettinger, 2020) that are generally preserved through fine-tuning for semantic tasks like paraphrasing (Pérez-Mayos et al., 2021). However, Hessel and Schofield (2021) find that on the GLUE tasks (Wang et al., 2018), BERT is relatively insensitive to shuffling of the input sentences, which removes many syntactic clues in English. For ASAG, this behaviour is double-edged: On the one hand, ASAG focuses on scoring answer content over answer form, so insensitivity to shuffled (or syntactically incorrect) input is an advantage. On the other hand, input words in truly random order would certainly be noticed by human graders and could indicate an attempt at manipulating the grade. Insensitivity to word order removes the system's ability to filter out such answers.

More problematic for the use of BERT-based models for ASAG are results from Ettinger (2020) that BERT is insensitive to negation in a word prediction task. For a task like ASAG, the removal or addition of negation to a student answer will likely immediately change the correct grade, so sensitivity to this information is vital.

Adversarial attacks specifically have been a fertile approach for studying neural networks in NLP in recent years (Zhang et al., 2020). Specifically for ASAG, Ding et al. (2020) found that attacks randomly generated from prompt specific words were more easily accepted by the system, more so if longer word sequences remained intact and most readily if the attack was generated by shuffling, since all lexical material is preserved. This is in line with the results by Hessel and Schofield (2021) and points to semantic association at the core of ASAG performance.

Filighera et al. (2020) identified a number of two-word trigger sequences that would frequently switch an ASAG grade from *incorrect* to *correct* when simply prepended to the student answers, increasing the misclassification rate of the attacked model by about 130-160%. This is a clear attack vector for grade manipulation, although it does not guarantee misclassification: Adding the triggers does not flip classification for any answer but only for ones that were already somewhat similar to the target answer.

3 Method

Data We work with two corpora that, together, constitute the standard English-language SemEval-2013[1] data set (Dzikovska et al., 2013), Beetle and SciEntsBank (SEB). The corpora contain student answers to science domain questions; Beetle (3.6k answers) was collected from interactions with a tutoring system, while SEB (4.5k answers) stems from a conventional test setting.

Evaluation Both corpora offer in-domain and out-of-domain test sets. For the in-domain test sets, additional *unseen answers* (UA) to questions from the training set are presented. In addition, there are also test sets containing completely new questions and their answers, called *unseen questions* (UQ). Finally, for SEB, there are also questions from an *unseen domain* (UD).

The task is to determine the human-annotated grade for a student answer by comparing it to a given correct reference answer. In the literature, Beetle is rarely used, since it provides several reference answers per question. Here, we append these reference answers into a single input.

We report Macro F_1 scores (for comparison to the literature state of the art) and Accuracy (for experimental evaluation) on the test sets, using the binary classification labels. In addition to overall Accuracy, we also break down the results into label-wise Accuracy. Across all data sets, the `incorrect` answers are the majority class (consistently at about 60% across all data subsets).

Model We aim to create a model close to the state of the art. Given the results in Camus and Filighera (2020), RoBERTa$_{base}$ as well as models pre-trained on the MRPC paraphrasing task (RoBERTa$_{MRPC}$) and the MNLI Natural Language Inference task (RoBERTa$_{MNLI}$) were separately fine-tuned on SEB and Beetle.

On a development set comprising 10% of the training data, we determined the optimal number of training epochs and compared the results for three versions of each RoBERTa model based on different random seeds. The models received a maximum of 256 tokens per input sentence. We used the Adam optimiser with an initial learning rate of 5e-5, and ϵ of 1e-8; batch size for training was 8. RoBERTa$_{MNLI}$ consistently outperformed the other model instances on the development set, so this model (with seed 100 and 6 epochs of training for SEB and seed 1 or 100 and 6 epochs of training for Beetle) was chosen.

Table 1 shows that we have succeeded in training a model that closely matches or numerically outperforms the state of the art for both corpora using macro F_1: We compare to Saha et al. (2018) on SEB.[2] and report the first results for 2-way Beetle since SemEval-2013[3].

[1]Available from `https://www.cs.york.ac.uk/semeval-2013/task7/index.php%3Fid=data.html`.

[2]Ghavidel et al. (2020) achieved a slightly higher F_1 score for UA at 79.7, but lower scores for UQ and UD.

[3]Results for the best model for each test set from the top-

	Beetle		SEB		
	UA	UQ	UA	UQ	UD
best SemEval-13	83.3	72.0	76.8	73.7	70.5
Saha et al. 2018	–	–	78.6	73.9	70.9
RoBERTa$_{MNLI}$	**89.7**	**78.1**	**82.2**	**74.1**	**72.1**

Table 1: Macro F_1 on the test sets for literature benchmarks and RoBERTa$_{MNLI}$.

Adversarial Attacks We modify the SEB and Beetle test data in different ways and compare model performance on the original and modified data using the difference in overall and label-specific model accuracy. This strategy allows us to both show the effect of the attack and to factor in imperfect model performance on the original data.

We will create attacks to evaluate the model's reliance on syntactic and semantic cues. In both cases, we will remove information from the student answers in the official test sets. For syntactic information, this means removing word order by shuffling and removing function words (as identified by the NLTK[4] tagger). For semantic information, we remove different content word classes (nouns, verbs, adjectives and adverbs). Since our strategy shortens the original student answers, we also closely look at the influence of answer length (by duplicating the original answers and by generating synthetic answers in different length bands).

If our attacks impair the model's ability to recognise the correct student answers, we expect a drop in overall prediction Accuracy, and more specifically, a strong decrease in prediction Accuracy for originally *correct* items (below, Acc$_{corr}$) and possibly an increase in Accuracy for originally *incorrect* items (Acc$_{incorr}$). If the model's ability to recognise *incorrect* answers suffers, overall prediction Accuracy will drop as well, but this time driven by lower Acc$_{incorr}$.

4 Experiment 1: Syntax

Our first experiment tests the impact of deleting syntactic information from the student answers. We try two strategies: Shuffling the input data (so word order information is lost), and deleting all tokens not belonging to the noun, verb, adjective and adverb classes: for example, pronouns, determiners, prepositions or conjunctions. In a third attack, we delete non-content tokens *and* shuffle. Sample attack items can be found in Table 2.

ranked Heilman and Madnani (2013) and Ott et al. (2013).

[4] https://www.nltk.org/

Table 3 shows the results: Shuffling and deleting non-content words both lead to lower Accuracy scores for both corpora (the table shows Δ Accuracy to the unaltered test data). The effect increases when we combine the attack strategies *and* the student answers are reduced to bags of content words.

Interestingly, the Beetle model is much more sensitive to the attack than the SEB model. Inspection of the data shows that Beetle contains many questions on opened and closed electrical circuits, where the direction of relations like *connected-to* is highly relevant and often signalled through syntactic means. Possibly, this is why model performance is hurt so much when syntactic signals are removed.

We look at the label-specific Accuracy results (see Table 6) to determine the cause of the observed drops in overall Accuracy. The results can be summarised as follows: As hypothesised, the drop in overall Accuracy is driven for both corpora and all test sets by a strong shift towards always predicting *incorrect*. For instance, looking at the most extreme attack of *shuffle+content only*, the label-specific Accuracy for *correct* instances drops by 50 percentage points for Beetle-UA while the label-specific Accuracy for *incorrect* rises by almost seven percentage points. The picture for Beetle-UQ is similar, and while the drops are generally less dramatic for SEB, the pattern is the same. Acc$_{corr}$ drops by about 13 points for SEB-UA and -UD (and by 33 points for SEB-UD), Acc$_{incorr}$ rises by 2-3 percentage points. This means that almost half of the bags of content words created by the attack are now so dissimilar to the reference answers that the models no longer recognise them as a correct answer.

In sum, the impact on the Accuracy of grading *correct* student answers is quite strong across all test sets, demonstrating that the RoBERTa models do use syntactic information in their decision-making. However, for the SEB model, the lack of syntactic cues is never catastrophic: The ma-

Syntax and Semantics Attacks		Length attacks	
Original	there is a damaged bulb	Original	there is a damaged bulb
Syntax: Shuffle	bulb there damaged is a	Rand. Short	was path in is or is closed has incorrect
Syntax: delete Non-Content	is damaged bulb	Rand. Avg.	a affect terminal terminal by bulb [...] (34 words)
Semantics: delete Nouns	there is a damaged	Rand. Long	a and c path state difference bulb [...] (93 words)
Semantics: delete Verbs	there a bulb	Duplicate	there is a damaged bulb there is a damaged bulb

Table 2: Adversarial attack items for syntax, semantics and length (Rand: randomly generated) attacks (Beetle).

	Beetle		SEB		
	UA	UQ	UA	UQ	UD
Test data	89.7	78.1	82.2	74.1	72.1
Shuffle	-9.3	-7.2	-3.7	-2.2	**-1.8**
Content only	-9.5	-6.4	**-4.4**	-0.3	+0.5
Both	**-16.1**	**-11.2**	-3.7	**-7.3**	**-1.5**

Table 3: Exp.1: Removing syntactic information: Shuffling and removing non-content words from the SEB and Beetle Unseen Answer (UA), Unseen Question (UQ) and Unseen Domain (UD) test sets, overall Δ Accuracy (lowest result in boldface).

	Beetle		SEB		
	UA	UQ	UA	UQ	UD
Test data	89.7	78.1	82.2	74.1	72.1
No Adj	-7.7	-4.8	-7.6	-1.7	-2.1
No Adv	-5.2	-2.2	-1.5	-3.0	-0.2
No Nouns	**-10.2**	**-14.5**	**-8.3**	**-3.8**	-2.3
No Verbs	-4.3	-0.7	-4.8	+0.4	**-3.5**

Table 4: Exp.2: Removing various content word classes from the SEB and Beetle Unseen Answer (UA), Unseen Question (UQ) and Unseen Domain (UD) test sets, overall Δ Accuracy (lowest result in boldface).

jority of correct student answers is still recognised based on shuffled content words only. For ASAG this means that a relevant combination of content words still has a chance of being recognised as a correct answer even if it is not syntactically correct. This potentially helps non-native speakers and is in line with the focus on content in ASAG. Looking at the attack items in Table 2, it is likely that human graders would be able to interpret some of these answers and grade them as *correct*, as well - we did not investigate this point further, however.

5 Experiment 2: Semantics

In Exp. 1, we probed the influence of syntactic information by excluding all non-content words. In Exp. 2, we ask about the relative importance of the different classes of content words instead. We create four different sets of attack items by selectively removing all nouns (or verbs, adjectives or adverbs) as identified by the NLTK tagger. We hypothesise that nouns and verbs furnish the most crucial information for correct grading, so removing them from the test set answers should affect grading Accuracy most. Negation expressed by "not" will be removed with the adverbs, so grading may suffer in this case, as well (since the meaning of the student answers will be substantially changed by the deletion).

We find a clear impact of removing content words (see Table 4), with the greatest effect from deleting nouns (while the SEB-UD model does worst without verbs). For three out of five test sets (Beetle-UQ and SEB-UA and -UD), the performance drop from removing nouns is larger than when syntactic information was removed. This performance drop is again caused by a tendency of the models to label the attack items as *incorrect*, which is visible in Table 6 across all data sets and for all content-word classes. This is plausible, as the student answers become very hard to interpret for humans, as well (cf. the sample item "there is a damaged" in Table 2).

Removing adverbs, and thereby negation expressed by "not", at first glance seems to be less damaging than removing adjectives and much less so than removing nouns and verbs. However, note that not all student answers contain adjectives and adverbs in the first place, so fewer changes are made to the test data. The fact that we still see a noticeable effect speaks to the semantic importance of these word classes in the student data. As for the syntactic attack items, it would be interesting to see whether humans and the models accept and reject the same attack items to gauge the importance of the word classes to human interpretation versus machine grading.

We also see that model performance strongly

	Beetle		SEB		
	UA	UQ	UA	UQ	UD
Test data	89.7	78.1	82.2	74.1	72.1
Repeat 1x	-9.1	-6.8	-5.2	-4.1	-4.8
Repeat 2x	**-14.3**	**-10.8**	**-9.6**	**-14.1**	**-8.5**
Rand. Short	–	97.5	–	–	95.5
Rand. Avg.	–	89.9	–	–	83.0
Rand. Long	–	**43.0**	–	–	**33.0**

Table 5: Exp.3: Testing the influence of answer length: Repeating answers from the SEB and Beetle test sets and randomly generated input sequences in three length bands; overall Δ Accuracy to test data (absolute Accuracy for randomly generated input).

deteriorates in the UA setting for both corpora (and for Beetle-UQ). We hypothesise that performance in the UA setting, where the model sees new answers to questions encountered in training, depends on keyword spotting more than in the UQ and UD settings. This is consistent with the well-established deterioration of performance on the unaltered test sets when moving away from the UA setting.

The model's remaining robustness towards removal of content words (after all, about 50% of correct answers are still recognised by the SEB RoBERTa model even if nouns are removed) may be rooted in RoBERTa's masked pre-training task which specifically teaches the model to reconstruct missing input.

Again, this result is reassuring in the context of ASAG: The model uses information from all groups of content words and is more likely to reject as *incorrect* inputs with some missing content words.

6 Experiment 3: Input Length

When we remove content words, we also shorten the input. At the same time, answer length is correlated with grade in the training data: *correct* Beetle answers have a median length of 54 characters (min: 3, max: 367), while *incorrect* answers are only 41 characters long in the median (min: 0, max: 256). For SEB, the numbers are 60 characters (min: 4, max: 532) for correct and 51 (min: 2, max: 413) for incorrect answers. Therefore it is relevant to ask whether the models pick up on this correlation.

We use two strategies to probe sensitivity to length while keeping the meaning of the utterances constant: One is to repeat the student answer, thus doubling or tripling the input in length without making a change to its meaning. The other is to randomly generate synthetic test items of different lengths (but without discernible meaning). More specifically, we build an attack set with synthetic length-controlled items generated randomly from the vocabulary of the Beetle-UQ and SEB-UD test sets (which are most different from the training data). We generate 200 attack items for each of three length classes: Short attack items are in the range between the minimum and median length of all relevant answers, average-length items are in the range of the first to third quartile and the length of long items is between the median and maximum lengths for the test sets. All of these attack items should be rejected as *incorrect* by the model since they are nonsensical (see Table 2 for sample items).

The results are shown in Table 5. Repeating each student answer once (doubling the answer length) or twice (tripling the answer length) clearly reduces model Accuracy. However, the result pattern at label level is inverted to the first two experiments (see Table 6). Now, Acc_{corr} increases for double- and triple-length answers, while Acc_{incorr} drops by more than 20 percentage points for all corpora. The model now *accepts* answers more easily the longer they are, although their content has not changed.

We turn to the length-controlled synthetic items to gauge the effect of submitting short items (which we could not probe in the replication attack without modifying answer meaning). The synthetic items show that the shortest inputs are in fact labelled *incorrect* even more frequently than the average length ones, so short items are somewhat at a disadvantage (the table shows absolute overall Accuracy). Long items are again labelled *correct* with very high probability (leading to low Accuracy, since all synthetic items are *incorrect*), and this effect is much stronger than the disadvantage for short items. This is a concerning finding for ASAG, since item length can easily be influenced by test-takers independent of their understanding of the task.

7 Word Deletion Attacks and Length

Given the results from Exp. 3, we need to reconsider our strategies and results in Exp. 1 and 2, where our attacks rely on deleting words from

	Beetle				SEB					
	UA		UQ		UA		UQ		UD	
	corr	incorr	corr	incorr	corr	incorr	corr	incorr	corr	incorr
Test data	88.6	90.5	62.5	89.5	75.1	87.6	86.6	74.7	73.4	74.5
Shuffle	-30.1	+5.5	-23.3	+4.4	-4.7	-2.9	+0.2	-3.2	-1.0	-3.0
Content only	-31.8	+5.3	-25.	+2.0	-10.7	+0.3	-19.3	+3.8	-7.8	+3.1
Both	**-50.6**	+6.8	-37.5	+7.8	-12.6	+2.3	-32.8	+1.2	-13.0	+3.5
No Adjs	-22.7	+2.2	-16.0	+3.1	-19.7	+2.6	-31.1	+9.8	-15.8	+4.5
No Advs	-14.8	+1.7	-8.1	+2.0	-1.3	-1.6	-22.1	+1.0	-6.1	+0.7
No Verbs	-13.0	+1.5	-7.3	+4.0	-11.6	-1.0	-20.5	+5.6	-21.8	+6.5
No Nouns	-30.6	+2.2	**-39.2**	+3.3	**-22.7**	+2.6	**-36.4**	+9.6	**-27.4**	+12.5
Repeat 1x	+2.3	-16.7	+11.9	-20.4	+7.9	-15.0	-4.5	-13.1	+5.4	-15.6
Repeat 2x	+6.3	**-28.1**	+16.2	**-30.6**	+13.8	**-27.0**	+1.6	**-23.0**	+10.6	**-25.8**

Table 6: Exp.1-3: Label-wise Δ Accuracy for different types of answer manipulation on the SEB and Beetle Unseen Answer (UA), Unseen Question (UQ) and Unseen Domain (UD) test sets (lowest result per column in boldface).

the student answers, thereby shortening them. Indeed, we found for both experiments that the models showed a tendency to reject the modified student answers, which could now also be explained by their shorter length. Recall, however, that the results for deleting non-content words in Exp. 1 were backed up by the shuffle attack, which preserves length.

In order to gauge the effect of length reduction in the word deletion attacks, we re-ran the experiments after replacing each non-content word rather than deleting it – e.g., nouns by "thing", verbs by "do", and non-content words by the particle "to" or, alternatively, any deleted word by "—" The attack items kept their length in this way.

Across all data sets and attacks, we found that replacing content words with valid lexical items generally further reduces model performance. Replacing words distorts the sentences even more strongly than just deleting them, because no guessing or filling in the blanks is possible (which is the task RoBERTa was trained to do during pre-training). There is very little difference between deleting words and replacing them by "—" placeholders, except that the extremely low performance for Beetle-QA in Exp. 2 is mitigated to something closer to the SEB performance. We therefore conclude that any length effect confounded with the deletion attacks is minor. This is supported by our observation that short answers are somewhat more likely to be graded `incorrect`, while long answers are much more likely `correct` (so the effect is smaller for shorter answers). Therefore, we believe that the results from Exp. 1 and 2 are not due to the length effects of the word deletion strategy but indeed to the loss of syntactic or semantic information from the student answers.

8 Conclusions

Across our three experiments, we have observed the performance of the RoBERTa$_{MNLI}$ model on the SAG task using the SEB and Beetle corpora.

A first, striking insight across all three experiments is that the size of the impact of our attacks differs strongly between corpora, while the general patterns stay the same. Removing syntactic information causes the models to label previously *correct* student answers as *incorrect*, but the model fine-tuned on SEB is much more forgiving and ready to retain the *correct* label than the Beetle model. The same is true for removing semantic information. This result shows how much of SAG model performance depends on the fine-tuning and test data and how misleading it can be to generalise insights from one data set to another.

Second, we saw clear evidence of RoBERTa's sensitivity to syntactic information in Exp. 1 – removing structural and word order clues causes the model to no longer accept originally correct student answers in many cases. This is plausible, since the student answers also become harder to interpret for humans. Model performance is not completely impaired, however, so slightly imperfect syntax will likely not preclude a *correct* grade.

Removing semantic information (even when utterance length is preserved) in Exp. 2 is similar. When nouns are removed, only about 50% of all *correct* student answers are still recognised (for both Beetle and SEB) – understandably so, as the meaning of the answers is strongly distorted also to humans. Removing all other classes of content words showed similar effects; normalising the results by the number of affected student answers per manipulation in order to more accurately weight the influence of the word classes remains for future work.

Confirming that the RoBERTa models are sensitive to the syntax and semantics of student answers is reassuring in the context of ASAG. However, the strong length effect shown in Exp. 3 is very concerning for a SAG model, since it is clearly independent of content and could be used to gain an unfair advantage. Any serious use of the models as they stand should therefore install safeguards, for example a human review of all unusually long answers. In the long run, adversarial training (Madry et al., 2017) could be employed to mitigate the length effect.

While we carry out our experiments on one specific model (RoBERTa), the effects we find are likely to generalise to other Transformer-based ASAG models because they appear to stem from the training data and training regime. Further, the effect of insensitivity to word order (Hessel and Schofield, 2021) has been observed for another semantic task in previous work and the importance of semantic information (in terms of the choice of question-relevant lexical material) is also observed in (Ding et al., 2020).

In both Exp. 1 and 2, we were as yet unable to answer the question whether the attack items that were still accepted as *correct* by the models would also be acceptable to human graders or whether they are completely spurious. Comparing human and machine grades for these attack items is another interesting avenue for future work.

Acknowledgments

The authors acknowledge support by the state of Baden-Württemberg through the bwHPC high-performance computing infrastructure. N.W. was supported by AraCom IT Services AG for the duration of his Master's thesis.

References

Marie Bexte, Andrea Horbach, and Torsten Zesch. 2022. Similarity-based content scoring - how to make S-BERT keep up with BERT. In *Proceedings of the 17th Workshop on Innovative Use of NLP for Building Educational Applications (BEA 2022)*, pages 118–123.

Steven Burrows, Iryna Gurevych, and Benno Stein. 2015. The eras and trends of automatic short answer grading. *International Journal of Artificial Intelligence in Education*, 25:60–117.

Leon Camus and Anna Filighera. 2020. Investigating transformers for automatic short answer grading. In *Artificial Intelligence in Education AIED*, Lecture Notes in Computer Science, pages 43–48.

Jacob Devlin, Ming-Wei Chang, Kenton Lee, and Kristina Toutanova. 2019. BERT: Pre-training of deep bidirectional transformers for language understanding. In *Proceedings of the 2019 Conference of the North American Chapter of the Association for Computational Linguistics: Human Language Technologies, Volume 1 (Long and Short Papers)*, pages 4171–4186, Minneapolis, Minnesota. Association for Computational Linguistics.

Yuning Ding, Brian Riordan, Andrea Horbach, Aoife Cahill, and Torsten Zesch. 2020. Don't take "nswvtnvakgxpm" for an answer –the surprising vulnerability of automatic content scoring systems to adversarial input. In *Proceedings of the 28th International Conference on Computational Linguistics*, pages 882–892, Barcelona, Spain (Online). International Committee on Computational Linguistics.

Myroslava Dzikovska, Rodney Nielsen, Chris Brew, Claudia Leacock, Danilo Giampiccolo, Luisa Bentivogli, Peter Clark, Ido Dagan, and Hoa Trang Dang. 2013. SemEval-2013 task 7: The joint student response analysis and 8th recognizing textual entailment challenge. In *Second Joint Conference on Lexical and Computational Semantics (*SEM), Volume 2: Proceedings of the Seventh International Workshop on Semantic Evaluation (SemEval 2013)*, pages 263–274, Atlanta, Georgia, USA. Association for Computational Linguistics.

Allyson Ettinger. 2020. What BERT is not: Lessons from a new suite of psycholinguistic diagnostics for language models. *Transactions of the Association for Computational Linguistics*, 8:34–48.

Anna Filighera, Tim Steuer, and Christoph Rensing. 2020. Fooling automatic short answer grading systems. In *Artificial Intelligence in Education AIED*, Lecture Notes in Computer Science, pages 177–190.

Hadi Abdi Ghavidel, Amal Zouaq, and Michel C. Desmarais. 2020. Using bert and xlnet for the automatic short answer grading task. In *Proceedings of the 12th International Conference on Computer Supported Education (CSEDU)*, pages 58–67.

Ian Goodfellow, Jonathon Shlens, and Christian Szegedy. 2015. Explaining and harnessing adversarial examples. In *Proceedings of the International Conference on Learning Representations*, San Diego, CA, USA.

Michael Heilman and Nitin Madnani. 2013. ETS: Domain adaptation and stacking for short answer scoring. In *Second Joint Conference on Lexical and Computational Semantics (*SEM), Volume 2: Proceedings of the Seventh International Workshop on Semantic Evaluation (SemEval 2013)*, pages 275–279, Atlanta, Georgia, USA. Association for Computational Linguistics.

Jack Hessel and Alexandra Schofield. 2021. How effective is BERT without word ordering? implications for language understanding and data privacy. In *Proceedings of the 59th Annual Meeting of the Association for Computational Linguistics and the 11th International Joint Conference on Natural Language Processing (Short Papers)*, pages 204–211. Association for Computational Linguistics.

John Hewitt and Christopher D. Manning. 2019. A structural probe for finding syntax in word representations. In *Proceedings of the 2019 Conference of the North American Chapter of the Association for Computational Linguistics: Human Language Technologies, Volume 1 (Long and Short Papers)*, pages 4129–4138, Minneapolis, Minnesota. Association for Computational Linguistics.

Sepp Hochreiter and Jürgen Schmidhuber. 1997. Long short-term memory. *Neural Computation*, 8(9):1735–1780.

Boh Young Lee and Sang Keun Shin. 2020. Doable and practical: A validation study of classroom diagnostic tests. *Journal of Asia TEFL*, 17(2):349–362.

Yinhan Liu, Myle Ott, Naman Goyal, Jingfei Du, Mandar Joshi, Danqi Chen, Omer Levy, Mike Lewis, Luke Zettlemoyer, and Veselin Stoyanov. 2019. Roberta: A robustly optimized BERT pretraining approach. *CoRR*, abs/1907.11692.

Aleksander Madry, Aleksandar Makelov, Ludwig Schmidt, Dimitris Tsipras, and Adrian Vladu. 2017. Towards deep learning models resistant to adversarial attacks. In *Proceedings of ICLR*.

Niels Ott, Ramon Ziai, Michael Hahn, and Detmar Meurers. 2013. CoMeT: Integrating different levels of linguistic modeling for meaning assessment. In *Second Joint Conference on Lexical and Computational Semantics (*SEM), Volume 2: Proceedings of the Seventh International Workshop on Semantic Evaluation (SemEval 2013)*, pages 608–616, Atlanta, Georgia, USA. Association for Computational Linguistics.

Laura Pérez-Mayos, Roberto Carlini, Miguel Ballesteros, and Leo Wanner. 2021. On the evolution of syntactic information encoded by BERT's contextualized representations. In *Proceedings of the 16th Conference of the European Chapter of the Association for Computational Linguistics: Main Volume*, pages 2243–2258, Online. Association for Computational Linguistics.

Brian Riordan, Andrea Horbach, Aoife Cahill, Torsten Zesch, and Chong Min Lee. 2017. Investigating neural architectures for short answer scoring. In *Proceedings of the 12th Workshop on Innovative Use of NLP for Building Educational Applications*, pages 159–168, Copenhagen, Denmark. Association for Computational Linguistics.

Swarnadeep Saha, Tejas I. Dhamecha, Smit Marvaniya, Renuka Sindhgatta, and Bikram Sengupta. 2018. Sentence level or token level features for automatic short answer grading?: Use both. In *Artificial Intelligence in Education*, pages 503–517.

Archana Sahu and Plaban Kumar Bhowmick. 2020. Feature engineering and ensemble-based approach for improving automatic short-answer grading performance. *IEEE Transactions on Learning Technologies*, 13(1):77–90.

Chul Sung, Tejas Indulal Dhamecha, and Nirmal Mukhi. 2019. Improving short answer grading using transformer-based pre-training. In *Artificial Intelligence in Education AIED, Proceedings*, Lecture Notes in Computer Science, pages 469–481.

Ian Tenney, Patrick Xia, Berlin Chen, Alex Wang, Adam Poliak, R Thomas McCoy, Najoung Kim, Benjamin Van Durme, Sam Bowman, Dipanjan Das, and Ellie Pavlick. 2019. What do you learn from context? Probing for sentence structure in contextualized word representations. In *Proceedings of the International Conference on Learning Representations*.

Alex Wang, Amanpreet Singh, Julian Michael, Felix Hill, Omer Levy, and Samuel Bowman. 2018. GLUE: A multi-task benchmark and analysis platform for natural language understanding. In *Proceedings of the 2018 EMNLP Workshop BlackboxNLP: Analyzing and Interpreting Neural Networks for NLP*, pages 353–355, Brussels, Belgium. Association for Computational Linguistics.

Joshua Wilson, Yue Huang, Corey Palermo, Gaysha Beard, and Charles A. MacArthur. 2021. Automated feedback and automated scoring in the elementary grades: Usage, attitudes, and associations with writing outcomes in a districtwide implementation of mi write. *International Journal of Artificial Intelligence in Education*, 31(2):234–276.

Wei Emma Zhang, Quan Z. Sheng, Ahoud Alhazmi, and Chenliang Li. 2020. Adversarial attacks on deep-learning models in natural language processing: A survey. *ACM Trans. Intell. Syst. Technol.*, 11(3).

Towards a Verb Profile: distribution of verbal tenses in FFL textbooks and in learner productions

Nami Yamaguchi[1,2], **David Alfter**[1], **Kaori Sugiyama**[2] and **Thomas François**[1]
[1] Université catholique de Louvain, Belgium
[2] Seinan Gakuin University, Japan
first.last@uclouvain.be, sugiyama@seinan-gakuin.jp

Abstract

Morphological inflection is known to be difficult to master for L2 learners. In this paper, we examine the state of the use of inflection in the verbal tense system among learners of French, and contrast it with the use in FFL textbooks. The objectives of our study are threefold: 1) To establish the distribution of verbal tenses on French textbooks in an automatic way, in order to obtain the first fully empirical and extensive resource on French verbal tenses; 2) To objectively describe the use of verbal tenses by learners of different CEFR levels; 3) To identify the tenses that learners struggle with. Through the description of the use of the tenses in the learners, we found that they had difficulty with the past perfect indicative, even at advanced levels. The proposed Verb Profile summarizes which tenses should be understood at which level, and as such can guide teachers and learners, as well as help pinpoint tenses that learners are underperforming on.

1 Introduction

In second language acquisition (SLA), the construct of complexity is frequently used to measure learner development (Bulté and Housen, 2012; Pallotti, 2015) and has been mainly addressed through lexicon and syntax. Measures of morphological complexity, on the contrary, have been overlooked to some extent, as argued by De Clercq and Housen (2019). Yet studies remind us that learning morphological inflection remains a challenge even for advanced learners (DeKeyser, 2005; Larsen-Freeman, 2010; Lardiere, 2016), and, for morphologically rich languages such as French, the use of morphological complexity measures seems even more justified (Brezina and Pallotti, 2019).

Furthermore, beyond the field of complexity, there are a number of studies and theories that focus on morphological development of learners and discuss the development of language and its order of acquisition (Dulay and Burt, 1974; Pienemann, 1998; Bartning and Schlyter, 2004). For French, a large part of the morphological complexity lies at the level of the verbal system and the inflectional morphology of verbs (De Clercq and Housen, 2019, p. 76). Among the many features of verbal inflection, the verb tense is one of the main components of the complexity of the system. Therefore, in this study, we focus on the acquisition of morphological inflection in relation to verbal tenses in learners of French as a foreign language (FFL).

Here is a list of the tenses existing in French (Grevisse and Goosse, 2007) and the moods that invariably accompany them:

- Indicative: present, imperfect, simple past, past perfect, double compound past, pluperfect, double compound pluperfect, anterior past, simple future, anterior future or future perfect, and double compound future perfect;
- Conditional: present and past;[1]
- Imperative: present and past;
- Subjunctive: present, past, double compound past, imperfect, and pluperfect;
- Infinitive: present, past, and double compound past;
- Participle: present, past, past perfect, and double compound past;
- Gerund: present and past.

For second language learning, it is clear that one cause of difficulty is related to L1 interference;

[1] Grevisse and Goosse (2007, p. 980) classify the tenses of the conditional mood within those of the indicative, following the tendency of the linguists. However, in this article, we distinguish them, because this is normally the case in the FFL textbooks.

Nami Yamaguchi, David Alfter, Kaori Sugiyama and Thomas François. Towards a Verb Profile: distribution of verbal tenses in FFL textbooks and in learner productions. *Proceedings of the 11th Workshop on Natural Language Processing for Computer Assisted Language Learning (NLP4CALL 2022).* Linköping Electronic Conference Proceedings 190: 123–142.

however, examinations of learners' actual use of the language have revealed that many errors come from the target language itself, not from the L1 (Richards, 1970). Since then, the focus has been on the similarities that L2 learners have, regardless of their L1 (Spada and Lightbown, 2020, p. 118).

There are many theories about the learning steps that learners are generally expected to follow. One of the most representative theories is the *Processability Theory* (PT) proposed by Pienemann (1998). It is a theory that formally predicts which structures can be processed by the learner at a given level of development based on human psycholinguistic constraints on language processing. Table 1 presents the order of development according to this theory:

Order of development	Processing procedures	Structural outcome
5	Subordinate clause procedure	Main and subordinate clause
4	S-procedure	Interphrasal information exchange
3	Phrasal procedure	Phrasal information exchange
2	Category procedure	Lexical morphemes
1	Word or lemma access	Words

Table 1: Processing procedures and their structural outcome according to PT (based on Tables 1 and 2 in Pienemann and Håkansson (1999))

However, it is not possible to explain in detail the sequence of acquisition of each linguistic phenomenon (or grammatical rule), because PT only has five steps and therefore lacks granularity for this purpose. For example, if we apply this theory to verbal tenses, which are the focus of this paper, simple tenses – composed of a single verb – belong to the second stage, because they are processed in the word category. On the other hand, compound verbs, which are composed of an auxiliary and a verb, are at stage 3 (sentence level, beyond the word category). Therefore, according to PT, simple verbs are acquired at an earlier stage than compound verbs. The fact that the French indicative present is easier than the indicative past perfect is indeed consistent with FFL teachers' practices. However, it is unlikely that all simple tenses, such as the simple past, are easier than the past perfect. In addition, PT does not tell us which tense is acquired first among simple or compound tenses.

Pragmatically, what L2 teachers and learners are interested in is to know which linguistic elements should be mastered at what stage of learning. After the introduction of the Common European Framework of Reference for Languages (CEFR; Council of Europe 2001) in 2001, this framework became widely used in Europe as well as the proficiency scale of the CEFR. The CEFR scale provides "can-do" descriptors for the five skills (listening, reading, two subcategories for speaking, and writing) spread over six levels (A1 to C2). However, since the CEFR was developed to be compatible with different European languages, these "can-do" descriptors remain rather general and do not specify the details corresponding to each language (Hawkins and Buttery, 2010, p. 2). As a result, a number of research projects have attempted to link precise lexical or grammatical elements to the CEFR scale for various languages, as outlined in Section 2.

In the present study, we attempt to explain the acquisition of morphological inflections of verbal tenses by FFL learners. We use an empirical approach that relies on two datasets (textbooks and learners essays) and natural language processing (NLP) techniques to automatically annotate the large amounts of data. We hope that this approach will lead to more robust and generalizable results. Our research questions are:

1. **In the corpus of FFL textbooks, which verb tenses appear at which CEFR level?** Based on analysis of a textbook corpus, we will study the distribution of tenses according to the CEFR levels. Then, we will propose a "Verb Profile", a resource which will be the first fully empirical and extensive resource describing the distribution of verbal tenses in FFL pedagogical texts.[2]

2. **How do learners at different levels use verbal tenses?** In the long term, we plan to also establish the

[2]The name "Verb Profile" was chosen based on existing *grammar profiles*, of which it can be seen as a subcomponent.

"Verb Profile" of learners based on a large amount of written production data. In this paper, as a first step, we attempt to describe the use of tenses by FFL learners using a manual annotation of a small corpus of written productions. We will also discuss the challenges of using NLP for the automatic identification of verbal tenses.

3. **Which tenses do learners have difficulties with?**
   Inspired by the CEFR-J project (Tono, 2013), in case the learners have made some errors with the tense forms, we will also annotate the form that they should have written. These annotations will allow us to identify the tenses causing the most difficulties to learners.

The next section (Section 2) describes previous work on grammatical profiling of learners and on the acquisition steps of the morphology of verb tenses. It is followed by Section 3, which describes our research object, the corpus used, and the two annotation methods (automatic and manual). Section 4 presents the results of the textbook and learner data analysis respectively. Then, in Section 5, we enter into a discussion of the results and future research perspectives, and we conclude this paper in Section 6.

2 Related work

In both SLA and NLP, English is the dominant language in research, and this is also the case for grammar profiling projects. We can therefore mention several projects for English, such as the Core Inventory for General English by British Council (North et al., 2010), the English Grammar Profile[3] (O'Keeffe and Mark, 2017), the Pearson's Global Scale of English[4], and CEFR-J (Tono, 2013).

For French, there is a limited amount of work, including the study of Bartning and Schlyter (2004), the reference level descriptors (RLD) of Beacco and his collaborators (Beacco, 2008; Beacco and Porquier, 2007; Beacco et al., 2011, 2004; Riba, 2016) and the reference level descriptors of North (2015).

Bartning and Schlyter (2004) are among the first that summarized the acquisitional stages in the style of a grammatical profile, by analyzing a corpora of Swedish FFL learners' oral production with an empirical perspective. Based on these stages, they described French grammatical phenomena from the morphosyntactic point of view, specifying the phenomena expected at each developmental stage, from beginners (level 1) to Quasinatives (level 6).

As mentioned in the introduction, it is worth remembering that the CEFR descriptors lack a detailed description of acquisitional stages for the linguistic phenomena. To overcome this problem, the Council of Europe, which published the CEFR, also supported the creation of Reference Level Descriptions (RLDs) with the aim of offering more detailed language guides (Abel 2014, p. 112; Dürlich and François 2018, p. 873). The French version of the RLD is the referentials of Beacco and collaborators (Beacco, 2008; Beacco and Porquier, 2007; Beacco et al., 2011, 2004). Their RLD describe, for each level of the CEFR, the linguistic phenomena that are supposed to be mastered, and organize them within several distinct categories (basic lexicon, specialized notions, syntactic structures, phonemes, graphemes, functions, etc.). However, in the end, the knowledge of experts seems to often have been the primary criterion influencing the decision to assign a given language item to a given level (Dürlich and François, 2018).

According to North (2015, p. 5), what we teach, what learners can do, and what we measure in exams are not the same. Beacco et al.'s RLD have not sufficiently resolved the teachers' question about what content to teach at what level of the CEFR (North, 2015, p. 5), as they focus more on what learners are supposed to be able to do. North's work, then, focused on activities within the classroom. With the goal of making the CEFR accessible to teachers and learners, he established the linguistic inventory of key content for levels A1 to C1. These key elements were determined through the analysis of several types of data: the CEFR descriptors, some curricula, the French RLD and other similar sources, as well as a survey addressed to FFL teachers. By outlining these key contents, North's work provides teachers with support for selecting classroom activities and learners with support for independent learning.

In Appendix A, we have summarized the acquisitional stage of the French moods and tenses

[3]http://englishprofile.org

[4]https://www.pearson.com/english

as described in these three studies. Based on the comparison of these resources, we can say that Bartning and Schlyter (2004)'s study is interesting in that the results are based on actual learner data. However, because the tenses discussed are not comprehensive, we cannot see the overall picture of verb acquisition for French. In addition, the results are not aligned with the CEFR scale, so they do not address recent needs. In contrast, being based on the CEFR, Beacco and North's RLD are more applicable to practical situations. In addition, they cover many elements. Nevertheless, their inventories are based on various sources of information, including expert or teacher opinion, but not on large corpora. References of this nature are very informative in some respects, but it is not clear whether that they accurately reflect usage in textbooks and by learners. Thus, to the best of our knowledge, there is no study that is at the same time data-driven, comprehensive, and based on the CEFR scale. This study attempts to fill this gap by applying NLP to this challenging issue.

3 Methodology

In this section, we first describe the study proper (3.1). We then give an overview of the corpora used (3.2), the automatic annotation pipeline (3.3), and conclude with a description of the manual annotation process (3.4).

3.1 Overview of the study

Our study focuses on the use of verbal tenses in French. It is therefore necessary to define our object of study, that is, the tenses that will be the subject of our analysis. Among the tenses we presented in the introduction, the double compound tenses, the participles and the gerund have been excluded from our study for the following reasons:

- Double compound tenses: They are almost never used and are not taught in French textbooks.
- Participles: Present and past participles belong to one of the grammatical categories that are difficult to classify because of the ambiguity between the participle and the adjective, when they are in epithet (after nouns) or predicate position (after the verb *être* 'to be').[5] Moreover, by performing tests that we will detail later, we observed that parsers/taggers sometimes detect nouns that end in *ant* (e.g. étudiant 'student', enseignant 'teacher', etc.) as present participles, which would bias the results. Therefore, the present participle was also excluded.
- Gerund: The gerund consists of the preposition *en* and a present participle. It is difficult to find the link between these two elements automatically. This is an area for improvement that can be explored in the future.

Thus, we look at 18 tenses in this paper.

3.2 Corpus

In this study, we use two corpora: the first one is a FFL corpus of textbooks, and the second one is a French learner corpus.

The textbook corpus is identical to the one used in the study by Yancey et al. (2021). The corpus contains 20 textbooks published since 2015, as well as the *Annales du niveau C* publicly available on the Internet.[6] The selected texts target reading comprehension tasks, and the CEFR level assigned to them is that of the textbook from which they were taken. In total, the corpus contains 2769 texts distributed over five levels (A1 to C) – levels C1 and C2 having been merged –, for a total of 369,170 words, as detailed in Table 2.

Level	Texts	Words	Books
A1	764	48,639	6
A2	865	77,255	6
B1	507	82,728	4
B2	345	81,171	3
C	288	79,377	3
Total	2769	369,170	22

Table 2: Number of texts, words and textbooks by level in the textbook corpus

The learner corpus includes written productions from the TCF exam (Test de connaissance du français).[7] In this exam, candidates respond to three tasks, which are varied in topic and can be given to candidates of any level. Such a corpus

[5] "The past and present participles, which by their nature can be used as epithets, are often confused with adjectives" (Grevisse and Goosse, 2007)

[6] `https://www.france-education-international.fr/diplome/dalf/exemples-sujets` `http://www.delfdalf.fr/exemples-sujets-dilf-delf-dalf.html`

[7] The data was obtained through an agreement with France Education International and currently cannot be published.

is advantageous in that we can compare data produced by learners of various levels on the same tasks. First of all, it should be noted that each answer was evaluated by two or three trained evaluators, which provides a reliable CEFR level for each production. Moreover, the corpus also includes the candidates' usual language. We selected texts written by learners of five common but different languages, namely Arabic, Chinese, English, Russian and Spanish. Then, we extracted prototypical productions, i.e. those productions whose levels assigned by the two evaluators are the same and whose rounded Multi-faceted Rasch Analysis values correspond well to the level assigned by the evaluators.[8] Concerning the levels, having combined the C1 and C2 levels which were poorly represented in some of our five languages, we obtain five different levels (A1, A2, B1, B2 and C), following the example of the textbook corpus. Finally, as the topic of the tasks can influence the use of verbal tenses, we controlled for the number of tasks oriented towards the past (e.g. telling about one's last weekend), the present (e.g. talking about one's preferences about something such as how to shop (online or on the spot)) and the future (e.g. proposing an activity to friends). In concrete terms, in the 25 prepared sub-corpora (i.e. five levels for each of the five common languages), we randomly selected texts from a larger corpus and retained texts until we had two per task type (past, future and present).[9] Table 3 gives an overview over the learner corpus used.

Level	Texts	Words
A1	26	1253
A2	30	1452
B1	30	2793
B2	30	3002
C	30	2943
Total	146	11,443

Table 3: Number of texts and words by level in the learner corpus

[8]Multi-faceted Rasch Analysis (Linacre, 1989) is used to calculate an adjusted score for each production which takes into account rater severity and test taker competence.

[9]On the lowest level A1, there were not enough future-oriented tasks. This is why the number of texts in this level is 26 instead of 30.

3.3 Automatic annotation

In order to process large amounts of data, we created a script that identifies verbal tenses automatically based on several automatic language processing tools that we evaluated. We first performed a preliminary evaluation with five popular parsers and taggers, namely Stanza (Qi et al., 2020), UDpipe (Straka and Straková, 2017), spaCy (Honnibal et al., 2020), TreeTagger (Schmid, 1994), and RNNtagger (Schmid, 2019). In this preliminary study, we noticed that both UDpipe and RNNtagger failed at detecting several verbs. TreeTagger seemed promising, but its main limitation lies in the fact that it is a tagger and not a parser (i.e., it lacks the dependency information which is necessary to detect compound tenses). Following this preliminary analysis, we performed a more detailed evaluation of Treetagger, Stanza and spaCy. For this purpose, we prepared 10 sentences for each tense to be detected. The sentences were selected from French grammars (Asakura, 2002; Beacco et al., 2004; Cherdon, 2005; Grevisse and Goosse, 2007; Machida, 2015); we choose sentences that were as diverse as possible at the lexical level (both verbs and auxiliaries), at the usage level (complex sentences, as well as basic sentences that are suitable for language learners) and at the syntactic level (with or without adverbs such as negation, and inversion).

However, none of the taggers and parsers used in this study can detect French compound tenses, and, except for a system described in de Alencar (2017) that focuses on identifying the past perfect and passive constructions, but seems to be unavailable at the time of writing, we are not aware of previous work focusing on the detecting of composed tenses in French. Hence, we created a custom script that identifies compound tenses based on dependencies and part-of-speech information. The script identifies dependencies between auxiliary verbs and participles and uses a set of rules to derive the composed tense. While not a focus of this study, we included the detection of passive tenses, since they sometimes resemble active tenses and thus might lead to erroneous counts.

Based on this comparative evaluation of the three tools, we chose spaCy as main parser, TreeTagger for the present conditional and imperfect subjunctive, and Stanza for the past imperative. Table 4 shows the recall, precision and F1 score of the final script. The script can be accessed through a dedicated web interface.[10] The low precision for ind_pres and sbj_pres may be due to the fact that many verb forms of these tense have identical surface forms (e.g., *qu'il marche*-SBJ_PRES and *il marche*-IND_PRES). Furthermore, we noticed that sbj_pres was often mistagged as sbj_imp.

Tense	Recall	Precision	F1 score
Simple tenses			
ind_pres	1	0.56	0.71
ind_imp	1	1	1
ind_ps	0.8	1	0.89
ind_fs	1	1	1
cnd_pres	1	1	1
impe_pres	0.7	0.85	0.78
sbj_pres	0.8	0.5	0.61
sbj_imp	0.9	1	0.95
inf_pres	1	1	1
Compound tenses			
ind_pc	1	1	1
ind_pqp	0.9	1	0.95
ind_pa	0.9	1	0.95
ind_fa	1	1	1
cnd_pass	1	1	1
impe_pass	1	1	1
sbj_pass	0.9	0.9	0.9
sbj_pqp	1	1	1
inf_pass	1	1	1

Table 4: Precision, recall and F1 score on the different tenses

3.4 Manual annotation

We will first perform the annotation of verbal tenses in both corpora using our script. However, since automatic language processing tools are developed on the basis of well-formed data, it is to be expected that learner corpora, due to the inclusion of errors, will lead to annotation errors (Granger, 2011; Štindlová et al., 2011; Krivanek and Meurers, 2013; Rubin, 2021; Volodina et al., 2022). Therefore, we decided to also manually annotate the learner corpus.

According to Volodina et al. (2022, p. 152), a common pitfall when annotating learner corpora is to start by annotating what the learners meant, which is subjective in nature, rather than objectively describing what was used. Therefore, we started with manual annotation by scrupulously respecting the forms that the learners produced. That is to say, when we found a correctly written verb whose conjugated form exists, we annotated this verbal tense in square brackets ([ ])[11], regardless of whether its usage in relation to the context is correct or not. In this step, we did not take into account the learners' intention in order to capture only what they are able to produce.

(1) Je vous écris [ind_pres] pour vous informer [inf_pres] que la fête du sport aura [ind_fs] lieu dans ma ville le 01/04/2022. (C-fut-chi2)[12,13]

As has been done in the CEFR-J project, it would also be interesting to clarify what the learners wanted/needed to produce. In addition to the annotation that was based purely on form, we chose to include additional information. In some cases, it is clear that the verb form used was not the one that the learners were trying to use. That is, when the verb is in a form that exists but its usage is grammatically incorrect, due to errors such as a spelling mistake and/or a lack of grammatical competence, we added the error label *E!* or *E*. The former was added when the conjugated form that the learner wanted/needed to write was identifiable. In this case, we added next to it the tense they would have wanted/needed to write in curly braces ({ }).The second was used when the learner's intention was not certain or when the verb has no subject, except in the imperative form. As explained above, the present and past participles are not included in this study. However, it happens that the learner writes a verb in the participle when they probably wanted to form another verbal tense. In this case too, we annotated it with these labels.

(2) Après j'ai [ind_pres_E!] fais [ind_pres_E!] {ind_pc} le longue couries (B1-pre-ang1)

(3) Bonjour, moi ecrîte un proposer [inf_pres_E] pour tu. (A1-fut-ang1)

[10]https://cental.uclouvain.be/verbprofile

[11]See Appendix B for tense abbreviations used in the annotation.

[12]The label identifies the learners; it is composed of their level (A1, A2, B1, B2, C), the task orientation (*pas* for past, *fut* for future and *pre* for present), and their everyday language (*ang* for English, *ara* for Arabic, *chi* for Chinese, *esp* for Spanish and *rus* for Russian, followed by the id (1 or 2).

[13]Since most of the presented examples contain errors that make their translation difficult to impossible, we have opted not to gloss the sentences in English.

(4) J'aime [ind_pres] mangé [prt_pass_E!] {inf_pres} dans le restaurant familial (B2-pre-ang2)

Sometimes, a conjugated form corresponds to more than one tense. This is mainly the case of ambiguity between the present indicative and the present subjunctive. The subjunctive is mainly used with the conjunction *que*. When this ambiguous case occurs without such markers in the situations mentioned just before (annotation *E!* or *E*), the present indicative was noted as a temporary annotation before the correction. The reason is that it is evident from previous research and our textbook corpus results presented later that the present subjunctive is taught and learned later and is much less frequent than the present indicative.

(5) je aime [ind_pres] bien reste [ind_pres_E!] {inf_pres} avec soliei du campagne (A2-pas-ang2)

When a misspelled word is found that can be assumed to be a verb, we have annotated $\emptyset$ plus the correction between curly braces ({ }). This annotation is only used when the learner's intention is deemed sufficiently certain. In the opposite case, i.e. when we cannot determine the tense the learner has used, we used the annotation <E>.

(6) Donc j'ai [ind_pres_E!] règardè [$\emptyset$] {ind_pc} le netflix (B1-pas-ang-2)

(7) Nous fair <E> le skis fon avec mes enfants. (A1-pre-rus1)

In cases where it is impossible to tell whether a word is a verb or another part-of-speech, we added the label <NV>.

(8) L'ecole est [ind_pres] pas lion pour enfant, just marche <NV> (A1-pre-chi1) [The word *marche* can be a noun or a verb.]

Our correction (between { }) acts on the change of form and mode of the verbs if we can formulate a hypothesis based on what the learners have written. The choice of tense is linked to the writing style and it is therefore delicate to determine whether a tense is appropriate or not (e.g. use of the present tense instead of the past tense). Therefore, in general, our correction does not change the tense that the learners used.

As mentioned above, the passive is not included in our analysis, so we had to distinguish between passive and active cases. In situations where it was difficult to judge whether it was a passive or active voice, we asked three experts to decide. These experts are native French speakers and have already worked on projects that also encountered this difficulty. They annotated one of the two voices, following the annotation guide we had prepared based on the definition of voices according to the Bon Usage (Grevisse and Goosse, 2007) and the annotation guide of the French Treebank (Abeillé et al., 2003).

4 Results

In this section, we first describe the results from the textbook corpus (4.1). We then focus on the learner productions (4.2), including an in-depth analysis of both the automatic (4.2.1) and manual (4.2.2) annotation.

4.1 Textbook corpus

Table 8 in the appendix presents the results of the automatic analysis of the textbook corpus. To attach a level to a phenomenon, several approaches have been used, like the first occurrence (Gala et al., 2014; Alfter et al., 2016), but also threshold methods (Hawkins and Filipović, 2012; Gala et al., 2014; Alfter et al., 2016), and since we are dealing with learner language, observing a phenomenon only once or twice at a certain level is not sufficient to claim that it is of this level (Hawkins and Filipović, 2012; Alfter, 2021). In order to assign a level to each tense, we looked both at frequency and dispersion: we only took into account frequencies of tenses that occurred in *all* textbooks of that level; indeed, if only one textbook introduces a tense at a certain level, it is less likely to be globally of this level than if multiple/all textbooks introduce it. For frequency, we explored threshold methods, with thresholds of 1,3,5,10, and found that for our corpus, a threshold of 5 gives consistent results.

For the tenses that have not been sufficiently covered in some textbooks up to level C, namely the anterior past, the anterior future, the past imperative, the past subjunctive, the imperfect subjunctive, and the pluperfect subjunctive, it is very unlikely to find them in learner production tasks, and we can assume that their learning is a very low priority. For all the other tenses, we can observe that they are used a certain number of times until level B1, and more prominently at level B2.

The proposed Verb Profile based on the number of occurrences in the textbooks is shown in Table 5. Light colored cells indicate levels at which the tense may be observed sporadically, while dark shaded cells indicate levels at which the tense should be understood by learners of the corresponding level.

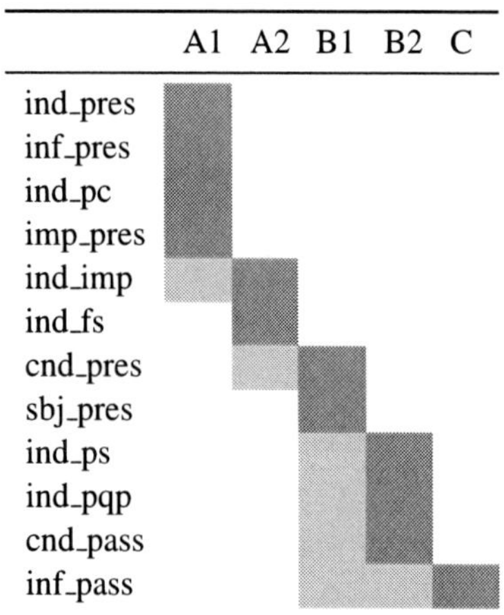

Table 5: Proposed textbook verb profile

4.2 Learner productions

In this section, we first describe the automatic analysis of learner productions, followed by the manual analysis of learner productions.

4.2.1 Automatic analysis

After the textbook corpus analysis, we performed an automatic analysis of the learner corpus. Several problems were identified, especially in the lowest CEFR level productions. This is due to the fact that the syntactic parser is misled by learner errors. By trying to interpret the texts despite its errors, our script will try to recognize as verbs words that are not, but that are in the expected position for a verb. In the following examples, the tense in parentheses is the one identified by the script.

(9) elle ne pa (ind_pres) de grave. (A1-pas-ang-1)

This "feature" causes other misidentifications. For example, it tends to judge words ending in *er* or *ir* as present infinitives. This error is probably caused by the fact that verbs of the first and second groups, which represent the majority of French verbs, end with these suffixes respectively.

(10) ôûî je puex alleer (inf_pres) al aniversarie de paula (A2-fut-esp1)

(11) j' ai more rir (inf_pres) pour lui (A1-pas-ara1)

We have observed this same phenomenon for other tenses. For example, when there are erroneous words that end with a suffix of a certain verb conjugated to a certain tense, the script can identify that tense, even though the word does not exist. Here are some examples that were misidentified as *simple past*, whose conjugated form of the first group verbs end with *ai*, *as*, *a*, *âmes*, *âtes*, and *èrent* depending on the person.

(12) Bonjour Maris ! sava (ind_ps) toi (A1-pas-ang2)

(13) j aimrai (ind_ps) bien passe mon anniversaire a la maison (A1-pre-ara2)

(14) Les doctors dirent (ind_ps) regarder le télé deux heures par jours par plus, (A2-pre-rus2)

Misidentifications of the *past perfect* have also been frequent. This tense consists of the auxiliary *avoir* 'to have' or *être* 'to be' conjugated in the present indicative and a past participle verb. However, when the word that follows the auxiliary is close to or identical with a certain verb form, the script may identify it as *past perfect*.

(15) çava matte noi, j'ai trie (ind_pc) mal lu venti. (A1-pas-ang1)

(16) Après j'ai fais (ind_pc) le longue couries (B1-pre-ang1)

(17) Et pour le dessert j'ai preparer (ind_pc) gâteux au framboise au créme anglaise. (A2-fut-rus2)

Likewise, the scripts assign a certain tense to verbs even if the accent is missing or on the contrary with an accent added in a wrong way.

(18) la concentration à pris (ind_pc) place. (A2-pas-esp2) [expected form: a pris]

(19) je vousley achèter (inf_pres) une pair de nouveau chausseurs. (A2-fut-ang2) [expected form: acheter]

(20) sa me fe reflechir (inf_pres) bocou (A1-pas-esp2) [expected form: réfléchir]

Thus, the script tends to infer irrelevant results by interpreting erroneous data, which would lead to an over-assessment of learners' results. To clarify the picture, we performed annotation manually as detailed below.

4.2.2 Manual analysis

The results from the manual analysis are presented in Table 9 in the appendix. Colored zones reflect the results from Table 8.

The percentages of each verbal tense were calculated on the basis of the numbers found in **Total 1**, which are the sums of all correctly conjugated verbs. The "other" values correspond to the numbers of words we labeled ∅, <E>, <NV>as well as words accidentally formed as past/present participles. Except for <NV>labels, which are infrequently present, all other words that are classified as "other" could be considered errors. The percentages found in the "others" row were calculated on the total numbers including these errors, i.e., the **Total 2** row. It is important to note that this percentage is considerably high at the lower levels. In particular, at level A1, we see that half of the verbs that learners tried to produce are there, and were not included in the first part of the table, the one showing the distribution of tenses.

We can observe tenses that are present in the textbooks, but which are not produced by the learners, even at the higher levels, namely the past simple, the indicative pluperfect, the anterior future, the past conditional and the past infinitive. This does not necessarily mean that they are not acquired, but it may simply mean that they are used less frequently in the everyday context corresponding to the tasks that the TCF exam calls for. For example, in tasks describing a past weekend, the imperative is expected to appear less frequently. In addition to the influence of opportunity, it is not excluded that learners avoid certain grammatical elements as a consequence of an avoidance strategy (Granger, 2011). As O'Keeffe and Mark (2017, p. 462) point out, zero occurrences in the native speaker data can be interpreted as resulting from choice, whereas in the learner data, this can be seen more as due to lack of proficiency. It is therefore important to be careful about the interpretation of the absence of a feature in a learner corpus. To know when they are learning the tenses, we will need other tests such as a grammaticality test. But here, our results are interpretable in the sense that we were able to observe the use of tenses for written production in a context with few constraints, thus with freedom of choice for the learner.

We see several uses of the present conditional and present subjunctive at a level below that expected according to the Verb Profile. For the first of these two tenses, all five uses were relevant. However, they were only *je voudrais*, a boilerplate that shows a modal value for politeness. This is consistent with what previous work had mentioned (Bartning and Schlyter, 2004; Beacco et al., 2004; Beacco and Porquier, 2007; Beacco, 2008; Beacco et al., 2011; North, 2015).

(21) Je voudrais [cnd_pres] visiter à Paris, (A1-fut-esp1)

(22) Je voudrais [cnd_pres] manger les repas typics (A1-fut-esp1)

(23) je voudrais [cnd_pres] faire amies là bas, (A1-fut-esp1)

(24) Je voudrais [cnd_pres] participé à activité pour marcher en samedi, (A2-pas-chi2)

(25) tu voudrais [cnd_pres] participé avez moi? (A2-pas-chi2)

Regarding the other tense, the present subjunctive, we observed three uses at the A1 level, whereas this tense was used very little in the textbooks at this level and not often at the next level either. These three uses are as follows:

(26) j' ai [ind_pres_E!] sorte [sbj_pres_E!] {ind_pc} avec Mohammed a jaddhe (A1-pas-ara1)

(27) il set sorte [sbj_pres_E] son ficag Parsra les basa bonne (A1-pas-ara1)

(28) J' aime ma ville ,paccquc avec juli montange , vive [sbj_pres_E!] {inf_pres} est facile , magasins es a cote ,la lac pas trop lion , (A1-pre-chi1)

In fact, these three uses are the results of a spelling error and/or chance. We cannot therefore consider that the learners were able to produce it.

In the annotation so far presented, we annotated by respecting the form of the verbs that the learners wrote. This allowed us to know what they wrote without overestimating their skills, which was one of the problems in the previous results with the automated approach. Moreover, thanks to this annotation, we were also able to better identify erroneous verbs by level, which was not the case in the automatic annotation. On the other hand, as we have just shown via the three examples of incorrect use of the present subjunctive, there are sometimes cases where verbs are not assigned to the correct verbal tense. However, it would be interesting to know what the learners wanted to write. This would allow us to clarify the difficulties they have in producing certain forms. Therefore, we prepared another table that was modified by the correction made with our estimation. Table 10 in the appendix shows the results of our correction hypotheses. As for Table 9, the colored areas reflect the results of Table 8.

Here, *correction* refers to the fact that we have removed the number of verbs annotated with *E*, *E!* and ∅. Moreover, for the last two, it is the learner's intended tense (and not the tense detected in the previous manual annotation) that is counted in Table 10.

Table 6 below shows the percentage change between the original and corrected annotation. For example, -11.22% in the present indicative in level A1 represents the percentage difference between the original table (Table 9, 73.50%) and the corrected table (Table 10, 62.29%).

	A1	A2	B1	B2	C
ind_pres	-11.2	0.3	-3.4	-3.99	0.2
ind_imp	0	-1.44	-0.15	-0.57	0.27
ind_ps	0	0	0	-0.22	0
ind_pc	5.15	7.31	3.13	2.09	-0.02
ind_pqp	0	0	0.39	0.2	-0.03
ind_pa	0	0	0	0	0
ind_fs	-0.28	-0.33	-0.56	0.36	-0.13
ind_fa	0	0	-0.02	0	0
cnd_pres	0.29	-0.16	-0.19	0.01	-0.08
cnd_pass	0	0	-0.02	-0.03	0
imp_pres	0	0.47	0.6	0.54	0.18
imp_pass	0	0	0	0	0
sbj_pres	-1.99	0.47	-0.32	0.09	0
sbj_pass	0	0	0	0	0
sbj_imp	0	0	0	0	0
sbj_pqp	0	0	0	0	0
inf_pres	8.05	-6.61	0.57	1.54	-0.38
inf_pass	0	0	-0.02	-0.04	-0.01

Table 6: Change in percentage before and after correction

We would like to draw attention to the past perfect (*passé composé*), whose numbers generally increase even at the higher levels, meaning that learners wanted to use and should have produced more past perfect but failed to do so. We have therefore studied the case where learners failed to produce the past perfect although they intended to do so.

As mentioned earlier, the past perfect is composed of the auxiliary *avoir* 'to have' or *être* 'to be' conjugated in the present indicative and a verb in the past participle. At A1 level, they had construction problems where the auxiliary was missing.

(29) je parti [prt_pass_E!] {ind_pc} week-end à la compagne chez ma grand parents. (A1-pas-ang2)

(30) Nou bian sortie [prt_pass_E!] {ind_pc}. (A1-pas-rus1)

Être and *avoir* are verbs that are learned from the beginning. From level A2 on, the construction is stabilized. The auxiliary was present and the learners were generally able to conjugate it correctly. However, we found that they had difficulty conjugating the second part, the past participle.

(31) les enfants se sont [ind_pres_E!] amuser [inf_pres_E!] {ind_pc}, (A2-pas-ara1)

(32) pour le dessert j'ai [ind_pres_E!] preparer [∅] {ind_pc} gâteux au framboise (A2-fut-rus-2)

(33) parceque j ai [ind_pres_E!] remarquer [inf_pres_E!] {ind_pc} (B1-pas-ara1)

(34) s'il y a quelqu'un qui dèja a [ind_pres_E!] connais [ind_pres_E!] {ind_pc}, (B1-pre-esp2)

(35) le film dont tu m'a [ind_pres_E!] parler [inf_pres_E!] {ind_pc} la semaine dèrnière. (B2-fut-ara1)

(36) Le chef nous a [ind_pres_E!] preparé [∅] {ind_pc} le plat japonais (B2-pas-rus1)

We can see that it was the inability to correctly conjugate the past participle that prevented the realization of the past perfect. In the first manual annotation, in Table 9, we annotated the well-conjugated auxiliary as being in the present indicative instead of assigning it to the past perfect.

This partly explains the drop in the percentages of the present tense after the correction. In addition, as we see in the examples above, there are many cases where the present indicative or present infinitive, the tenses we learn right at the beginning of the learning process (see Table 5 and 8) was used in place of the past participle. This also contributed to the decrease for these two tenses. Moreover, the proportion of errors in relation to the total number of verbs in the past perfect tense decreases as learners progress. But it is important to note that this type of error is still present at the higher levels.

Comparing the numbers of different levels in Table 6, the decrease of the present indicative tense in A1 is noticeable. In order to create Table 10, we have deleted error-labeled verbs to avoid counting verbs whose verbal tense used is too difficult or impossible to estimate in its context. The written productions of low level learners are not always comprehensible because of incorrect construction and wrong words. At A1 level, this tendency was obviously pronounced and a large proportion of verbs in the indicative present tense labeled as errors were observed. In addition to the difficulty of the past perfect tense, this could be a factor in the marked decrease. It is interesting, however, that even after eliminating the inappropriate use of the present indicative tense, its presence remains dominant at low levels and decreases as learners' level increases. This is consistent with the trend observed in the textbook data.

5 Discussion

Our automated annotation of a corpus of FFL textbooks made it possible to create a Verb Profile based on a large amount of data. It is an indicator that represents a form of consensus in the teaching of FFL, as it was created by considering the number of occurrences of verbal tenses in a large sample of textbooks, which may have different characteristics and objectives. The Verb Profile clearly indicates which elements are taught at which level. It can therefore be useful for teachers and those creating computer-based learning systems, such as an intelligent tutoring system, to select texts and the right tenses to cover, and to think about how much time to spend on explanations.

From a didactic point of view, we found that the indicative past perfect continues to cause errors from the beginning of learning to a fairly high level in learners. As our study has validated, it is a tense used quite frequently in the textbook corpus, as well as in the learner corpus. It is therefore necessary to teach it strategically to learners. For example, A1 learners were found to have difficulty producing the correct form of the past perfect. Therefore, it would probably be effective to offer them tasks that focus on its structure. From A2 onward, their difficulty is with the second verb, which is supposed to be conjugated as a past participle. Multiple-choice questions requiring them to select the past participle from several options would allow learners to practice the correct conjugation. Later, tasks that require them to spell the verbs themselves would further anchor their use.

To see how our results relate to existing studies, we compared our textbook and learner profiles to previous studies based on the CEFR, i.e., Beacco et al. (2004); Beacco and Porquier (2007); Beacco (2008); Beacco et al. (2011) as well as North (2015). Specifically, we checked whether the first level in which each of the two references marks a given tense as acquired corresponds (1) for the textbooks, to the first level we indicated with the dark shade in Table 8, and (2) for the learners' productions, to the first level in which we checked the usage of a given tense by five learners in Table 10 after correction. For both the textbook profile as well as the learners' profile, we find that they are closer to North than to Beacco. For our textbook profile, this trend makes sense, as North's inventory is more oriented towards reception. For learner production, on the other hand, we expected it to be closer to the inventory of Beacco et al. that describes the acquisition of tenses from a production point of view. We therefore need a more detailed interpretation of our results and also of these referentials.

Finally, from a NLP perspective, through our study, we confirmed that analyzing learner data in an automatic way is not easy. One way to improve on the study would be to integrate existing dictionaries into the script. As shown in Section 4.2.1, it is the overly bold assumptions of the parser that lead to errors. It is likely that most of these problems can be solved by adding a check against dictionary entries. However, even with this improvement, the problem of undesirable identification that leads to the over-estimation of verbal tense usage remains when a word is accidentally conjugated to an existing verbal form as a result of learner error. As we can see from the example of the present subjunctive, discussed in Section 4.2.2, when a tense appears when it should not yet have been learned in a textbook at a given level, it is likely to be an inappropriate use. If a semi-automatic approach is considered, manual verification could make the results more reliable when a learner is using a tense that they are not yet expected to know at their current level. The Textbook Verb Profile could serve as a reference resource for estimating the tenses known at a given CEFR level and therefore usable by learners.

We would like to mention some limitations of our study and suggest directions for further research. First, we studied only the tenses found in the verb conjugation table. Thus, the periphrastic near future tense *futur proche* (e.g., *je vais manger* 'I'm going to eat') and the recent past tense *passé récent* (e.g., *je viens de manger* 'I just ate'), both constructed with the verb *venir* 'to come', are counted as two separate verbs in this study – instead of as a compound tense – even though they behave like compound tenses. In addition to the passives and the gerund, which we excluded from the analysis, these automatic identifications and examinations must be addressed.

Second, the sampling was done with the aim of being able to generalize the results, therefore the impact of the learners' native language was not examined. In view of previous studies on the acquisition stages, the consensus is that language acquisition is not affected by the learner's native language. On the other hand, many teachers and researchers are empirically or intuitively convinced that L1 influences L2 acquisition (Izumi et al., 2005; Spada and Lightbown, 2020, p. 119). Therefore, the impact of the language used by the learner (and possibly the language of instruction, although this information is not present in our data) should be taken into account in the analysis.

Third, the present research was conducted from a purely morphological perspective and therefore remains at a one-dimensional level. The English Grammar Profile, for example, provides, in addition to a CEFR level assigned to the items concerned, much more in-depth information such as lexical range. In the future, we would like to also create a Verb Profile for learners, taking into account the lexical and syntactic difficulty of a given verbal tense.

Finally, our attempt to apply automatic analyses to learner data has again highlighted the difficulties of automatically processing data containing errors. However, manual annotation is time consuming and necessarily involves subjective judgments; it seems inevitable to use NLP to treat large amounts of texts in order to produce a Verb Profile for learners, which would give a robust and generalizable perspective based on a large amount of data. Two observations arise from these statements: first, there is a need for a more systematic and in-depth analysis of taggers and parsers in order to tackle the problem of correctly identifying verb tenses in learner language; second, we should seek ways in which to handle learner language in order to make it compatible with our scripts. A potential solution to these problems may lie in the normalization of learner productions, either manually, semi-automatically or automatically.

6 Conclusion

Thanks to our script that automatically identifies verbal tenses we have made it possible to process a large amount of data to establish a Verb Profile of FFL textbooks. It can serve as a resource in a different way from others that already existed, as it is purely data-driven, and thus does not rely on (subjective) human judgments as to which tenses ought to be known at which levels. Another remarkable aspect of this resource is the comprehensive treatment of tenses. Tenses that are not covered in the existing resources, i.e., those that were thought not to need to be taught or were not considered to be used by learners, were also included in the study. This allowed us to verify whether or not these tenses were covered in the textbooks that underpin learners' learning. That said, biases inherent in the data may affect the analyses. Therefore, it should be noted that the quality of our resources depend on the nature of the data used in this study.

Our two methods of analyzing learner productions, one that shows what they wrote and another that shows what they would have wanted/needed to produce, allowed us to describe the state of the use of verbal tenses according to CEFR levels. Furthermore, the comparison of the two annotations revealed that learners, even at advanced levels, had difficulties with the past perfect. We also found a gradation in difficulty, depending on the level, meaning that learners at A1 level had difficulties with the auxiliary verb, while learners at

A2 level had more difficulties with the inflection of the main verb. These results can help teachers focus on areas that need addressing in learners of different levels.

7 Acknowledgement

This study was enabled through a research agreement with France Education International. We would like to express our deepest gratitude to Eva Rolin and Adeline Müller, who willingly accepted to help us during the annotation process. Nami Yamaguchi is supported by the Japan Student Services Organization (JASSO). David Alfter is supported by the Fonds de la Recherche Scientifique de Belgique (F.R.S-FNRS) under grant MIS/PGY F.4518.21.

References

Anne Abeillé, Lionel Clément, and François Toussenel. 2003. Building a treebank for French. In *Treebanks*, pages 165–187. Springer.

Andrea Abel. 2014. A trilingual learner corpus illustrating european reference levels. *RiCOGNIZIONI. Rivista di Lingue e Letterature straniere e Culture moderne*, 1(2):111–126.

Leonel Figueiredo de Alencar. 2017. A computational implementation of periphrastic verb constructions in French. *Alfa: Revista de Lingüística*, 61(2):437–467.

David Alfter. 2021. *Exploring natural language processing for single-word and multi-word lexical complexity from a second language learner perspective*. Ph.D. thesis, University of Gothenburg, Sweden.

David Alfter, Yuri Bizzoni, Anders Agebjörn, Elena Volodina, and Ildikó Pilán. 2016. From distributions to labels: A lexical proficiency analysis using learner corpora. In *Proceedings of the joint workshop on NLP for Computer Assisted Language Learning and NLP for Language Acquisition*, pages 1–7.

Sueo Asakura. 2002. *Dictionnaire des difficultés grammaticales de la langue française (Shin Furansu bunpō jiten)*. Hakusuisha, Tokyo.

Inge Bartning and Suzanne Schlyter. 2004. Itinéraires acquisitionnels et stades de développement en français L2. *Journal of French language studies*, 14(3):281–299.

Jean-Claude Beacco. 2008. *Niveau A2 pour le français*. Didier.

Jean-Claude Beacco, Béatrice Blin, Emmanuelle Houles, Sylvie Lepage, and Patrick Riba. 2011. *Niveau B1 pour le français*. Didier.

Jean-Claude Beacco, Simon Bouquet, and Rémy Porquier. 2004. *Niveau B2 pour le français: utilisateur-apprenant indépendant: textes et références*. Didier.

Jean-Claude Beacco and Rémy Porquier. 2007. *Niveau A1 pour le français*. Didier.

Vaclav Brezina and Gabriele Pallotti. 2019. Morphological complexity in written L2 texts. *Second language research*, 35(1):99–119.

Bram Bulté and Alex Housen. 2012. Defining and operationalising L2 complexity. *Dimensions of L2 performance and proficiency: Complexity, accuracy and fluency in SLA*, pages 23–46.

Christian Cherdon. 2005. *Guide de grammaire française*. De Boeck.

Council of Europe. 2001. *Common European Framework of Reference for Languages: Learning, Teaching, Assessment*. Press Syndicate of the University of Cambridge.

Bastien De Clercq and Alex Housen. 2019. The development of morphological complexity: A cross-linguistic study of L2 French and English. *Second Language Research*, 35(1):71–97.

Robert M DeKeyser. 2005. What makes learning second-language grammar difficult? a review of issues. *Language learning*, 55(S1):1–25.

Heidi C Dulay and Marina K Burt. 1974. Natural sequences in child second language acquisition 1. *Language learning*, 24(1):37–53.

Luise Dürlich and Thomas François. 2018. EFLLex: A graded lexical resource for learners of English as a foreign language. In *Proceedings of the Eleventh International Conference on Language Resources and Evaluation (LREC 2018)*.

Núria Gala, Thomas François, Delphine Bernhard, and Cédrick Fairon. 2014. Un modèle pour prédire la complexité lexicale et graduer les mots. In *TALN'2014*, pages 91–102.

Sylviane Granger. 2011. How to use foreign and second language learner corpora. *Research methods in second language acquisition: A practical guide*, pages 5–29.

Maurice Grevisse and André Goosse. 2007. *Le bon usage*. De Boeck, Duculot.

John A Hawkins and Paula Buttery. 2010. Criterial features in learner corpora: Theory and illustrations. *English Profile Journal*, 1.

John A Hawkins and Luna Filipović. 2012. *Criterial features in L2 English: Specifying the reference levels of the Common European Framework*, volume 1. Cambridge University Press.

Matthew Honnibal, Ines Montani, Sofie Van Landeghem, and Adriane Boyd. 2020. spaCy: Industrial-strength Natural Language Processing in Python.

Emi Izumi, Koyotaka Uchimoto, and Hitoshi Isahara. 2005. Investigation into Japanese learners' acquisition order of major grammatical morphemes using error-tagged learner corpus (erā tagu tsuki gakushūsha kōpasu wo mochiita nihonjin eigo gakushūsha no shuyō bunpō keitaiso no shūtoku junjo ni kansuru bunseki). *Journal of Natural Language Processing*, 12(4):211–225.

Julia Krivanek and Detmar Meurers. 2013. Comparing rule-based and data-driven dependency parsing of learner language. *Computational dependency theory*, 258:207.

Donna Lardiere. 2016. Missing the trees for the forest: Morphology in second language acquisition. *Second language*, 15:5–28.

Diane Larsen-Freeman. 2010. Not so fast: A discussion of L2 morpheme processing and acquisition. *Language Learning*, 60(1):221–230.

John Michael Linacre. 1989. *Many-faceted Rasch measurement*. Ph.D. thesis, The University of Chicago.

Ken Machida. 2015. *Compendium de la grammaire française (Furansugo bunpō sō kaisetsu)*. Kenkyusya, Tokyo.

Brian North. 2015. Inventaire linguistique des contenus clés des niveaux du cecrl.

Brian North, Angeles Ortega, and Susan Sheehan. 2010. Eaquals core inventory for general english.

Anne O'Keeffe and Geraldine Mark. 2017. The english grammar profile of learner competence: Methodology and key findings. *International Journal of Corpus Linguistics*, 22(4):457–489.

Gabriele Pallotti. 2015. A simple view of linguistic complexity. *Second Language Research*, 31(1):117–134.

Manfred Pienemann. 1998. *Language processing and second language development*, volume 10. Amsterdam: John Benjamins.

Manfred Pienemann and Gisela Håkansson. 1999. A unified approach toward the development of Swedish as L2: A Processability Account. *Studies in second language acquisition*, 21(3):383–420.

Peng Qi, Yuhao Zhang, Yuhui Zhang, Jason Bolton, and Christopher D. Manning. 2020. Stanza: A Python Natural Language Processing Toolkit for Many Human Languages. In *Proceedings of the 58th Annual Meeting of the Association for Computational Linguistics: System Demonstrations*.

Patrick Riba. 2016. *Niveaux C1/C2 pour le français*. Paris, Didier.

Jack C Richards. 1970. A non-contrastive approach to error analysis. In *TESOL Convention*, pages 1–37.

Rachel Rubin. 2021. Assessing the impact of automatic dependency annotation on the measurement of phraseological complexity in L2 Dutch. *International Journal of Learner Corpus Research*, 7(1):131–162.

Helmut Schmid. 1994. Probabilistic part-of-speech tagging using decision trees. In *International Conference on New Methods in Language Processing*.

Helmut Schmid. 2019. Deep learning-based morphological taggers and lemmatizers for annotating historical texts. In *Proceedings of the 3rd International Conference on Digital Access to Textual Cultural Heritage*, pages 133–137.

Nina Spada and Patsy M Lightbown. 2020. Second language acquisition. In Norbert Schmitt and Michael P.H. Rodgers, editors, *An introduction to applied linguistics*, third edition, chapter 7, pages 172–188. Routledge, London and New York.

Barbora Štindlová, Svatava Škodová, Jirka Hana, and Alexandr Rosen. 2011. CzeSL – an error tagged corpus of Czech as a second language. In *PALC*, pages 13–15.

Milan Straka and Jana Straková. 2017. Tokenizing, POS Tagging, Lemmatizing and Parsing UD 2.0 with UDPipe. In *Proceedings of the CoNLL 2017 shared task: Multilingual Parsing from raw text to universal dependencies*, pages 88–99.

Yukio Tono. 2013. *The CEFR-J Handbook : a resource book for using CAN-DO descriptors for English language teaching*. Taishukan Shoten.

Elena Volodina, David Alfter, Therese Lindström Tiedemann, Maisa Susanna Lauriala, and Daniela Helena Piipponen. 2022. Reliability of automatic linguistic annotation: native vs non-native texts. In *Selected papers from the CLARINAnnual Conference 2021*. Linköping University Electronic Press (LiU E-Press).

Kevin Yancey, Alice Pintard, and Thomas Francois. 2021. Investigating readability of french as a foreign language with deep learning and cognitive and pedagogical features. *Lingue e linguaggio*, 20(2):229–258.

A Link between tense/mood and learner proficiency levels according to previous studies

Bold-faced tenses and moods show newly introduced tenses/moods at this level. An asterisk indicates that usage is sporadic at this level according to the original study. Underspecified tenses in the original study such as "future" or "past" are indicated in double quotation marks.

A.1 Summary of moods and tenses by levels according to Bartning and Schlyter (2004)

Stage	Mood and tense
Stage 1	Indicative: **past perfect***
Stage 2	Indicative: past perfect, **imperfect***
Stage 3	Indicative: **future simple***
	Subjunctive*
	"Past"
Stage 4	Indicative: **pluperfect**
	Conditional
	Subjunctive
Stage 5	Indicative: pluperfect, future simple
	Conditional
	Subjunctive
Stage 6	"stabilized inflectional morphology"

A.2 Summary of moods and tenses by levels according to Beacco et al. (2004); Beacco and Porquier (2007); Beacco (2008); Beacco and Riba (2011)

Level	Mood and tense
A1	Indicative: **present**, **imperfect***, **past perfect***
	Infinitive
	Imperative
	Conditional: present
A2	"Main tenses for certain verbs"
	"imperfect"*
	"future"*
B1	Indicative: present, imperfect, past perfect, **pluperfect**, "future"
	Conditional: present
	Subjunctive: present*;
	Imperative: present
	Infinitive: present
	Participle: present*, **past***
B2	Indicative: present, imperfect, past perfect, "future", **future anterior**
	Conditional: present, **past**
	Subjunctive: present, **past**
	Imperative : present, **past**
	Infinitive : present, **past**
	Participle: present, past, **past perfect**

A.3 Summary of moods and tenses by levels according to North (2015)

Level	Mood and tense
A1	Indicative: **present**, **imperfect***, **past perfect***
	Conditional: **present***
	Imperative: **present***
	Infinitive: **present**
A2	Indicative: present, imperfect, past perfect, **simple future**
	Conditional: present*
	Imperative: present
	Subjunctive: **present***
	Infinitive: present
B1	Indicative: imperfect, **pluperfect**
	Conditional: present, **past**
	Imperative: present
	Subjunctive: present
	Infinitive: present, **past**
B2	Indicative: **simple past**, pluperfect, **anterior future**
	Conditional: present, past
	Subjunctive: present, **past (receptive)**
	Infinitive: past
C	Indicative: simple past
	Subjunctive: present, past

B Tenses and their abbreviations

Tense	English name	Abbreviation
Indicatif présent	Indicative present	ind_pres
Indicatif imparfait	Indicative imperfect	ind_imp
Indicatif passé simple	Indicative simple past	ind_ps
Indicatif passé composé	Indicative past perfect	ind_pc
Indicatif plus-que-parfait	Indicative pluperfect	ind_pqp
Indicatif passé antérieur	Indicative anterior past	ind_pa
Indicatif futur simple	Indicative simple future	ind_fs
Indicatif futur antérieur	Indicative anterior future	ind_fa
Conditionnel présent	Conditional present	cnd_pres
Conditionnel passé	Conditional past	cnd_pass
Impératif présent	Imperative present	impe_pres
Impératif passé	Imperative past	impe_pass
Subjonctif présent	Subjunctive present	sbj_pres
Subjonctif passé	Subjunctive past	sbj_pass
Subjonctif imparfait	Subjunctive imperfect	sbj_imp
Subjonctif plus-que-parfait	Subjunctive pluperfect	sbj_pqp
Infinitif présent	Infinitive present	inf_pres
Infinitif passé	Infinitive past	inf_pass
Participe présent	Participle present	part_pres
Participe passé	Participle past	part_pass

Table 7: Tenses and abbreviations

C Textbook and learner corpus annotation results

C.1 Textbook corpus annotation results

	A1		A2		B1		B2		C	
	A1	A1%	A2	A2%	B1	B1%	B2	B2%	C	C%
ind_pres	4501	66.81	5334	49.81	5262	49.63	4725	47.38	4318	48.31
ind_imp	88	1.31	492	4.59	414	3.90	504	5.05	216	2.42
ind_ps	3	0.04	8	0.07	34	0.32	185	1.86	85	0.95
ind_pc	459	6.81	1018	9.51	913	8.61	702	7.04	591	6.61
ind_pqp	1	0.01	29	0.27	74	0.70	48	0.48	24	0.27
ind_pa	1	0.01	0	0	1	0.01	4	0.04	1	0.01
ind_fs	35	0.52	274	2.56	227	2.14	185	1.86	285	3.19
ind_fa	0	0	1	0.01	14	0.13	14	0.14	3	0.03
cnd_pres	51	0.76	128	1.20	180	1.70	203	2.04	170	1.90
cnd_pass	0	0	0	0	27	0.25	23	0.23	16	0.18
imp_pres	233	3.46	476	4.44	201	1.90	121	1.21	290	3.24
imp_pass	0	0	1	0.01	10	0.09	1	0.01	0	0
sbj_pres	3	0.04	34	0.32	139	1.31	135	1.35	82	0.92
sbj_pass	0	0	1	0.01	14	0.13	5	0.05	6	0.07
sbj_imp	0	0	0	0	0	0	0	0	0	0
sbj_pqp	0	0	0	0	0	0	3	0.03	0	0
inf_pres	1361	20.20	2902	27.10	3052	28.78	3087	30.96	2832	31.68
inf_pass	1	0.01	11	0.10	41	0.39	27	0.27	19	0.21
Total	6737		10709		10603		9972		8938	

Table 8: Results of the textbook corpus analysis. Light shaded cells indicate levels at which the tense was used at least once in all of the textbooks of this level. Dark shaded cells indicate levels at which the tense was used at least five times in all of the textbooks of this level.

C.2 Learner corpus annotation results (original)

	A1				A2				B1				B2				C			
	V	V%	C	C%	V	V%	C	C%	V	V%	C	C%	V	V%	C	C%	V	V%	C	C%
ind_pres	86	73.50	25	96.15	105	57.38	30	100	192	49.61	30	100	205	44.28	30	100	164	36.36	29	96.67
ind_imp	0	0	0	0	12	6.56	5	16.67	18	4.65	9	30	27	5.83	10	33.33	24	5.32	10	33.33
ind_ps	0	0	0	0	0	0	0	0	0	0	0	0	1	0.22	1	3.33	0	0	0	0
ind_pc	2	1.71	2	7.69	13	7.10	6	20	42	10.85	13	43.33	40	8.64	16	53.33	68	15.08	17	56.67
ind_pqp	0	0	0	0	0	0	0	0	4	1.03	4	13.33	0	0	0	0	4	0.89	3	10
ind_pa	0	0	0	0	0	0	0	0	0	0	0	0	0	0	0	0	0	0	0	0
ind_fs	1	0.85	1	3.85	4	2.19	2	6.67	15	3.88	9	30	18	3.89	9	30	20	4.43	8	26.67
ind_fa	0	0	0	0	0	0	0	0	1	0.26	1	3.33	0	0	0	0	0	0	0	0
cnd_pres	3	2.56	1	3.85	2	1.09	1	3.33	9	2.33	6	20	14	3.02	10	33.33	12	2.66	8	26.67
cnd_pass	0	0	0	0	0	0	0	0	1	0.26	1	3.33	2	0.43	2	6.67	0	0	0	0
imp_pres	0	0	0	0	0	0	0	0	5	1.29	4	13.33	5	1.08	4	13.33	5	1.11	4	13.33
imp_pass	0	0	0	0	0	0	0	0	0	0	0	0	0	0	0	0	0	0	0	0
sbj_pres	3	2.56	2	7.69	0	0	0	0	4	1.03	3	10	8	1.73	6	20	0	0	0	0
sbj_pass	0	0	0	0	0	0	0	0	0	0	0	0	0	0	0	0	0	0	0	0
sbj_imp	0	0	0	0	0	0	0	0	0	0	0	0	0	0	0	0	0	0	0	0
sbj_pqp	0	0	0	0	0	0	0	0	0	0	0	0	0	0	0	0	0	0	0	0
inf_pres	22	18.80	9	34.62	47	25.68	24	80	95	24.55	28	93.33	140	30.24	29	96.67	153	33.92	29	96.67
inf_pass	0	0	0	0	0	0	0	0	1	0.26	1	3.33	3	0.65	3	10	1	0.22	1	3.33
Total 1	117				183				387				463				451			
part_pres	0				1				0				0				0			
part_pass	12				10				10				3				1			
∅	76				56				55				39				9			
E	25				17				6				1				0			
NV	8				2				0				0				2			
Other	121	50.84			86	31.97			71	15.50			43	8.50			12	2.59		
Total 2	238				269				458				506				463			

Table 9: Results of the original learner corpus annotation. V: counts for a given tense; V%: percentage of V with regards to all verbs, i.e., Total 1; C: number of learners who produced this tense; C%: percentage of C with regards to all learners (26 for level A1, 30 for the other levels)

C.3 Learner corpus annotation results (corrected)

	A1				A2				B1				B2				C			
	V	V%	C	C%	V	V%	C	C%	V	V%	C	C%	V	V%	C	C%	V	V%	C	C%
ind_pres	109	62.29	25	96.15	124	57.67	29	96.67	195	46.21	29	96.67	199	40.28	30	100	170	36.56	29	96.67
ind_imp	0	0	0	0	11	5.12	5	16.67	19	4.50	9	30	26	5.26	9	30	26	5.59	11	36.67
ind_ps	0	0	0	0	0	0	0	0	6	1.42	5	16.67	1	0.20	1	3.33	4	0.86	3	10
ind_pc	1	0.57	1	3.85	4	1.86	2	6.67	14	3.32	8	26.67	21	4.25	10	33.33	20	4.30	8	26.67
ind_pqp	0	0	0	0	0	0	0	0	1	0.24	1	3.33	0	0	0	0	0	0	0	0
ind_pa	0	0	0	0	0	0	0	0	0	0	0	0	0	0	0	0	0	0	0	0
ind_fs	1	0.57	1	3.85	4	1.86	2	6.67	14	3.32	8	26.67	21	4.25	10	33.33	20	4.43	8	26.67
ind_fa	0	0	0	0	0	0	0	0	1	0.24	1	3.33	0	0	0	0	0	0	0	0
cnd_pres	5	2.86	2	7.69	2	0.93	1	3.33	9	2.13	6	20	15	3.04	11	36.67	12	2.58	8	26.67
cnd_pass	0	0	0	0	0	0	0	0	1	0.24	1	3.33	2	0.40	2	6.67	0	0	0	0
imp_pres	0	0	0	0	1	0.47	1	3.33	8	1.90	6	20	8	1.62	7	23.33	6	1.29	5	16.67
imp_pass	0	0	0	0	0	0	0	0	0	0	0	0	0	0	0	0	0	0	0	0
sbj_pres	1	0.57	1	3.85	1	0.47	1	3.33	3	0.71	2	6.67	9	1.82	7	23.33	0	0	0	0
sbj_pass	0	0	0	0	0	0	0	0	0	0	0	0	0	0	0	0	0	0	0	0
sbj_imp	0	0	0	0	0	0	0	0	0	0	0	0	0	0	0	0	0	0	0	0
sbj_pqp	0	0	0	0	0	0	0	0	0	0	0	0	0	0	0	0	0	0	0	0
inf_pres	47	26.86	19	73.08	41	19.07	20	66.67	106	25.12	27	90	157	31.78	29	96.67	156	33.55	29	96.67
inf_pass	0	0	0	0	0	0	0	0	1	0.24	1	3.33	3	0.61	3	10	1	0.22	1	3.33
Total	175				215				422				494				465			

Table 10: Results of the corrected learner corpus annotation. V: counts for a given tense; V%: percentage of V with regards to all verbs, i.e., Total 1; C: number of learners who produced this tense; C%: percentage of C with regards to all learners (26 for level A1, 30 for the other levels)

Association for Computational Linguistics
209 N. Eighth Street
Stroudsburg, Pennsylvania 18360

ISBN 978-1-7138-9143-7

CURRAN ASSOCIATES INC.
proceedings.com